**Does ANY a This CRAP Make SENSE
ta Ya, OR Am I Jest FUNNIN' Ya...**

YOU DECIDE !!!

authorHOUSE®

AuthorHouse™
1663 Liberty Drive
Bloomington, IN 47403
www.authorhouse.com
Phone: 1-800-839-8640

Published by AuthorHouse 3/19/2013

ISBN: 978-1-4817-2666-5 (sc)
ISBN: 978-1-4817-2667-2 (e)

Library of Congress Control Number: 2013904207

Any people depicted in stock imagery provided by Thinkstock are models,
and such images are being used for illustrative purposes only.
Certain stock imagery © Thinkstock.

This book is printed on acid-free paper.

Because of the dynamic nature of the Internet, any web addresses or links contained
in this book may have changed since publication and may no longer be valid.

The views expressed in this work are solely those of the author and do not necessarily reflect
the views of the publisher, and the publisher hereby disclaims any responsibility for them.

Does ANY a This CRAP Make SENSE ta Ya, OR Am I Jest FUNNIN' Ya...

YOU DECIDE !!!

A Rather HUMOROUS (In MY "Opinion"…..the ONLY One That Counts)

"Politickin' and Religiousmess" Satire

of OUR Time (the "Last Days")

by

A. L. "BIG AL" Nolram

THE Bombastic and Beaudacious Mouth-of-the-South

(and Curmudgeon @ Large)

from Beauregard, AL

This Page Has Been "INTENTIONALLY" ("RIGHTly") "LEFT" BLANK.

(Exceptin' Fer THIS Line, And the Text Above, AND The Text Below THIS Line)

(ta HONOR the Makers of "ZORK",.the Very 1st ARPAnet (Before "Internet") Game I Ever LOVED)

Corporate Sponsors

(Since These Corporate Sponsors Have Been KIND Enough ta Assist with the "Creation" of My Little "Baby", Please Be KIND Enough ta at Least "Consider" Givin' Them Yer Business…..Tell 'em "BIG AL" Sent Ya and They'll Treat Ya "Extra Special")

Animal Health Center

Address/Phone: 1520 2nd Ave, Opelika, AL 36801 **(334) 745-0060**

WebSite: **http://www.animalhealthctr.vetsuite.com/Templates/ModernElegance.aspx**

AboveBoard Roofing

Address/Phone: 801 S. Railroad Suite 201, Opelika, AL 36801 **(334) 741-4253**

WebSite: http://www.aboveboardroofingal.com   **Toll Free: 888-214-9988**

Lee County Feed & Seed

Address/Phone: 7747 AL Highway 51 (Marvyn Parkway), Opelika, AL 36804 **(334) 741-5320**

WebSite: **Check with "Gary Cooper" (Like the Actor)**   **Nutrena Feed Dealer**

And LASTLY, BUTT "Definitely" NOT Leastly (In The Position of HONOR), All of The Producers, Distributors, AND Marketers of Dr Pepper, (RKC) Rice Krispies Candy, AND WhoEVER is CRAZY Enough ta Publish This Here "Baby" a Mine (Like Mr Tim Murphy of AuthorHouse). PLEASE Stop By Yer Local Supermarket, Grocery Store, AND/OR Bookstore (Along with Yer Local "Mental Health" Facility) and Give 'em ALL Yer Business (Or "The Business", Or ……..AHHHH, HELL…… Y'all KNOW What I Mean……Jest Give 'em ALL a Yer Money, and Be DONE with it….. Before Ole OBAMMA RAMMA's "BIG Government" Steals it ALL Away from Ya…..). Have a BLESSED "the REST of Yer LIFE"… AND DON'T Y'all DARE Fergit……..If'n Ya DON'T Send a Little "VALUE" ta P.O. Box 2149, Tuskegee, AL 36083… Then MY GOD's Gonna GIT Ya Fer THAT !!!.... Have FUN !!!!!!!.....I DO !!!!!!

Individual Sponsors

(These is the OTHER Folks Who Put UP with My Crap ta Git This Here Danged Book Published, SOOOOO Be Kind ta THEM When Ya See 'em on the Street)

M. P. Gosda – Executive Assistant to A. L. "BIG AL" Nolram (the BEST Little Tit-Turd I Know)

R. M. Gosda – Wife (and GOOD Lady Fer Puttin' Up with His Crap) of My Executive Assistant

Mr Bryant Lewis – the Team Leader Extrordinaire of My Little Tit-Turd Executive Assistant

Ms Cecelia Pitts – the Executive Assistant Extrordinare that MY Exec Assistant Larned From

Tim Murphy – the AuthorHouse Publishing Consultant that Worked with My Executive Assistant

Table of "Outlandish" Contents

(Chapters 1 - 66)

Chapter # and Name (THAT's So's Y'all Can FIND it Later ON)   **Page #**

1. What's "WRONG" with AMERICA, What's "RIGHT" with AMERICA, And HOW Can I CHANGE That ???   1

2.   WHAT the Heck IS a NIPer Anyway, and WHAT Do I Have to DO to BECOME One ???   4

3. WHAT is a "CALL to Service", and HOW Can I GIT One ???   12

4. WHY Do Pro-LIFE Folks Kill Doctors and Bomb Abortion Clinics ???   21

5. How CAN We NIPers Git Prayer BACK inta the Schools ???   25

6.   WHAT Do We DO About Them Thar GOD DAMNED godLESS Atheists ???   28

7.   What IS Rice Krispies Candy (RKC) fer the SOUL ???   29

8.   WHO the Heck AM I, and WHY the HELL Should YOU Care ???   31

9.   How the HECK Can We NIPers SOLVE AMERICA's Immigration Problem ???   36

10. What IS the "User's Guide and Maintenance Manual for a Human Life" ???   38

11. WHAT's the "DIFFERENCE" Between a "Hoe" and a "Culler" ???   40

12. What's the "DIFFERENCE" Between an AFRICAN-American And an AMERICAN-African ???   42

13. WHO's Tryin' ta START a "NEW" AMERICAN Revolution in This GREAT GOD-Fearin" NATION of OURS (One Voter at a Time) ???   44

14. WHAT's the "DIFFERENCE" Between "Leadership" and "Management" ???   48

15. If the "Pen" is Mightier than the "Sword", is a "Word Processor" More Powerful than an "Atomic Bomb" ???   53

16. Are Ya the "Git 'er Dun" Type, OR is There a "BETTER" ("BEST" ??) Way ???   56

17. How CAN We REFORM the Tax System, AND, Pay Off the National Debt at the SAME TIME ???   57

18. How CAN the NIPers "Convince" Ms Sarah Palin ta Be OUR Presidential   59
Candidate and Mr Herman Cain ta Be OUR Vice-Presidential Candidate ???

19. Why WOULD Bill O'Reilly, Glen Beck, AND Rush Limbaugh Make GOOD   64
SPIN Controllers ??

20. Why WOULD "The Fox and Her Friends" (Little Gretchen and the Boys) Make   67
Really GREAT Media Consultants ???

21. WHY Do We Hafta Call Them "Secretaries", And Can We Pleeease NOT ???   69

22. WHY Do the NIPers Want to Take 13 Bomb-Bustin' Buses Across ALL of the   70
50 GREAT GOD-Fearin' United States THREE Times ???

23. How CAN Ya Make Over $10 Million in ONE Month ???   74

24. Do Y'all Have Jest ONE God, or a "Family" of GODs Like MINE ???   75

25. What Ever HAPPENED ta Noah's Ark, AND Why Cain't We FIND it ???   76

26. WHY is the RAPTURE Due to Occur in the Spring of 2033 and ARMAGEDDON   79
in 2040 ???

27. Are YOU a "miss, Miss, MISS" Type or a "make it, Make It, MAKE IT" Type ???   82

28. WHY Do the 4 Houses of Hogwarts School of Witchcraft and Wizardry Conform   83
So PERFECTLY with the 4 Quadrant Leadership Model ???

29. HOW is SPANKING My Kids EVER Gonna SAVE THEIR LIVES ???   85

30. I May NOT Be "76....AND TIRED" Like Bill Cosby, BUTT Why DO Kids Tattoo   87
and Pierce TheirSelves ???

31. Do Ya Really OWN Yer Home And Have "Money" in the "BANK" ???   89

32. If'n Ya Can Laugh ALL the Way ta the Bank, Cain't the NIPers HOPE ta Laugh   91
ALL the Way t' the White House ???

33. Do Y'all REALLY Know Who Yer "Neighbor" is, or Do Ya Even CARE ???   92

34.   If'n the "Definition" of INSANITY is ta Do the SAME Thing Over and OVER   95
Again And Expect "DIFFERENT" Results, WHY Do Y'all KEEP Electing Those Lousy
LEFT-Leaning Liberal Damn Democrats AND Rascally Radically Religious RIGHT-Wing
Republicans Over and OVER Again….. When There is a BEST "Third Party" CHOICE
Out There ???

35. If'n "COMMON Sense" = "Universal TRUTH" = "GOD's WORD", Then   96
WHY Doesn't "GOD's Word" Make Any SENSE ???

36. IS the "GIFT o' Tongues" Alive and Well Today, AND Do I HAVE it ???   99

37. ARE We Here ta LEARN What We Need to Learn, DO What We Need ta Do, and TEACH What We Need ta   Teach, or NOT ???   100

38. What's the "DIFFERENCE" Between "Bits", "Bytes", and "MBs" (And….. NO Puppies, I Don't Mean "Milky Bones") ???   102

39. If'n Dr Pepper Tastes Like Carbonated PRUNE JUICE, Then HOW Can "They" Git it PAST the Federal Inspectors (DAMN Revenoors) ???   105

40. How Long DOES it Take ta Git a "NEW" Political Party Started, And HOW Can I HELP ???   106

41. WHY Would Arnold Be a GOOD FBI Man AND Jessie Be a GREAT Head of the (CIA)…… (SHHHHHH…... It's a "Top Secret SCI KYDEOI "……… Don't TELL Nobody!!!) ???   108

42. WHY Haven't We WON a War Since WWII ???   109

43. HOW Can We Convince ALL o' Them Thar RIGHT-ta-LIFErs that "Capital Punishment" is a "Good Thing" (NO…."Verry GOOD Thing"…NO….."EXTREMELY GOOD Thing")???   112

44. Did Ya KNOW that a Sadomasochistic Dominatrix (with Very HIGH Moral Character) in Skin Tight Red Leather is Called a "Mord Sith" ???   113

45. HOW Can We NIPers RESOLVEe the Conflict Between Creationists and Evolutionists ???   115

46. How DO Ya "Effectively" and "Efficiently" Take the MEASURE of a Man/Person ???   117

47. WHAT's the "DIFFERENCE" Between a "Value Added Tax" (VAT) and a FREEDOM Tax ???   119

48. WHY Do We NIPers FEEL that When Ms Barbara Walter's Put Together Her Little "MOST Fascinating People" Specials, She MIGHT've Missed Jest ONE or TWO of Us Out Here ???   120

49. How WOULD the NEW Independence Party Handle Foreign Relations ???   124

50. HOW Can Y'all "Beat" ANY Lie Detector Test EVER Created ???   126

51. Why Do "THEY" Say "Y'all Can't Take it WITH Ya", When There's at LEAST 3 (a Trinity) Things that Y'all CAN Take with Ya ???   128

52. Is Jehovah, Allah, and GOD Almighty Jest the SAME "Supreme Being" Doin' a Little "RE-BRANDING" Fer a "Bit" a FUN in a Pretty BORIN' Universe ???   130

53. What IS the "DIFFERENCE" Between Righteousness /Justice and "LEGALITY" ???   131

54. WHY is the WORST Thing Y'all Can Do TO Someone AND the BEST Thing   132
Y'all Can Do FOR Someone the SAME Damn THING ???

55. HOW Can I Find My SOUL Mate and WHAT Does it MEAN ta be "Mates" ???   133

56. If'n Y'all Cain't "BEAT 'em", WHY the in the HELL Would Ya Want ta "JOIN 'em" ???   136

57. What's the "DIFFERENCE" Between "Good" LUCK and "Bad" LUCK ???   138

58. Why WAS Jesus CHRIST SOOOO Dog Goned DEPRESSED All of the Time ???   139

59. Why Do SOME Folks Treat Their GOD Like Their Mother-OUT-Law ???   141

60. Y'all MIGHT Have Heard of the "12 Days of CHRISTmas", BUTT …..Have Ya   143
Ever HEARD of the "12 Answering Machine Messages of the Year" ???

61. WHY Do Bears DEFECATE in the "National Park Service" FORESTS ???   147

62. If'n We TRUELY Live Our Lives the SAME Way Jesus CHRIST Did, Does   149
THAT Mean We Will ALL End Up Being CRUCIFIED fer OUR Beliefs TOO ???

63. WHY Did David CHOOSE 5 Smooth Stones, And HOW Does That Apply ta ME ???   150

64. WHY Do Us NIPers "HOPE for the BEST", "EXPECT the WORST", and   151
"PREPARE Ourselves" fer WHATEVER Comes in Between ???

65. Why IS a Raven Like a Writing Desk ???   152

66. And FINALLY (Thank GOoDness), "WHERE" Do We GO from "HERE" ???   153

For More Information on These and Other Topics, Please Review the Collected Wit, Wisdom, and Outlandish Opinions of A. L. Nolram, the Bombastic and Beaudacious Mouth-of-the-South from Beauregard, AL on www.YouTube.com

Future Projects:

Several Words to the "WISE" (Gentle Editors):

Before I Tell Y'all About My Future Projects, I Need to Make This Point VERRY Clear: My Little Book is My Little "Baby", and I Dearly HOPE that Y'all Treat it as Such. PLEASE DON'T Try ta Perform Any Heart or Brain Surgery on My "Baby". I Have Poured MY Heart and SOUL….Mind and SPIRIT into My "Baby" and I Don't WANT Any Invasive Surgery to Disturb That Delicate Balance…..a Little Cosmetic Surgery to Coorect (Like "Coorect" to "Correct") a Physical Defect is Acceptable…………

HOWEVER What Y'all MAY See as a Physical Defect, I May See as a Disfiguration of a Very Unique and Vital Part of My Baby's Appearance (My Baby has a Lazy Eye…My Baby has a Hooked Nose…My Baby has a Cleft Pallet…My Baby has Worts, and Moles All OVER it's Body…My Baby has a Twisted Spine…and My Baby has Downs Syndrome….BUTT to Me My "Baby" is the Most Wonderful Thing I Have EVER Created…..Remember THAT as You Read ON…..). In Case Y'all Haven't Noticed, I Have a Rather "Unique" Way of Using CaPiTaLiZaTiOn, Punc?ua?!on, and Grammar (GOD Rest Her Ornery SOUL) that I NEED to be Retained. I Use Frequent and Fluent Use of, Alliteration, Simile, Metaphor (Mixed and Otherwise), Homily, Rhyme, and MANY Other Literary Techniques that I Use in "Unusual" Ways to Achieve "Unusual" Results in the Hearts and Minds (Sublininally) of My Readers (i.e., I Mix My Metaphors, I Shuffle My Similes, I Pervert My Punctuation ,and I Catastrophize My Capitalization, Along with Causin' My Grammar t' Spin Like a Pin Wheel in Her Grave, in Addition t' Causin' Them Thar Dictionary and Thesaurus Writers to BellyFlop inta THEIR Graves.)

I Also Prefer to Use 11 Pitch "Times New Roman" Typeface Because I Feel that it is the Most Versatile and Easily Read of the Ones I Have Seen. Be VERRY Careful with the "Red Ink" so as NOT ta Scar or "Bloody" My Baby Too Much. I PREFER that My Manuscripts be Edited Manually with a Red Pen and NOT "Massaged" with a Word Processor: It 's TOO Difficult for Me ta Detect Minor Word Processing Changes on My Baby. I PREFER t' Review the Suggested Red Ink Changes and Perform the Surgery MySelf Because SOMETIMES, in the Process of Making a Cosmetic Change, I May Notice a Heart Arrhythmia/Palpitation or a Brain Embolism/Tumor that I Hadn't Noticed Before and Needs Correcting (And of Course, Every Once in a While I Have to Surgically Remove My Foot from My Mouth).

 I WELCOME ALL Suggestions Intended to Improve My "Baby", BUTT Jest Keep in Mind that I AM the Parent...it IS MY "Baby", and When ALL is Said and Done (And the "Smoke" from Yer "Raging OUT of Control Temper" Has Cleared) I NEED ta Be the "FINAL" AUTHORity on Which Changes are Performed and Which are NOT. I Sincerely HOPE that Y'all (Gentle Editors) Have as Much FUN Reviewing/Revising My "Baby" as I Have Had Bringing it to "LIFE".

Back to Future Projects:

An EXTRA Ordinary Life - The UNAuthorized AutoBiography of A. L. Nolram by His Executive Assistant M. P. Gosda

The Holy Bible Companion Series from an Information Technology Perspective, The First Book of Moses Called GENESIS – "How it ALL Began"

The Holy Bible Companion Series from an Information Technology Perspective, The Second Book of Moses Called EXODUS – "Let's Get the Flock Outta Here"

The Holy Bible Companion Series from an Information Technology Perspective, The Third Book of Moses Called LEVITICUS – "What the Heck IS a LEVITE Anyway ???"

The Holy Bible Companion Series from an Information Technology Perspective, The Fourth Book of Moses Called NUMBERS – "Count 'em Up, and TAX to the MAX"

The Holy Bible Companion Series from an Information Technology Perspective, The Fifth Book of Moses Called DEUTERONOMY - ....

    Well, Y'all Get the "General" (or "Corporal", or "Sergent") Idea and Tone of My Work. My MAIN Goal is to ENTERTAIN: I Take a Little Information and Graft it to a Little Inspiration (a VERY Volatile Combination, Used Effectively by Everyone from Hitler to Gandhi) and Wrap it in a Sugar-Coating of Humor (So it Goes Down Easier AND is in a Form that MOST People Can Swallow) OR I Wrap it in a "Trojan Horse" of Humor and Shoot it Through Yer Defenses and Capture Yer Heart Before Y'all Even Realize What's Happenin'.......

Christopher Paolini (One of My Favorite Writers) MAY Have Had 4 Books in His "Inheritance" (Dragon Rider) "Trilogy" that Expanded "Itself" into a 4 Book Series, AND

J. K. Rowling (Another of My Favorites) MAY Have Had 7 Books in Her "Harry Potter" Series, AND

Terry Goodkind (Who SHOULD be Named "Terry BadEvil", BUTT I Love His Work Anyway) MAY Have Had 11 Books in His "Sword of Truth" Series, BUUUTTTTT (And THAT's a VERRY BIG BUTT)

There are 66 Books in the Standard "Holy Bible" (the SAME as the Number of Chapters in MY "Baby"). Now of Course, Several of "The Holy Bible" (Anthology) Books are Too Short and Would Need to be Lumped Together with Others to Fit into a Good Commentary Volume of the "Holy Bible (or UGMMHL, I Haven't Decided Yet) Companion Series from an Information Technology Perspective", BUTT it Would STILL Be MORE Volumes in the Series than ANY (and Even ALL) of the Previously Mentioned Famous (and Wealthy) Authors. Consider the "Commissions"......Think About it.....I HAVE......

A "Point" to Know About Me, I Am VEERRRY LOYAL (24 Years with the US Air Force, 13+ Years with the Department of Veterans Affairs, and 27+ Years with My Lovely Wife) and I Would Be JUST as LOYAL to ANYONE Who Helped Me Publish My Little Book(s). Just Imagine the Profits (and

"Commissions") on My "Future" Projects, IF I Can Get My "Baby" Published (and it Makes a "Healthy" Profit) Successfully.

Think about it..........

Whatever Assistance Y'all Can Provide to Help Ne Git MY Little Book "Baby" Published Successfully Would Be Greatly Appreciated, and "Appropriately Compensated".

Thankee Fer Yer Time And Consideration.

M. P. Gosda, Executive Assistant for A. L. "BIG AL" Nolram

"Bye, Bye fer Now. Y'all Take Care a Each Other Out There. Don't Be Doin' TOO Much Fussin' and Feudin'. Be KIND ta Each Other, AND "Above it All".......GOD BLESS AMERICA!!! as Quoted from the Collected Wit, Wisdom, and Outlandish Opinions of A. L. Nolram, the Bombastic and Beaudacious (YES, I MISSpelled "Bodacious" on Purpose) Mouth-of-the-South (And Curmudgeon at Large) from Beauregard, AL on www.YouTube.com

Hold onta Yer Derriere 'Cause Hyar We GOOOOO!!!

Chapter 1

What's "WRONG" with AMERICA, What's "RIGHT" with AMERICA, And HOW Can I CHANGE That ???

Many Folks've Tried ta Tell Me What's WRONG with America and What's RIGHT with America and Some of it Makes Sense t' Me, BUTT MOST of it Doesn't, So in THIS and MANY Other Chapters in This Little Book ("Baby") a Mine, I'm a Gonna Do My "BEST" ta Try t' Give Y'all My "UNIQUE" Perspective (and "Outlandish" Opinions) on This and MANY Other Topics. I Might PISS Y'all OFF (Probably).....I Might MAKE Ya Laugh (in Spite a YerSelf)..........I Might Even Make Ya THINK (OOHHHH LORDY, ANYTHING BUTT THAT !!!).......BUTT My GREATEST HOPE is That Y'all Will Be Able t' Say that Y'all Were....... ENTERTAINED ('Cause Y'all "SURELY" Can Use a Little Bit a Entertainment in These Tough Times...... and Don't Y'all DARE Accuse Me a Callin' Ya "Shirley"....).

In MY Opinion, There's a VERY Simple Way ta Discover What's RIGHT and WRONG with This Here GREAT GOD-Fearin' NATION of OURS All at ONCE.....Look in a Mirror. Lookin' Back at Ya Will Be Everything that's RIGHT with AMERICA (e.g., Individuality, the NEED to SUCCEED, the Ability to Endure Pain and Suffering, Patriotism, Intolerance for Injustice, the Desire to Make the World a Better Place fer YerSelf and Posterity, HOPE, etc.) AND Y'all Will See Everything that's WRONG with AMERICA (e.g., Intolerance fer Others; Social, Political, Ethnic, Religious, and Financial Prejudice; Despair; Mistrust; Apathy; and HELPLESSNESS, etc.), AND (to Top it All) Y'all Will See the ONLY Person Who Can Do ANYTHING About it AND the ONLY Person in the ENTIRE WORLD that Ya Have the "ABILITY" ta Change.

Do Ya LIKE Who Ya See Lookin' Back at Ya Out o'that Mirror??? Is there Anythin' Y'all'd Like t' Tell or Teach 'em??? Did the Person Ya See Vote FOR the "CURRENT" Administration a This GREAT GOD-Fearin' Nation o' Ours (FOUR MORE YEARS, Jest Like the Last Four), or Did that Person NOT Do ENOUGH ta Vote OUT the Current Yahoo, or Did that Person Even BOTHER to VOTE at ALL??

The Next Time Ya Look inta a Mirror, Don't JEST Check Out the Status o' Yer Latest Zit, or Try ta Decide Whether t' Shave or Not, OR Check t' See if'n Yer Makeup's on Straight, BUTT Take a GOOD LONG Look and Decide if'n THAT's the Person Ya WANNA Be (a Person to be Treated With Respect, Kindness, and Courtesy.....a Person t' be Proud of.....a Person Ya Would WANT as a Friend and Ally) or IF Maybe.... Jest MAYBE.....a Few Changes Wouldn't Hurt Ya (So Go Ahead and POP that Zit, or Shave OFF that Stubble, or STRAIGHTEN that Makeup and "Git On" with Yer Day...and Doncha Pay No NeverMind t' THIS Tired "Old Fart" from Beauregard, Alabama).

I've Heared Tell that There are 2 Topics Y'all Should NEVER Discuss: Religion and Politics, SOOO THEREFORE, This Book is Everything Y'all NEVER Wanted t' Know About BOTH, BUTT it's NOT a Discussion....YOU Have NO Say (Except ta Close This Book and Throw it Away). I Will be Doin' ALL of the Talkin' (Writin') and Y'all Will be Doing ALL of the Listenin' (Readin'), IF and ONLY IF, Yer BRAVE Enough (and Intelligent Enough) ta Read ON............HOWEVER, I Am WARNIN' Ya NOW: I'm IRREVERENT, I'm IRRASCIBLE, I'm IRROOT..TOOT..TOOT..TOOT..TOOTY...TOOTIOUS

(WHATEVER the HELL That Means…… Sorta Like That Thar "SuperCaliFragilistic ExpiAlaDocious" Word from "Mary Popins" that Can Mean ANY Damn Thing that Ya WANT it to). It Kindly a Sounds Like the NEW Independence Party (NIPer) Train Getting' Ready ta Leave the Station, or Maybe a 13 Bomb-Bustin' Bus CONVOYYYYY About t' Set Out on the First of 3 Fifty State Campaigns Across the Good Ole US of A in an Attempt t' Git Ms Sarah Palin and Mr Herman Cain Elected President and Vice-President (Respectively) o' These Here GREAT GOD-Fearin' NATION of OURS on the NIPer Ticket Fer Them Thar Nov 2016 Elections.

If'n That LAST Statement Happened t' Catch Yer Attention (Kindly a Like Hittin' a MULE Between the Eyes with a 2x4, Baseball Bat, or Axe Handle t' Git Their Attention Before Ya Ask 'em ta Do a Little GEEin' and HAWin' Fer Ya (Now Fer Y'all Out There Who Are as STUBBORN as MULES, BUTT Ya Don't Know NUTHIN' About 'em…..GEEin' Means Steerin' ta the "RIGHT"….NOT ta Be Associated with Them Thar Radically Religious RIGHT-Wing Republicans…..And HAWin' Means Steerin' ta the "LEFT"….NOT ta Be Associated with Them Thar LEFT-Leanin' Liberal DAMN Democrats…...Cause We NIPers Would NEVER Want ta "CONFUSE" Ya By Thinkin' That We'd "ASSOCIATE" ANY o' Them Thar "FINE" Folks with STUBBORN MULES……Maybe….."NOT") , THEN Y'all Jest MIGHT Find a Little Somethin' Fer Ya "Between the Sheets" of This Book (My Little "Baby").

Now I'm Givin' Ya "ANOTHER" WARNING: My "Baby's" Appearance is a Bit of a Shock t' MOST Folks (i.e., My Baby Has a Lazy Eye…My Baby Has a Hooked Nose…My Baby Has a Cleft Pallet…My Baby Has Worts, and Moles All OVER it's Body…My Baby Has a Twisted Spine and a CLUB Foot….. and (On Top a it ALL) My Baby Has Downs Syndrome….BUTT ta Me, My "Baby" is the Most Wonderful Thing I Have Ever Created………..Remember THAT as Ya Read ON, Gentle Reader…..). In Case Y'all Haven't Noticed, I Have a Rather "Unique" way o' Using CaPiTaLiZaTiOn, PUNC?UA?!ON, And GRAMMAR (GOD Bless Her "Ornery" SOUL). I Use Frequent and Fluent Use of: Alliteration, Simile, Metaphor (Mixed and Otherwise), Homily, Rhyme, and MANY Other Literary Techniques in "Unusual" Ways to Achieve "Unusual" Results in the Hearts and Minds of My Readers (e.g., AND i.e, ………I Mix My MANY Metaphors, I Shuffle My Silly Similes, I Pervert My Particlary Preposterous Punctuation , I Catastrophize My Cantancerous Capitalization, AND I Even "Precariously Dangle" My "By-Danged Participles" Along with Causin' My Poor Ole GRAMMAR t' Spin Like a Pin Wheel in Her Grave, in Addition t' Causin' Dictionary/Thesaurus Folks t' BellyFlop inta "Their'ns.)

My Intent is ta Try and SLOOOWWWW Ya Down and Read the Way I Talk (Which is Purtty Dog Gone SLLOOWWWWW….MOST of the Time…..UnLESS I'm in a "Manic" Phase, Like Right NOW… OR…..I've Had a Little TOO Much GOOD Sippin' Whisky in Me, Like Right NOW….OR…..Well, I Figger Ya Git the General Idea). I TRIED ta Explain it t' My Brother-in-Law Like This: You Have ta Treat My Book Like a "FINE Wine or a Gormet Meal" and Chew Each Word and Concept Until Ya Git The FULL Flavor of it……And Then I Came ta My Senses and Said "Fergit That CRAP…..This Book is 190 Proof MoonShine, and If'n Ya Try ta GULP it Down Like a Soda Pop, Yer Gonna REALLY HURT YerSelf……This is FINE Sippin' Whiskey ("Shine") and Ya Need ta Take it in SLLOOWWWWWLY, So's Ya Don't Go inta Anaphalactic Shock , or Fallin' Down Drunk and Passed OUT. SLOOOWWWW Down and Enjoy Life and Treat My Little Book ("Baby"), as If There Was a VERRY Deep Dark Secret Hidden in Each Word (Because There IS)……AND Because I GuaranDagGumTee Ya I'm FULL of It.

ALSO, I'm a "Bit" Deef in One Ear, And I Cain't HARDLY Hear Otta the Other'n, SOOOOOO I "WRITE" REAL "LOUD" (With LOTS a "CAPITAL" Letters, So's I Can HEAR MySelf "THINK"). I Been Taught in EVERY "Effective Writin' Course" That I Ever TOOK, ta "Write the Way Ya TALK", SOOOOOO (Since I ALWAYS Like ta Be "Effective" and "Affective" When I Take the Time ta Write) I "WRITE" EXACTLY the Way I Talk……..If'n Y'all'd EVER Bother ta Check Out My Little YouTube Videos, Then Y'all Would KNOW That……BUTT…..Y'all Jest WON'T DO it WILL Ya?? AND Yer Probably NOT Gonna Buy the "Companion" CD Version a My Little "Baby" Either (ta HEAR This Book Read from My OWN Virtual Lips……Since Nobody ELSE Can Seem ta Read My Writin' Like I CAN), So I Don't Even KNOW Why I Should Bother ta Even MAKE It Fer Ya….BUTT I WILL…..

Now I HAVE ta Tell Ya That I WOTE My "Baby" on My HP Pavilion dv7-3188cl Entertainment 17 inch Notebook with the "Cheap ASS" (NO……I Meant ta Say VERRY "Inexpensive" High Quality) Copy a MicroSoft Office Word 2010 that I Bought Fer Little a NUTHIN' on the Home Use Program (HUP) That MicroSoft Offers Through the "BIG Government" Organization that I Work (Like a DOG) Fer, SOOOOOO It is "Designed" ta Be "Viewed" in a 8 ½ by 11 inch Page Format (AND Speakin' a "FORMATTIN'"……It Took Me One HELL of a Time ta "KILL" That Dad Burned "Gremlin Demon" That Kept Tryin' ta "REFORMAT" My Typin' ALL a the Time……Like When I JEST Wanted ta Type a '1' Follered by a "." And Two Spaces…….And Dog Gonned If'n EVERY TIME that Dad Blamed Little "Gremlin Demon" Would Try ta "Indent" it inta Some DAMN Formatted "Numbered" List….), SOOOO If'n Yer a Readin' This in Any "OTHER" Way……Like One a Them Thar "Kindlin's" Some "OTHER" Electronic Gizmo, Then Yer NOT Gonna Unnerstand the "Reason" Fer the "Blank" Pages (in HONOR of the Makers a "ZORK"…..One a the "FIRST" Roll Playin' Games on the "ARPAnet"….Which was the Danged "Parent" a That "OBNOXIOUS" Little "Know-it-ALL" BRAT Called the "Internet"…That I Ever "LOVED"). AND Theres a WHOLE HEEP a "OTHER" Little Subliminal "Easter EGGs" That Are a Gonna Fall "FLAT" If'n I CAIN'T Convince the AuthorHouse Folks NOT Ta MESS with My Little "BABY'S" Formattin'……Like My "Unique" Method of Page Numberin' Fer Instance….Oh WELL….

I'll REMIND Y'all o' This a Little Later, BUTT (THIS May BE the First Time Y'all Have Noticed My BIG "BUTT", BUTT it Won't Be the LAST, I'm Here ta Tell Ya) If'n Y'all REALLY Wanna Git ta' KNOW Me, Check Out My Little www.YouTube.com Videos Out There. My Book Has the SAME Kindly a Crap in it, BUTT Y'all Will Hear it a Comin' Outa My OWN Virtual Lips. Ain't Nobody ELSE Lookin' at 'em, And I was Kindly a HOPIN' that They'd "Go Viral" Last Year or So When I Put 'em Out There. Please Do This Old Fart from Beauregard, AL a Favor (Dear Readers) and Give 'em a Little Peek. I SHORELY Would Appreciate it. ALSO Remember, Jest Like That Thar Bill O'Reilly Fella, and Steve Doocy, and Sarah Palin, I Wanna Git My Little "Baby" Out Thar on One o' Them Thar CD Thing-a-ma-Jigs, and I Don't Figger NoBody BUTT ME Could READ it "RIGHT" (NO, I Meant "CORRECTLY" ….. Don't Y'all DARE Be a Confusin' Me with'n Any o' Them Thar Radically Religious RIGHT-Wing Replublicans….NOR Any o' Them Thar LEFT-Leanin' Liberal DAMN Democrats…..I'm a NIPer Tried and TRUE……Now, Where was I??... Oh Yeah, I Remember Now…..) Exceptin' ME (Because MOST Folks CAN Read Readin' When it's Writ, BUTT They Have a Bit o' Trouble Readin' Writin' When it's Wrote……OH HELL…..Y'all Know What I Mean…….Lighten UP and Have FUN with My "Baby"…..I DID!!! Y'all SAY that Ya Don't KNOW What a NIPer IS???...........WEELLLL Then……Read On, Gentle Reader….. READ ON !!

Did THAT Crap Make ANY Sense to Y'all On Pages 1-3, or Am I JEST Funnin' Ya…..YOU Decide!!!

Chapter 2

WHAT the Heck IS a NIPer Anyway, and WHAT Do I Have to DO to BECOME One ???

This Chapter Contains Everything Y'all NEVER Wanted ta Know About NIPers (and THEN Some). The "shrt" Answer is: a NIPer is a NEW Independence Party (NIP) Thinker/Member (NIPer), So if'n Yer NOT Interested in Knowin' ANYTHING About the NEW Independence Party (NIPers), Jest SKIP This Chapter (AND MOST of The WHOLE DAMN Book 'Cause References ta the NEW Independence Party are Peppered Throughout), BUTT if'n Y'all WANT t' Know More, Here's the "LONNGGGG" Answer:

The NEW Independence Party (NIPer), Like This Little Book, is Another One of MY Little "Babies", and LIKE This Book, I Would HOPE that Y'all Treat My Little "Baby" with the Respect, Kindness, and Courtesy (RKC) that it Deserves. I AM the "Founding Father" of the NEW Independence Party....I Am THE Charter Member of the NEW Independence Party... AND Currently (Except fer My Little Tit-Turd Executive Assistant) I AM the ONLY Member of the NEW Independence Party (NIPers).

Let Me Give Y'all a Little History Lesson if'n I May. "Back in the Days" When This GREAT GOD-Fearin' NATION o' OURS Was Jest Gittin' Started (Like MY Little "NIPer") a Bunch o' Fellas Got Together and Had a Little "Tea Party" in Boston Harbor. They Dressed Up in Disguises and Got a Bit Rowdy and Had Some FUN, BUTT a Short While Later Some a Them SAME Folks "Sobered Up" and Decided ta Git a Little More Organized. They Got Together in a Little Place Called Independence Hall and Hammered Out a Little Document (Perhaps Y'all've Heared of it and Perhaps NOT) So VERRRY Appropriately Called "The Declaration of Independence" AND Jest a Short Time Later They Got BACK Together and Hammered Out "ANOTHER" Little Document (Perhaps Ya've Heared of it and Perhaps NOT) Called "The CONSTITUTION of the UNITED STATES of AMERICA".

Now I Told Y'all THAT ta Tell Ya THIS: Fast Forward ta Today (or Yesterday, or Tomorrow, or WHENEVER, Jest Make Sure it's Pretty "Close" ta Today), Because I Wanna Talk t' Y'all About a NEW AMERICAN Revolution.....No, Wait a Minute, That's Chapter 5, I'm Gittin' Ahead o' Myself....Where WAS I??..... Oh Yeah, I Remember Now....We've HAD Our Little "Tea Party" (Perhaps Y'all've Heared of 'em and Perhaps NOT), BUTT .....NOW it's Time ta "Git DOWN" t' Business and Start the "NEW" Independence Party (NIPers).

Like Every GREAT Movement in History, the NIPers Have the Following (BUTT UNlike the "Tea Party", the NIPers Have ME as Their Founder/Leader to Give 'em Purpose, Direction, and Focus (PDF) and That DOESN'T Mean Professional/Published/Portable Document Format):

A GREAT and HISTORIC Name: The NEW Independence Party

A "Cutesy" Little Acronym: NIPers (I'll Show Y'all HOW ta Use That in a Bit)

A Sign: (I'll Show Y'all THAT in a Bit Too, If'n Ya Stick WITH Me)

A Jingle: (Stand by for THAT.....Y'all Will Be Tickled "Purple")

A Theme Song: (THAT Otter Git Yer Corpuscles Corpusclin')

A Catch Phrase: (I Think Y'all Will Get a KICK Out of THAT)

Several Mottos: (They're Peppered Throughout This Book)

A Logo: (Under Construction…..We're Still Workin' on THAT)

AND a "Handbook" of OUR NIPer Values, Principles, and Standards (VPS)

In Accordance with the Values, Principles, and Standards (VPS) Contained in Our NIPer "Handbook", the "User's Guide and Maintenance Manual for a Human Life" (the "UGMMHL", Reference Chapter 10), Since it is LAST on the List, I'm Gonna Start with it FIRST. Perhaps Y'all've Heared of the "User's Guide and Maintenance Manual for a Human Life" and Perhaps NOT. There Are at LEAST Three (a Trinity) Main Versions of it Out There. Y'all Will Find, as Ya Read ON, that We Folks in the NEW Independence Party (NIPers) Like ta Deal in Threes (Trinity's) Because it Reminds Us of the Famous "BIG 3" Family Who's a Backing Us in THIS Little Venture: GOD the FATHER, GOD, the SON, AND ………GOD the FATHER's Significant "OTHER" -- More About THAT in Chapter 24).

I Don't KNOW if'n ANY a Y'all Folks Readin' This Try ta Work on Yer OWN Automobiles or NOT (I Find it DAMN Difficult MySelf Anymore with ALL a the Electronic DoDads and Paraphernalia Crap they Pack in There So Tight Ya Cain't Hardly Git a Finger in Edgewise), BUTT it is Kindly a Like There Are 3 MAIN Versions of Auto Maintenance Manuals (Chilton, Clymer, and Haynes), and Everyone has Their Preference; In the SAME Way There Are 3 MAIN Versions of the "User's Guide and Maintenance Manual for a Human Life" (UGMMHL): Ya Have Yer "Torah" that SOME Folks Subscribe to, Ya Have Yer "Koran" that a Few OTHERS (Especially in the "Middle EAST") Prefer, BUTT the Version that We NEW Independence Party Thinkers/Members (NIPers) Endorses is the Version Called "The Holy Bible", BUTT We Don't Call it THAT Because it Makes it SOUND Like Our GOD's Plan Has a Bunch a Dang HOLES in it And it DOESN'T. It's a PERFECT Plan, and We NIPers Foller it "Religiously".

We Believe that Our GOD's Plan is a PERFECT Plan, and Just Like a "User's Guide and Maintenance Manual" fer ANY o' Those Little Electronic Dodads Y'all are Buyin' these Days (that Tell Y'all "HOW TO" Use Them Efficiently and Effectively, and How ta Fix 'em Went They're Broke……. We Believe that Our NIPer "Handbook" the "User's Guide and Maintenance Manual for a Human Life" Does the SAME: it Tells Y'all How t' Operate Yer "Human Life" Efficiently and Effectively, and How t' Fix it When it's Broke. We in the NIPers Don't Really CARE Whether Y'all Use the Version Called the "Torah" or the "Koran" or the Version Most People Call "The Holy Bible" (or Even One of the MANY Other Versions), BUTT We DO Expect Y'all t' Foller Whatever YOUR God has Provided Y'all (Reference Chapter 6 on Them Thar GOD DAMNED godLESS Atheists).

That's Enough about Our Handbook fer Now. Y'all Can See References to it Throughout This Book (If'n I Haven't LOST Yer Interest and Attention ALREADY). Let's Move ON ta Some of Our Mottos:

How May I (We) Help Ya Today??

If'n Ya Cain't Beat 'em……..Then Yer NOT Tryin' HARD Enough!!!

If'n at First Ya Don't Succeed….Then YER NOT TRYIN' HARD "ENOUGH" !!!

Take the TIME to DO the Job "CORRECTLY" the VERY First Time.

Do the "Correct" Job, in the "Correct" Way, at the "Correct" Time. (Notice that We Use the Word "Correct" Instead of "RIGHT" ta Keep Them Thar Rascally Radically Religious RIGHT-Wing Republicans from Thinking that We MIGHT be Referring ta Them, Not t' Mention Them Thar Lousy LEFT-Leaning Liberal Damn Democrats, SOOOOOO...... Let's Not EVEN Mention Them Here at This Time EITHER)

Ya MIGHT Be a NEW Independence Party Thinker IF..... (Thanks Jeff Foxworthy)

Different "Strokes" Fer Different Folks (When Strokin' "EGOS", That is)

If'n it Ain't "LIVE", Y'all Better BELIEVE it's JIVE (Concernin' Media Interviews)

We NIP Things in the BUDS (We're GREAT "BUD" NIPers)

Constant Improvement Toward Goal-Achieving Excellence (OK...a Bit Uppeddy)

If'n it Ain't Broke.....Make it Better !!! (or Better YET....."BEST")

Always Give "Value for Value" (Thank Ya Mr Terry Goodkind, See Chapter 44)

Concentrate On the Solution, and NOT the Problem (Thanks Again Mr Goodkind)

AND Many, MANY More.....

I'm NOT Gonna Try ta Explain these Here. If'n Y'all Read ON, Y'all WILL Find Explanations and Examples in "Other" Chapters.

Our NIPer Catch Phrase is: "AMERICA Needs a Little Cream and Sugar (that's Ms Sarah Palin) WITH Yer Strong Black Coffee (that's Mr Herman Cain) to Wake Up to a Brand NEW Day in the USA, and a Little "NIP" (for the NEW Independence Party) Wouldn't Hurt Y'all a Bit". In Case Y'all Haven't Figured it Out Yet, the PRIMARY Goal of the NEW Independence Party (at THIS Time) is to Git Ms Sarah Palin and Mr Herman Cain Elected President and Vice-President (Respectively) of These Here GREAT GOD-Fearin' UNITED STATES on the NEW Independence Party (NIPer) Ticket in the Nov 2016 Elections. We TRIED ta Git 'em Elected in the Nov 2012 Elections, BUTT Not NEARLY Enough of Y'all Viewed My Collection o' Little YouTube Videos (ta Ensure They Went VIRAL), So We NEVER Managed ta Git Ms Palin's and Mr Cain's Attention to Git 'em On-Board the NIPer Train (OR the13 Bomb-Bustin' Bus CONVOYYYYYY, Reference Chapter 22) .

Our Jingle Goes Somethin' Like THIS (I'm Pretty SURE Ya'll Will Recognize the Tune Even Though There Ain't No Sound):

"I'm a NIPer, He's a NIPer, She's a NIPer, We're ALL NIPers, Wouldn't Ya Like to BE a NIPer Too?? BE a NIPer!!! And Drink DR PEPPER, the OFFICIAL Drink of the NEW Independence Party (NIPers), THAT There Carbonated "Prune Juice" Will KEEP Y'all Regular, I'm Here to Tell Ya."

Since We NIPers AIN'T Got NO Money, We're Kindly a Hopin' that Them Thar Dr Pepper Folks Will ALLOW Us ta Borrow Their Little Jingle, if'n We ENDORSE Their Product and Make it Our OFFICIAL

NIPer Drink. ALSO, We Heared Tell that Ms Sarah Palin Likes Them Thar Dr Peppers AND We're Kindly a Hopin' it Might HELP ta Git Her On-Board as Our Presidential Candidate (How About it Ms Palin???). Now, Ms Palin and Mr Cain MAY Take the SAME Ole Tired Attitude as ANOTHER Little Politician a Few Years Back ("If Nominated, I Will NOT Run; If Elected, I Will NOT Serve."), BUTT We're Gonna Try Throughout This Here Little Book a Mine t' Convince 'em (And Y'ALL) that THEY Are the "BEST" Choices fer President and Vice-President (Respectively) of These Here GREAT GOD-Fearin' United States AND that the NEW Independence Party (NIPers) Has the "BEST" Plan fer Makin' that HAPPEN (On or About Nov 2016…..If'n Not BEFORE…..) .

Our NIPer Theme Song is a Little Ditty that I Used ta Sing When I Was a "Little" NIPer in Grade School (BUTT I Don't Know WHAT the HELL Their Teachin' 'em t' Sing in School "These" Days…… If'n ANYTHING at ALL….). My Fergitter Has Been Workin' Overtime Lately, So I Cain't Remember the Name o' This Little Ditty, BUTT it Goes Somethin' Like This :

Make AMERICA Proud a YOU in Everything You SAY and DO.

Make AMERICA Proud ta SAY that You're a Son or a Daughter o' the USA.

In AMERICA You Are FREE to Write Yer Name in HISTORY..EE..Y,

So Now it's Up ta YOU, So WHAT are Ya Gonna DO

Ta Make AMERICA Proud of YOU ???

Whatever the GAME Ya Choose t' Play……..Play FAIR.

Whatever Ya ARE or HOPE ta Be…….Be SQUARE.

Whatever the ROAD Ya Choose t' Take……Take CARE,

And Walk it STRAIGHT with Your HEAD Up in the AIRRRRRR.

Make AMERICA Proud aYOU in Everything You SAY and DO.

Make AMERICA Proud ta SAY that You're a Son or a Daughter o' the USA.

In AMERICA You Are FREE to Write Yer Name in HISTORY..EE..Y,

So Now it's Up ta YOU, So WHAT are Ya Gonna DO

Ta Make AMERICA Proud of YOU !!!

I Don't KNOW About Y'ALL, BUTT THAT Kind of Patriotism Gits My Blood ta Pumpin' and My Corpuscles t' Corpusclin'. Now This "Baby" o' Mine Ain't DESIGNED ta Be NO Song Book, BUTT Fer Y'all Who REALLY Enjoyed That, We Got a Few More in Chapters 60 and 61.

Since We ALREADY Gave Y'all Our GREAT and HISTORIC Name and Our "Cutesy" Little Acronym UP Above, the Only Thing "Left" is ta "Rightly" Tell Y'all About Our SIGN (Y'all Know...... Like: Bill Engval's "Here's Yer Sign....", BUTT We're Still Workin' on Our LOGO). Every GREAT Movement Usually HAS a "Sign"..... Like the Vietnam Peace Movement Who STOLE Their Sign from the WWII "V" for "Victory" Sign....WWII Used it "CORRECTLY", the Vietnam Peace Movement Did "NOT", in the Opinion of the NIPers (AND We ALL Know About Opinions, Don't We??......DON'T WE???.......Well, Opinions are Like Anuses..... Everybody's Got One, They ALL Have Holes in 'em, and They ALL Stink.......Except'n ta the OWNER of the Anus.....Ta THEM it Smells Like a "Breath of Fresh Air".....Ta Everybody ELSE it Jest Sounds Like a FART.....). The "Sign of the NIPers" is a Little Tough ta Describe, BUTT Let's Give it a Shot ("BANG!!"....Weren't That 3 Shots???) Shall We??.....

Step 1. Raise the First 3 Fingers o' Yer Right Hand and Hold Down Yer Pinky with Yer Thumb (with Yer Palm Facin' Forward, Away from Yer Body) and Slightly Separate the 3 Fingers and Wiggle 'em Back and Forth in Recognition of Our Backers, the "Holy" (Remember.....No HOLES in THEIR Plan) Trinity (the "BIG 3"........GOD the FATHER, GOD the SON, AND........GOD the FATHER's Significant "OTHER"........Where Do Y'all THINK the Concept of Human Beings Living in Families CAME from Anyway.....Father, Mother, Children??). Anyhow Now....

Step 2. Snap Yer 3 Raised Fingers Together so that it Kindly a Looks Like the Sign of the Boy Scouts (a VERRY Fine and UP Standin' and OUTSTANDIN' Organization), and THEN.....

Step 3. Flip it Around BassAckerds (Now, "BassAckerds" is a "Technical" Term Meaning ta Flip Somethin' Around 180 Degrees, We NIPers are FAMOUS fer THAT....It's One o' Our BEST Magic Tricks, If Y'all Keep Reading Y'all Will SEE What I Mean)......

In Keeping with the NIPers Habit of Dealing in Trinity's (Notice the "3" Steps to Make the "Sign of the NIPers"), There are "Three" (Count 'em....."3") MAIN Uses fer Our NIPer "Sign":

1. Ta Show Support fer the NEW Independence Party (NIPers) in Our Goal ta Git Ms Sarah Palin and Mr Herman Cain Elected President and Vice-President (Respectively) of These Here GREAT United States on the NIPer Ticket in the Nov 2016 Elections (It's a Little Multiple-Choice Test They Give Us AMERICANS Every 2-4 Years or So, Where Yer SUPPOSED ta Pick or Write-In the "BEST" Answer, BUTT MOST Folks Screw it UP and Pick or Write-In the WRONG One.....Like THIS Year... Or LAST Year, Dependin' on HOW Long it Takes Yer Sorry ASS ta Git Around ta Readin' This Here Little "Baby" a Mine That I Been Pourin' My HEART and SOUL inta, and Ya DON't Appreciate it, And Ya DON'T Go ta www.YouTube.com and Watch My Little Videos, AND Ya DON'T Read or Reply ta My E-Mails, AND Ya AIN'T Sendin' NO Donations ta P.O. Box 2149 Tuskegee, AL 36083.....And I Ain't NEVER Gonna Git That Thar ROOF Fixed and My WIFE is Gonna "D-I-V-O-R-C-E" Me ANY Day Over it.....And I DON't Know WHY I Even BOTHER ta Try and Git ANYTHING Through Them Thar Dad Gummed THICK Sculls and HARD Heads o' Yours That I WISH I Had a BIG Enough 2x4, or Baseball Bat, Or AXE HANDLE That Could BEAT Some Sense inta Ya......OOPS !?!....Did I Type That Out LOUD !?!......Fergit What I JEST Said.......I Was JEST Funnin' Ya......MAYBE.....).

2. Ta Remind Everyone of the NIPer Motto "We NIP Things in the BUDS" (Y'all KNOW That's How Ya Turn a Stallion inta a GELDIN' or a Bull inta a STEER, Like We're Gonna HAVE ta Do with SOME o' Them Thar Senators and Congressmen Who Git in OUR WAY.......Ya NIP 'em in the BUDS). To Use THIS Form of the Sign, Ya Kindly a Have ta Combine the 3 Above Steps into ONE …Real Fast ....Like a Set of "BUD" NIPers…....Y'all Git the Idea.......Movin' ON.......

3. I Saved the "BEST" fer LAST (the Position of HONOR). I'd be Willin' to BET Y'all ANY Amount That THIS'll Be the Way Y'all 'r Gonna Use the "Sign of the NIPers" Every Dog Gone Day: Ms Palin....Listen Up, Dear Lady.....See If'n THIS Use of the "Sign of the NIPers" Wouldn't Have Come in Handy for Ya in Some of Yer PAST Dealings with the Press, Especially When Them DEBs (Demonic Evil Bitches) Ask Ya Those Penis-Suckin' Questions......CAN I Say Penis-Suckin'???.....Yeah, I Think it Was a "Different" Compound Word in the Late GREAT George Carlin's "List of 7 Words You Can't Say on TV"…....Well Hush My Mouth......I Ain't Even ON that Dad Blamed Babble Box'n BoobTube ….. ....YET.......Movin' On.....). Y'all Will NEVER Understand THIS Use of the NIPer "Sign", If'n I Don't Explain What We NIPers Mean by Penis-Suckin' Questions, so Kick Back and Take Yer Shoes Off..... We'll Git Back ta This "Third" (Trinity) Usage of the NIPer Sign after THIS Little "Public Service" Announcement from the NEW Independence Party (NIPers):

Ms Palin.....Dear Lady.....Please Sit THIS One Out While I Try ta Convince Mr Cain that the NIPers Jest MIGHT Have a Little Sumthin' to Entice "Him" inta Our Fold TOO......Mr Cain.....Listen Up, Kind Sir: Back in the High School Where I Gradiated Valedictorian (that's the "Top Dog" for Those of Y'all Who Don't Recognize the Term Because the Schools THESE Days Want EVERYONE to be "Equally" Mediocre.....More on That in Chapter 30) in the Boys Locker Room (Y'all Can SEE Where This is Goin' Cain't Ya.......SOME of Y'all DO.......Some of Y'all Don't….....BUTT MOST of Y'all Haven't Got a "CLUE".....) There Was This "Question" that "They" Liked ta Ask. I'm Gonna TELL Y'all "RIGHT" Up Front (So's Y'all Won't Be "LEFT" Out) that There is NO GOOD Answer ta THIS Question: It is Designed t' Be Inflammatory and Cause Conflict, and NOT ta Seek Quality Information (Kindly a Like MOST of the Questions the PRESS Asks Folks these Days........Except fer FOX Network.......THEY Don't Tend to Take "Cheap Shots".....They USUALLY Seek Quality, Fair and Balanced Information) and I THINK When Y'all Hear it, Y'all Will Understand WHY We NIPers Call it a Penis-Suckin' Question: Here it is: (Now Mr Cain......Ya Realize that This is Jest an Example and We in the NEW Independence Party (NIPers) Would NEVER Ask THIS o' YOU , or Anyone ELSE fer that Matter) "Would Ya Suck My Penis IF'n I Washed it??" Now, That's NOT the EXACT Phraseology "They" Used (I'm Jest a Paraphrasin' and Usin' More "Technical" Terms fer Propriety's Sake), BUTT I'm Pretty SURE that Y'all Can SEE that There is NO GOOD "Yes" or "No" Answer to THAT Question (Like MANY the "Press" Ask), BUTT For Those of Y'all Without a "CLUE": If'n Ya Answer YES, They Drop Their Drawers and Say, "Well Have AT it", and If'n Ya Say NO, They Say, "Well, I Wouldn't Want YOUR Mouth on MY Penis If Yer One o' Them Thar "DIRTY" Penis Suckers"......See What I Mean….. NO GOOD "Yes" or "No" Answer….(Jest Like Them Ones the "PRESS" Ask…Except'n Fer FOX Network That is…)…

Now I Told Y'all THAT One to Tell Ya THIS One........Where was I.......Oh Yeah, I Remember Now…. The 3rd (and MOST Valuable…..in the Position of HONOR) Use of the "Sign of the NIPers": Whenever the Press Asks Us NIPers One of Them Thar Penis-Suckin' Questions, Where They Try ta SPIN things t' the "LEFT" if'n They're One of Them Thar LEFT-Leaning Liberal Damn Democrats, or SPIN t' the "RIGHT" if'n They're One of Them Thar Radically Religious RIGHT-Wing Republicans.......

By the Way, We NIPers Stay in the "Neutral Zone" (Did Y'all HEAR That "Trekkies"??...Yes I HAVE Seen a Star Trek or 2....My WIFE Loves 'em and SO Do I.....), Straight Down the Middle of the Road, We NIPers Flip Them the "Sign of the NIPers" (Holdin' ROCK Steady on Step 3) as We Say: "Read Between the Lines and Spin on This .....READ Between the LINES and SPIN on THIS......I Say it 3 Times for the Trinity, READ BETWEEN THE LINES AND SPIN ON THIS !!!". We NIPers Find that THIS Political Tactic Works VERRY Well ta Put the KyBosh on ALL of Those Penis-Suckin' Questions from the Press. Since We NIPers Treat OUR Political Campaigns as if We were Goin' to WAR, We Have MANY Tactical and Strategic Plans fer Gittin' Y'all Elected. Ms Palin....Dear Lady.....And Mr Cain....Kind Sir.....Please Feel FREE ta Use the "Sign of the NIPers" as Y'all See Fit........a Little "GIFT" from the NIPers to Y'all in the HOPES That Y'all MIGHT Consider Bein' Our Presidential and Vice-Presidential Candidates (Respectively) on the NEW Independence Party (NIPer) Ticket for Them Thar Nov 2016 Elections.

One LAST Benefit of the NEW Independence Party is that Y'all DON'T Have ta Give UP Yer "CURRENT" Political Party Affiliation...as a Matter a FACT, We NIPers Want Y'all ta STRENGTHEN Yer Relationship with Yer "CURRENT" Political Party ta Draw Even MORE Folks Under the NIPer Umbrella.......Let Me Explain it ta Y'all in a Little "Different" Way........My Lovely Wife is a Medical Technologist, and She Has ALL o' These Little "Letters" After Her Name ta TELL Ya THAT......She Has a "MT" ta Indicate that She is a "Medical Technologist".....She Has a "CLS" ta Indicate that She is a "Clinical Laboratory Scientist".....She COULD Have a "BS" (Although She Doesn't TEND ta Be a BS'n Kind a Gal.....She's USUALLY Pretty Straight Forward......"Damn the Torpedos....And FULL Speed Ahead") ta Indicate that She has a "Bachelor's Degree in Biology".....She Has a "MS" ta Indicate that She Has a "Master's Degree in Hospital Administration", etc......I THINK Ya SHOULD Have Gotten the "Point" (Up Yer Anal Orifice) that Ya CAN Have MORE Than ONE Letter After Yer Name...... SOOOOO.......How Does This Apply ta Y'all??.....

Instead of Jest Havin' a BIG "R" or "D" (OR "I", "L", "G", "C", "S", or Even "T" Or WHATEVER "Other" Little Letter Y'all Use ta Indicate Yer "Current" Political Party of Choice....By the WAY, How's That Workin' OUT Fer Ya.....How's Yer "Current" Political Party been Treatin' Ya Lately??......Are Ya MAYBE Jest a Bit DISSatisfied with Their "Performance" Recently and MAYBE in the Market Fer Sumthin' "NEW") After Yer Name ta Indicate Yer Political Preference, ConSider THIS:

"Current LETTER", n	=	Someone with a "Little" NIPer Thinkin'
"Current LETTER", N	=	Someone with a "LOT" of NIPer Thinkin'
n, "Current LETTER"	=	Past the "Tippin'" Point, a "NEW" Little NIPer Member
N, "Current LETTER"	=	a STRONG NIPer Who "LEANS" to "Current Party"
N, "Current letter"	=	a STRONG NIPer Who "leans" to "Current Party"
N, "NO Other Letter"	=	a Tried and TRUE NIPer "ALL the WAYYYYYY"

This Would Give Yer Constituency a "Better" ("BEST"??) Idea of Yer Political "LEANin's" than the "Current" Method of ONLY Puttin' ONE Letter Behind the Names of "ELECTED" Representatives ta the Federal, State, and Local "BIG Governments".

One VERRY LAST Thing Before We Move On ta the NEXT Chapter in this Little Saga: A While BACK There Was This Little Lady Who Said, "It Takes a Village to Raise a Child", WELLLL….. I'm Here ta Tell Y'all, It's Gonna Take an "ENTIRE NATION" ta Raise MY Little "Baby"...........MY Little "NIPer"..... from Beauregard, AL to 1500 Pennsylvania, Avenue, Washington, D.C. AND If'n Y'all Don't THINK We Can Manage t' "PULL it" Off (Or "JERK Ya" OFF)….. You THINK AGAIN !!!

Did THAT Crap Make ANY Sense to Y'all on Pages 4-11, or Am I JEST Funnin' Ya....YOU Decide!!!

Chapter 3

WHAT is a "Call to Service", and HOW Can I GIT One ???

"Back in the Days", the Old Timey Churches Used ta Make "Calls to Service" t' Respected Members of the Community ta Serve as Deacons, Sunday School Teachers, Lay Pastors, etc. to "Pay Forward" the MANY Blessings that Their GOD Had Granted Them.

The NEW Independence Party (NIPers) Would Like ta "REVIVE" this "Time Honored" Tradition by Making a "CALL to Service" ta a Few AMERICANS Who We Feel Have Been "Graciously" Blessed by GOD, and We Think it's HIGH TIME that They "Pay Forward" that Blessing t' the AMERICAN Public in the Form of "Public Service". We Don't WANT Yer "MONEY" Folks…..We're Gonna Make a Pile of it Off'n This Here Little Book o' Mine (We HOPE Anyways). What We NIPers (and the ENTIRE AMERICAN PUBLIC, Who We HOPE Will ALL Want t' Become Our Little NIPers) WANT From ALL of Y'all (Who are Listed Below and Have Been BLESSED with FAME and FORTUNE by the GOOD LORD Above) is the BELIEF of Your HEARTS/SPIRITS, the Knowledge, Wisdom, and GOOD Judgment of Your MINDS/SOULS, and the ACTIONS/HARD WORK of Your Bodies. That's What's "Valuable" ta Us NEW Independence Party Thinkers/Members (NIPers).

I Heard Tell that There was ANOTHER Little Fella a Couple Thousand Years Ago Who Put Together a CORE Constituency of About 12 Community Leaders and Tried to Change the World, BUTT They Hung HIM on a CROSS……….We're Kindly a HOPIN' that Since We're ONLY Trying ta Jest "NEW" Revolutionize a "Single" GREAT GOD-Fearin' NATION (the Good Ole US of A), that Might NOT Happen ta Us (and ESPECIALLY t' ME)……We'll Hafta See……Hold onta Yer Derrieres 'Cause Here We GOOOOOO!!!…..

Sarah Palin: Yer Called ta Service by the NEW Independence Party (NIPers) as Our "Madam" Presidential Candidate. We Fersee "Tough Times" Ahead fer Our GREAT Nation and We Think YOU Would Be the "BEST" Suited to Steer Our Ship of State Through the Troubled Waters Ahead. You Was the Governor (Leader) of the GREAT State of Alaska (the Largest US State with One of the Most Inhospitable Environments on the Planet). Ya KNOW How ta Live off o' the Land by Shootin', Trappin', And "Hookin'" Yer Own Game and Fish, AND ta Survive Well WITHOUT the Technology that So Many AMERICANS Have Come ta DEPEND On (Reference Chapters 31 and 38). We NIPers Read (Welll….Not Really READ, We Listened to it on CD MANY Times) Yer Little Book (Baby) "GOING ROUGE" and TOTALLY AGREE with Yer Choices (Even Though a Few of Those LEFT-Leaning Liberal Damn Democrats AND Radically Religious RIGHT-Wing Republicans Tried to Brand Ya as a "Quitter"). As Far as THEY are Concerned, Yer"Damaged Goods" Dear Lady, BUTT that Makes Ya PERFECT fer the NIPers…….to Paraphrase Our NIPer Handbook, "The Stone Which the (OLD) Builders Rejected, We (the "NEW" Independence Party, NIPers) Have Made the Head of the Corner" …..Sound Familiar??? (Fer MORE Info See Chapter 18).

Herman Cain: Yer Called ta Service by the NEW Independence Party (NIPers) as Our Vice-Presidential Candidate. Yer Hard-Nosed Business Sense Coupled with Ms Palin's Political Savvy (Hard Earned), and the NIPers Marketing Skills and Support Will Make an UNBEATABLE Combination (Besides, We Heared Tell that When Y'all Have Our TRINITY "BIG 3" Backers on Yer Side, Ain't NO ONE Can Stand Against Ya), and We KNOW Ya Can Do a Better Job Than the "Current" VPOTUS (Who the HELL Couldn't???). Let Me Throw a Little Icin' on the Biscuit and Gravy on the Cake.......OR the Tother Way 'round if Ya'd Druther......We NIPers Have Found a Little "Loophole" in the Law that Could Keep YOU and Ms Palin in the White House fer as LONG as Y'all WANT.....You Listen Up TOO Ms Palin......the Damn Dems and the Radical Repubs Haven't Figured THIS One Out Yet......This is a NEW Independence Party (NIPer) "Revelation".....Grover Cleveland Alexander Showed Us the Way.......

    THIS is for the BOTH of Y'all (as a Tag Team), So we're Starting a NEW Paragraph: Plus it Helps ta Separate Y'all from the REST of the NIPer CORE Constituency Below. The KEY to UNLock That Thar Little "Loophole" is the Famous NIPer "BassAkerds Magic Trick" (AND as We Said a Little Bit Earlier, BassAkerds is a "Technical" Term Meaning ta "Flip" Something Around 180 Degrees), SOOOOO..... We Want ta Run Ms Palin fer President and Mr Cain fer Vice-President the FIRST Time Around ta Elect the FIRST "Lady" (and Remember there is a "BIG" Difference Between a "Woman" and a "Lady") "Madam President" And to Wash the "Taste" of the "Current" Administration from AMERICAN Minds, BUTT After Ms Palin's FIRST Term, She May WANT ta Take a Little Sabbatical as Vice-President to Mr Cain as President. We NIPers Don't WANT Another AFRICAN-American President (AMERICA has Had a BUTT Full of that).......So We Want YOU, Mr Cain to Re-Brand YerSelf (We Promise that it Won't Hurt a Bit) as an AMERICAN-African President. In the NEW Independence Party, We Like ta ALWAYS Put AMERICA "First" (I HOPE Ya Don't Mind, Reference Chapter 12). So Y'all See, If'n Mr Cain and Ms Palin Git Elected and CONTINUE ta Do a GOOD JOB fer the NIPers and the REST of AMERICA, They Can KEEP "Tag Teamin'" Each Other EVERY 4 Years fer as LONG as They WANT to (Don't Give Us NIPers a "Loophole" or We'll Drive a Truck Through IT........or MAYBE Even a 13 Bomb-Bustin' Bus CONVOYYYYY.....Reference Chapter 22).

    Barbara Walters: Yer Called ta Service by the NEW Independence Party (NIPers) as Our "Feminine" Representative to the More "Mature" Generations. We NIPers Like t' Stress Our "Family Values" and We Feel that There is NO BETTER Way than By Example, SOOOO We Would Like YOU t' Be the (as We Say in the South) G-Ma of the NEW Independence Party. You Would Be a Shinin' Example fer Them Thar More "Mature" Baby Boomers Out There t' Emulate. You ARE a LADY of the HIGHEST Caliber (Which Makes Me Think that "They" Must be Payin' Ya a BUTT Load a MONEY ta Be Seen by ALL AMERICA Sittin' with Some o' Them Thar DEBs on "The View"). If'n Y'all Fergot What DEBs Stands fer, Jest Back Yer Eyes Up the Road a Piece t' the LAST Chapter Where We was Talkin' About the "Third" Use of the "Sign o' the NIPers" (....Oh HELL.....I'll Jest GIVE it t' Y'all THIS Time, BUTT Pay Better Attention from Now ON......I Ain't Flappin' My Gums Jest t' Stir Up a Warm Breeze.....DEBs= Demonic Evil Bitches)......I Think It's About Time Fer Me ta Move ON.......

    Robert Duvall: Yer Called ta Service by the NEW Independence Party (NIPers) as Our "Masculine" Representative ta the More "Mature" Generations. Every GREAT LADY Should Have a

GREAT GENTLEMAN By Her Side (Like Me and My Wife…..He Said Humbly), and We NIPers Cain't Think a NO Better Fella t' Stand Next ta Ms Walters (as Our G-Ma Figure) that YOU (as Our G-Pa Figure). Now Y'all Ain't Gonna Be Expected ta "Get Physical"……This is Strickly a "Totally Platonic" Relationship fer the Sake o' the NEW Independence Party (NIPers). We NIPers Heard Tell that YOU Supported Ms Palin the LAST Time She Ran fer Public Office with That Thar Little McCain Fella, and So We was Kindly a Figgerin' that Ya Wouldn't Mind TOO Much Helpin Us NIPers Git Her Elected t' the Highest Office in the Land. Now I'm PROBABLY Gonna LOOSE a Lotta Ya Here, BUTT I Just Have ta Say This About Mr McCain: He Served Durin' the Vietnam Era Where They was Trained t' "Endure Torture" (Kindly a Like the Entire NATION is Gonna Have ta Endure the Torture of the NEXT FOUR YEARS), BUTT We NIPers Would Rather Return t' the Trainin' of the GOOD Ole Days of WWII (Where Ya Didn't "Endure Torture"……..Ya ESCAPED or Ya DIED TRYIN' ta ESCAPE, So Ya Could Come BACK with the CAVALRY and FREE Yer BUDDIES!!!.....Semper FI !!!!!).

We NIPers Have a PLAN (Laid Out "Between the Sheets" of This Little Book) Fer ESCAPIN' the SLAVE State o' MASSA President (and His Vile Adictive Drug Called "WELFAIR"…..the More Ya Git……the MORE Ya WANT/NEED), While He Attempts t' ENSLAVE the Nation Under the Auspices of the "NANNY State" and "BIG Government" (Which is Just ANOTHER Form of "Southern" Slavery, Where the Massa's Fed, Clothed, and Housed their Slaves…..BUTT at LEAST They Made Them Git Off'n Their DEAD ASSES and WORK fer a Livin') as We NIPers Take Our 13 (that Stands Fer 1 GOD in 3 PERSONS …..Our "LUCKy" Number) Bomb-Bustin' Busses (Like the Ones in Afghanistan, BUTT Modified t' NIPer Specifications for ADDed Safety and Comfort) Across ALL 50 of the GREAT United States (ta Stand Toe t' Toe with "Each and Every" AMERICAN Who Wants t' Take the Time and Effort t' Come OUT ta Meet Us) THREE TIMES (Planned in 2013….Our "LUCKy" Year and Executed , Even Better'n Better Each Year, in 2014, 2015, and 2016).

WHAT the HELL are Y'ALL THINKIN'……. Lettin' Me Git OFF Topic Like That….Now What the HECK Am I Supposed ta Tell Y'all in Chapter 22??? Wake UP PEOPLE !!! When I Git OFF Topic Like That…Don't Just Let Me Ramble ON…..Give Me a Good Ole Poke in the Ribs and Say, "Wasn't You SUPPOSED to Be Making a Few "Calls to Service" fer Them Thar CORE Constituency Positions You Had Mentioned Earlier???" So Now That We're ALL On the SAME Page……Let's TURN that Page and Move ON….

Before We Git inta The Nominations fer the Executive Cabinet Positions We NIPers Need t' Explain the Difference Between "Secretary" and "Executive Director", BUTT I Need ta Take a Potty Break, So Y'all Turn ta Chapter 21 (Since I Already Done Wrote That One and I Don't Like t' Chew My Cabbage Twicet By Reapeatin' it Here) and By The Time Y'all Git Done with Chapter 21, I'll Be Done with My Potty Break….the Good Lord Willin' and the Creek Don't Rise…..And We'll Meet Right Back Here…… GO ON…….GIT…..Y'all REALLY Do NOT Want t' BE Here Durin' My Potty Break……….I Can GaranDangGumTee it……..

WHEW!!! That Sure Did Take a Load OFF'n My Mind……My Dad Always Used t' Say That I Was Carryin' My Brains in My BUTT, and If'n He Kicked it HARD Enough, He MIGHT Jest Knock 'em BACK Up inta My Thick Scull Where They Belonged. It Musta Been a Bit Crowded in There, Because I Feel a WHOLE Lot Better Now…….And Now That Y'all Have Had a Chance ta Git that Picture of "Colin Powell in a MiniSkirt Bein' Chased Around the Oval Office Desk by Sarah Palin" Outta Yer Head

AND Know the Difference Between a "Secretary" And an "Executive Director", We Can Continue…..
ON……….SEE…..I TOLD Y'all ta Go Read Chapter 21 Whilst I Potty'ed, and Y'all Didn't DO it ……
DID Ya???……Maybe NEXT Time Y'all Will DO as Yer TOLD Instead o' Bein' Such Obnoxious
Folks……Go Ahead….... We'll Wait on Ya…………………………………………………………………………..
That Sure Took LONNGGG Enough…..Was You a Bit "Sloowwwww" in School???

     Oprah Winfrey: Yer Called ta Service by the NEW Independence Party (NIPers) as Our
Executive Director of the Department of State. We NIPers KNOW How GREAT Ya Are With Them
Funny Little Critters Called Human Beings that This Here Planet Seems ta Be "Infested" with, and We
Figger that Ya'd Do a Jam Bang Up Job o' Improvin' Our International Relationships with Some a OUR
More "Difficult" Customers (Ya Know…..the 10% a Yer Customers that Take Up 90% a Yer Time)….
AND We Figger Yer about the ONLY One Who CAN (or KNOWS aTEAM of Folks Who CAN) Hekp
US NIPers "Plan and Execute" a 13 Bomb-Bustin' Bus 50 State NIPer Campaign Tour 3 Years in a
ROW……WOW !!! (That's an Acronym Folks that Stands for "Wild Outlandish Wounderousness"). It's
Gonna Be a Friggin' Logistical Nightmare, BUTT (There I Am a Showin' Ya My BIG BUTT Again) We
New Independence Party Members Have FAITH and BELIEVE That YOU CAN DO IT !!! And If'n Ya
"Review" This Here Chapter, Ya Should Find: 3 (a Trinity) Ex-Governors ta HELP Ya Coordinate with
the 50 States, a Financial Wizard Who Can Help with the Funding, a TOP Notch Military Man Who Can
Help Us Secure Them Thar 13 Bomb-Bustin' Busses, a SUPER-DUPER Information Technology Man
Who can Help Us Be the MOST High Tech (Now as a High Tech Redneck Compter Network Manager, I
Know a "Fair" Bit About IT, BUTT the Guy I'm Talkin' About is MR IT…..When it Comes ta That Thar
"Information Technology" He IS "IT"….)….. AND Connected Bunch a Yahoos in the Whole Danged
NATION!!! And, of Course I'll Be There ta Help Out TOO, If'n Ya Think There's Anything a Poor Old
Fart from Beauregard Alabama Could DO ta Help. If Nuthin' ELSE, I'll Try ta Keep Ya Laughin'
Whenever We Hit a Little "Setback" That Makes Ya Want ta CRY…..OR a Soft Shoulder t' Cry
ON…..If'n Ya Prefer That…..Jest Don't Make My Lovely WIFE Jealous …..That Would Be VERRY
BAD (Fer My Health)……Ya REALLY DON'T Wanna Git on THAT Little Lady's BAD SIDE…..And
With HER MenoPause Reversin' ItSelf Lately……EVERY Side is Her "BAD SIDE"……'Nuff (And
Probably WAYYYY TOOO MUCH) Said….Movin' ON….

     Colin Powell: Yer Called ta Service by the NEW Independence Party (NIPers) as Our
Executive Director of the Department of Defense. We SAW How Ya Handled That Thar "Dessert
Storm" (or WAS That "Desert Storm"??….. Or Am I Gittin' Ya Confused With Ole"BIG BEAR",
"Stormin' Norman" Schwarzkopf ??) Task that President George Bush "The ELDER" Assigned Ya And
We NIPers was Pretty Impressed. We WAS Kindly a Dissapointed that Ya Stopped 'shrt' a the GOAL
Though, So That We Had ta Go BACK and Clean UP the Mess Under President George Bush "The
YOUNGER", BUTT That MAY Not o' Been Totally Yer Fault (We'd Like ta Discuss that With Ya, If'n
Ya Wouldn't Mind). ALSO, We Heard that a Couple a Years Ago (on NATIONAL TV No Less), Ya
Said Sumthin' Like, "There Ain't No ONE MAN Who Can Change the Political Landscape o' This Here
GREAT GOD-Fearin' Country of'n OURS", And Yer Probably "Correct" About That……Since I ("BIG
AL") Think It's Gonna Take an ENTIRE NATION (And THAT Includes YOU TOO Bubb) ta Raise Up

MY Little "NIPer" (Reference Chapter 2......DAMN Folks THAT Was Jest LAST Chapter......Have Ya Got the Attention Span of a TURNIP??.....Pay ATTENTION or I'm Gonna Quit Flappin' My Dad Gum Gums......JEESSHHH .....), BUTT (There I am Showin' Ya My BIG BUTT Again) That DOESN'T Mean that ONE MAN Cain't Git it STARTED.....Like the LAST Tiny "Flake" a Snow that Started the "AVALANCHE"...or the LAST Little "Pebble from the Pond" that Started the GREAT "LANDSLIDE" (of the NEW Independence Party inta the White House), or the LAST STRAW that Broke the Camels BACK (Who was Carryin' ALL o' OUR MONEY and BUSINESS ta CHINA).....WEELLLL ......I Think Ya Git the IDEA.......Movin' ON.....

Donald Trump: Yer Called ta Service by the NEW Independence Party (NIPers) as Our Executive Director of the Department of Commodities. WHAT!?! Ya Say Y'all've Never HEARD a the Department of Commodities......WEELLLLL.....PLEASE Let Me Explain......We NIPers Think that Yer a Pretty BIG MAN in Commodities, and a BIG MAN Needs a BIG JOB.......an We Ain't Heard Ya Doin' Much "APPRENTICIN'" Lately, SOOOOOO We Figger Ya MIGHT Be UP Fer a Little Bit o' a CHALLENGE.......On the "CURRENT" Administration's Cabinet, They Have These Three (Trinity) Departments: LABOR, COMMERCE, and TRANSPORTATION (Ya KNOW How We NIPers Like ta Pull the Famous "BassAkerds Magic Trick" and "Flip" Things Around 180 Degrees......Well THIS is Kindly a Like THAT......Our GOD is ONE in THREE PERSONS......and We NIPers Would Like ta Combine THREE Cabinet Positions inta ONE), And We NIPers Think it Would Be a GOOD Idea ta Combine These Three RELATED Cabinet Departments inta ONE and Put YOU in Charge of 'em..... Let Me Elaborate and Extrapolate (Now Ya KNOW the Difference Between Interpolation and Extrapolation Don't Ya......WELLL We Figgered Ya Did, BUTT Yer (HOPEFULLY) NOT the Only One Readin' This SOOOOOO......Let's "CLUE" in Those o' Y'all Out There Without One..."Interpolation" Means That If'n Ya Have 2 Points, Then There MUST Be an INFINITE Number of "Points" (or "Possibilities") Between Them, AND More IMPORTANTLY ta THIS "Little" Paragraph Here...."Extrapolation" Means that If'n Ya Have 2 Points, Then There MUST Be an INFINITE Number of "Points" (or "Possibilities") Beyond EACH o' Them Thar 2 Points ("OUT of the BOX" So ta Speak).....And THIS is What We're Tryin' ta Git Across t' Ya HERE).......I Think Y'all Need a "Little" Paragraph Break after THAT Mess.

Ain't That Thar Little Department of LABOR "Concerned" with the Manufacturin' and Distribution of COMMODITIES.......And Ain't That Thar Department of COMMERCE "Concerned" with the Buyin' and Sellin' of COMMODITIES.......AND Ain't the Department of TRANSPORTATION Supposed ta Be "Concerned" With the Movin' of People and COMMODITIES from Place ta Place (Now I KNOW that the "CURRENT Administration" Don't Seem ta be "CONCERNED" About NUTHIN', BUTT That's Not the "Point" I'm a Tryin' ta Make Here)..... If'n We Have These Here Three (3, a Trinity) Departments ALL Dealin' with COMMODITIES........Why Don't We Jest COMBINE Them inta ONE Department of COMMODITIES and Put Someone Like Donald Trump (LISTEN UP Son We're Talkin' About YOU) in Charge. Who KNOWS About ALL There IS ta KNOW about COMMODITIES??? We NIPers Give UP..... NO WE DON'T.....We Will NEVER GIVE UP!!!........We NIPers KNOW How the "GAME" of LIFE is Played......(and NO I Don't Mean That Stupid "Board" Game .....I Mean the REAL Game of LIFE)..... Ya Can NEVER Win......Ya Can NEVER Git EVEN......AND Ya Can NEVER Quit Playin' the GAME!!! ......Movin' ON.....

Bill Gates: Yer Called ta Service by the NEW Independence Party (NIPers) as Our Executive Director of the NEW Department of Information Technology. Since We Combined Them Thar 3 Cabinet Positions inta ONE ta Try ta Convince Donald Trump ta Climb on Board the NIPer Train (or 13 Bomb-Bustin' Bus 50 State Campaign Tour), We Got Some Room at the Table fer a "NEW" Department of Information Technology, and We Figgered Ya MIGHT a Got a Little Bored of Dominatin' the IT Market with That Little MicroSoft Company o' Yours (Which Reminds Me of a Little Story I Jest GOTs ta Tell Ya…….Yer Gonna Git a Kick in the Head Outta THIS One…..When I was Stationed in Germany Back in 1987-1991, the Captain of Our Little ADP, Automated Data Processin', Mainframe Programmin' Shop was Readin' These Damned Expensive Books He was Fond of about Emergin' Technologies and Startlin' Innovations, and He Told Us Troops "Have I GOT a DEAL Fer YOU"…..Yeah, "Right"……and He Said If'n We Wanted ta Make Some REALLY BIG BUCKS, We Should Invest in This Little Company that Was Bein' Started Up By a College Dropout "Bill Gates" Called MicroSoft……Now I Don't KNOW About ANY of Them Thar "Other" Troops, BUTT I was Young and Full of MySelf (or Full of "IT") and I "IGNORED" That GOOD Advice……Which is Why I'm Stuck Writin' This Little Book Fer Y'all and HOPIN' Ya Donate Enough Money ta P.O. Box 2149 Tuskegee, AL 36083 that I Can Afford ta Fix the Roof that My Wife has Been Complainin' About Ferever and a Day, Insteada Sittin' on a Pile a CASH) and Ya MIGHT Wanna Try Leadin' the NEW US Government Department "Concerned" (and as NIPers We ARE "Concerned" about IT) With IT and How IT Can be Used ta UPGRADE This GREAT GOD-Fearin' NATION of OURS ta FULL FUNCTIONALITY and IMPROVED PERFORMANCE Again.

Warren Buffett: Yer Called ta Service by the NEW Independence Party (NIPers) as Our Executive Director of the Department of the Treasury. Mr Buffett, I HOPE Ya Don't Take This the WRONG Way, BUTT We NIPers Think that You Eat, Drink, Breathe, Sleep, and DREAM Money, And That Yer JUST the Fella We NEED in the NEW Independence Party (NIPers) ta Handle ALL of Our Financial Transactions….AND ta Handle the Federal Government Finances as Head of the Department of the Treasury. We Figger that Ya MUST Know How ta Handle Yer Finances Efficiently and Effectively (Along with the GOOD LORD's Blessin' in Yer Life) ta Have Made Such a Wad of it, And We NIPers Feel that it's HIGH TIME Ya Put Yer Financial Wizardry t' Work Fer This GREAT GOD-Fearin' NATION of OURS. With the "Parin' Down" that Ms Palin Will Do as President, AND With Mr Cain's 9-9-9 Flat Tax Plan, And Our NIPer "Suggestion" of a FREEDOM Tax (See Chapters 17 and 47), We NIPers Feel That YOU Will Do a Jam Bang UP GOOD Job a Gittin' This GREAT GOD-Fearin' Nation BACK Our Triple "AAA" (a TRINITY) Credit Ratin'…..Dontcha Think???....Or DO Ya???.....

Note to SELF: Do MORE Research on the Cabinet Positions…..Try to Fill Them ALL…….
NAHHHHH…..Gots ta Leave SUMTHIN' Fer Ms Palin and Mr Cain ta DO ta Show the NIPers that We Didn't Make the WRONG Decision By Choosin' 'em………

Arnold Schwarzenegger and Jessie "The Body" Ventura: Yer Called ta Service by the NEW Independence Party (NIPers) as Our Heads of the FBI and CIA (Respectively). Mr Arnold "Terminator" Schwarzenegger, You Drammatically Expemplify the "Image" We NIPers Call to Mind When We Think of an FBI Man…."JUSTice" Like the "Special Agent" You Played in "True Lies"… We Think You Have the Correct "Mind Set" ta BE the Head of the Federal Bureau of Investigation. Anyone Can Learn a "Skill Set", BUTT Without the Correct "Mind Set", That "Skill Set" is Waisted. Now, Mr Ventura We NIPers Feel That Your "Attitude" and Navy SEAL Trainin' Make You a Better Choice as Head of the CIA. Like Yer Buddy Arnold…..Ya ARE Still Buddies Aren't Ya??…….Because This NIPer Plan o' Ours Ain't Gonna Be NEARLY as GOOD, If'n You and Arny's Done Had a Fallin' Out Lately and Ain't "GOOD Buddies" Anymore (Now We KNOW Ya Have This Problem a Thinkin' That Ms Palin is a "Quitter", BUTT Fer the Sake a the GOOD Ole US of A, PLEASE Let Us NIPers Try ta "Work it Out" Between Y'all Two). IF'n You and Arnold Are Still "GOOD Buddies" Then it "SURELY" Would Help This Nations Security Posture (and NO….I Ain't Tryin' ta Call Ya "Shirley") If'n the Head of the FBI and the Head of the CIA Could SHARE "Inteligent" Conversation Over Some Salted Nuts and a Couple a Beers……Dontcha Think??? …..WELLLL…..Think about it……We Have…….And WE NIPers Think AMERICA Needs Ya BOTH…..

Steve Doocy, Gretchen Carlson, and Brian Kilmeade ("The FOX and Her Friends", Little Gretchen and the Boys):   Yer Called ta Service by the NEW Independence Party (NIPers) as Our Media Consultants. AHHHHH….Come ON Folks……I Was Jest Joshin' Ya…..We KNOW that Yer Little Show is Called "FOX and Friends", BUTT (as I Tried ta Tell Ya LAST Year, When Ya WAS, and Still ARE….. NOT Readin' My E-Mails!!!) Ya Have ta WATCH What Ya Call YerSelves, Because an OLD Coot Like Me Don't Have Much ta DO ta Keep from Bein Bored t' Tears Other Than ta Try a Few "Variations" on a Theme (or Name)…….BUTT Seriously Folks…..Y'all Exemplify a "Standard" NIPer "Family"……Steve is the "Sage of the Age" FATHER Figure Who's Wisdom is Constantly Sought After, and Ms Gretchen is The Lovely and Nurtuin' MOTHER Figure Who is ALWAYS on the Side of the Same Heathen Children and Fools that My GOD is Always Lookin' Out For, AND THEN…We NIPers KNOW That it's a TOUGH Job (BUTT Somebody Has to DO it)…..That Leaves Mr Kilmeade ta Be the Figure of the OBNOXIOUS Little BRAT !!!…..Jest Kiddin'…..Maybe…..SSOOOOOO…..We NIPers Think That You 3 (a Trinity) Would Make Jam Bang UP GOOD Media Consultants Fer Us Poor Ignorant Media-Challenged NEW Independence Party Thinkers/Members……Although We DID Come Up with Some Pretty Good "Thoughts" that MIGHT be Considered Media SAVY in Chapter 48 Didn't We?????…… (For MORE Info See Chapter 20).

Bill O'Rielly, Glenn Beck, and Rush Limbaugh: Yer Called ta Service by US Here "NEW" Independence Party (NIPers) as Our SPIN Controllers. When "Combined", YOU Fellers Don't Let NO "Spin" (Whether it's ta the "LEFT" from Them Thar LEFT-Leanin' Liberal Damn Democrats NOR it's ta the "RIGHT" from Them Thar Radically Religious RIGHT-Wing Republicans) Git Past Yer SPIN-DETECTIN' Radar and We NEED That Kinda "Watch Dog" Attitude ta KEEP Us NIPers in the "Middle o' the Road" Where We Belong…..See Whatcha Think a THIS Idea Fellers: When That Thar Obamma Ramma Fella and His Family Git Kicked Outta the White House ta the Street, We NIPers Figger ta Offer

Him a "Job" That He Can Handle ta Keep Him Gainfully Employed Fer a While......We Want Him ta HELP Y'all Keep Us Straight (NO Spin).....Now We Cain't Speak Fer How Ms Palin and Mr Cain Will Feel about This, BUTT (Ya SHOULD Know By NOW That a BIG Ole "Brain Slap" is a Comin' When Ya See Me Showin' My BIG BUTT)......We Want Obamma Ramma ta Be a PAID "Watch Dog" of the Palin/Cain Administration.....AND The Entire NEW Independence Party in General......And HERE's How it's Gonna GO......If'n He Agrees.....And WE Think He WILL......Better Take a Paragraph Break after ALL a THAT.......It Even Wears ME Out.....

We NIPers Will Give Mr EX-(Thank GOoDness)-MASSA President Obamma Ramma a One Million Dollar a Year Salary WITH The Followin' Stipulations: Everytime He Cetches US NIPers Violatin' One of the Values, Priciples, and/or Standards of Our NIPer Handbook (the "User's Guide and Maintenance Manual for a Human Life", "Holy Bible" Version) "BEFORE" Any of the Three of Y'all Do, THEN He Gits a $100.000.00 Bonus.......BUTT.....If'n ANY of You Three Cetch it FIRST, Then He Gits a Little $100.000.00 Deduction Which the NIPers'll "Donate" Towards Payin' OFF That Thar "National Debt" that CHINA is So Fond a Holdin' Over Our Heads........Do Ya "SEE" the Beauty of This Plan??.....SOME a Ya DO......Some a Ya Don't......and as USUAL......MOST of Ya Don't Have a "CLUE"......Oh Well, ANYHOW NOW..... Let Me Make This VERRY CLEAR.............NO.....AND I Mean ABSOLUTELY NO US Government "HARD EARNED" Tax Payer Dollars Would be Involved......This Money Would ALL Come from the Coffers of the NEW Independence Party (NIPers) and If'n Ms Palin, Mr Cain,or ANY of My Little "NIPers" Don't WANT ta Have NIPer Funds Used in This Manner (Which I Would HOPE that They DID, BUTT Could Certainly Understand and Sympathise with'em If'n They Didn't), Then It Will Come ENTIRELY From the Coffers of "BIG AL" Nolram, If'n ANY Money Ever Comes inta P.O. Box 2149, Tuskegee, AL 36083.....Oh Well, I Can DREAM Cain't I.....Movin' ON......

I COULD Go inta Detail About How We was Plannin' ta Have Tiger Woods be Our NIPer "Prodigal Son" and Senator Dayh as Our Poor Demoralized and Dejected Little "Poster Child", and a WHOLE HEEP a Other Tails (Waggin' the Dog), BUTT.....It Would Jest Make This Here Chapter TOO Long and Y'all Would Skip it or Jest Not Bother ta Read it, and Nobody's Gonna Read This Here Dang Fool Thing ANYWAY.....And I Jest Git SOOOOOO Depressed Sometimes That I Jest Wanna....I jest wanna............BUTT.....Before I "End It ALL"......PLEASE Tell Me Ya Did NOT Think I Was Talkin' About Suicide.......WHAT the HELL Were Ya Thinkin'......I Only Have 37 Outta 66 Chapters of My "Baby" Writ So Far......I Gots a WHOLE HEEP More ta Try and Git Through Yer Thick Sculls and Damn HARD Heads Before Yer Even CLOSE ta Ready ta RETAKE that Little Multiple-Choice Test in Nov 2016 that Ya Failed So Miserably in Nov 2012......JEEZZZZ Folks.....Git a GRIP !!!......We Just Got ONE More (LAST, in the Position of HONOR, and Accordin' ta the UGMMHL NIPer "Handbook" Principle that "The FIRST Shall be LAST and the LAST Shall Be FIRST") "Call ta Service" t' Make...

The Father of Robert B. Thieme III: Yer Called ta Service by the NEW Independence Party (NIPers) as Our Spiritual Advisor. Since the Late GREAT Rev Billy Graham Ain't Available Any More (After His Little "Transfer to Heaven" Paperwork Got Processed), We NIPers (and This Entire GREAT GOD-Fearin' NATION of Ours) Have Been in Desperate NEED of Another GREAT Spiritual Leader t' Show Us that the "Slippery Slide Ride ta HELL" Ain't as FUN as Y'all Might Think, and That the

"Long, Hard, Steep Climb to HEAVEN" Ain't as Bad as it Sounds. Now, We NIPers KNOW Ya Have That Thar Little Congregation in Houston t' Think About and Ya Got Yer Very Loyal "Extended" Congregation Too, But it's HIGH Time They Quit Bein' So Dog Gone Selfish and Share Ya With the REST of the World. We NIPers TRUELY Feel That (According to the SOUND Business Strategy Endorsed by Mr Cain and the NIPers) it's HIGH Time that You "Pay Forward" ALL of the Blessin's and "Gifts" that the GOOD LORD's Given Ya, and CONSIDER Broadanin' Yer CUSTOMER Base to Include the ENTIRE AMERICAN POPULACE (One Voter…. One CHRISTian at a Time).

    The ONLY Escape Clause We're Offerin' Ya (Due ta the Fact that Yer Gittin' ON in Years and Are a Bit "Set in Yer Ways", AND That We NIPers Like ta Deal in Threes/Trnity's…..Do Ya "SEE" Were I'm a Goin' with This??.....SOME a Y'all DO……Some a Ya Don't …..And as USUAL……MOST a Ya Don't Have a "CLUE")…….The ONLY Way Ya Can AVOID Yer "Call to Service" is ta Pass it ON ta Yer (ONLY ???) SON, Robert B. Thieme, III (the THIRD….." Trinity"). He's a Bit Younger (Though I DOUBT, Stronger…..BUTT…I Ain't Met the Man in PERSON Yet ta Take the "Measure of the Man" Accordin' ta Chapter 46) And We NIPers Feel that He Would Be a "Suitable" Substitute in Yer Place… BUTT……YOU Will Have ta CONVINCE Him Because He Don't Seem ta LIKE Me Much Nun…… I'm a Bit of a "BURR Under His Saddle", I'm a Bit of a "Pebble in His Pond" (NO….That's Mr Terry Goodkind I'm a Thinkin' of….I MEANT ta Say "Pebble in His SHOE, or BOOT, or SANDAL……Or WHATEVER the HELL Kindly a FOOTWEAR He Prefers……. Y'ALL Git the General Idea…….), Needless ta Say I Rub Him RAW the WRONG WAY (ta Mix a Couple a My Favorite Metaphors)……So He's YOUR Problem and NOT MINE…..at This Time….. Unless Ya "Substitute" Him Fer YerSelf And THEN He's Gonna Be MY PROBLEM…..BUTT…..I Have the DISTINCT Feelin' That We'll Be Able ta Work Things Out Between Us…..HOPEFULLY……Some Day Soon……Maybe…..

    Before We Move ON……I Have ta Explain Somethin' ta Y'all That Yer NOT Gonna Understand…. BUTT…..at Least ONE of Ya Out There WILL……Like a Child "Screamin' Fer Attention"…..I Have Been "ACTING UP/OUT" Over the Last Couple of Years in the HOPES of Gittin' SOMEONE ta Open a Dialogue with Me ta "SET Me STRAIGHT"……BUTT….."OTHERS" Have Always Responded in HIS Place………..SOOOOOO……This is My LAST Attempt ta Git His "ATTENTION" (And If'n Y'all Believe THAT, I Have This Little Bridge in "Brooklyn" Fer Sale That I'd Like ta Talk t' Ya About….) ……I Have Four (Not 3, a Trinity) This Time, BUTT Four (4) Names that Can be "Connected" in ANY Order…..Two Are Current and Two Have a Bit of "AGE" on 'em, BUTT They're REALLY Good 'uns, Here They Are:

          Elijah……..Elisha……."BIG AL"……."Junior" (or a "Suitable" Substitute…Hint…HINT!!!)

According ta the "Message" I Got from "The Book of ELI" with Denzel Washington, the GOOD Lord is Gonna Do WHATEVER is Necessary ta Ensure that the "Correct" Information is Delivered ta the "Correct" Folks by the "Correct" TIME …….What Do YOU Think……."JUNIOR"…..???.....How's THAT Fer "Delusions of Grandeur" Dr "B"???.....UNLESS of Course it's TRUE…… If'n a "Pranoid/ Schitzophrenic Falls in the Woods" With Nobody Around ta Hear it, Does it REALLY Mean that Nobody is a Chasin' After Him???……. Movin' ON…..

Did THAT Crap Make ANY Sense to Y'all on Pages 12-20, or Am I JEST Funnin' Ya…..YOU Decide!!!

Chapter 4

WHY Do Pro-LIFE Folks Kill Doctors and Bomb Abortion Clinics ???

We in the NEW Independence Party (NIPers) Believe that the Reason SOME of Them Thar Pro-LIFE Folks Git So Hyped Up that They Fergit About the Sanctity of Life and Start Killin' Doctors (Life Savers, Like the Candy) and Bombin' Abortion Clinics (UNPlanned Parenthood Correction Facilities) is That They Have Been SOOOO Confused by Them Thar Catholic Folks (Who Have been SOOOO Confused by Their Stupid POOP....No that's Spelled POPE.... Fella's) that They Jest Don't KNOW Which Way to "Turn".....So They "Turn" to Violence. We in the NEW Independence Party (NIPers) Think We Have a Solution Which Will Clear EVERYTHING Up and Git Those Doctor Folks Out There Creatin' Cures from Fetal Tissue and Discarded Umbilical Cord Fluids instead of Bein' Killed by Them Pro-LIFER Folks.

First, Let Me Make ONE Thing Perfectly CLEAR.....We in the NEW Independence Party are PRO-Choice.....AND We are Pro-LIFE......AND There is ABSOLUTELY NO CONFLICT Between Those 2 Statements (Now HOW Am I Gonna Pull THAT One Out of My Anal Orifice???). The SECRET to it ALL is Knowin' EXACTLY When Human Life Begins, and We NIPers Think We Have it Figured Out ......Thanks to Our "Correct" Pastor Teacher (Who Shall Remain UnNamed at This Time).

HOWEVER......Y'all Ain't Ready to Believe THAT Just Yet, So We're Gonna Change the Subject for a While and Talk About Computers (While Y'all Settle Down a Bit). I May SOUND Like a "Hick from the Sticks", BUTT I'm ACTUALLY a High-Tech Redneck. I'm a Computer Local Area Network (LAN) Manager for a Rather "BIG Government" Organization. I Talk the Language of Them Thar Obnoxious Little Beasties, AND Can Make 'em Sit Up and Beg When I Put My Mind to it. I Used to AMAZE My Customers by Talkin' Trash t' Their Finicky Little Personal Computers (PCs) While I was Secretly Troubleshootin' the REAL Problem. I'd Say Things Like, "Have Y'all Been Talkin' UGLY t' This Sweet Little Darlin'???", "Ya KNOW This Baby is Sensitive and it Don't Take MUCH t' Hurt it's Feelin's???", "It's OK Sweet Heart, Daddy's Here t' Fix Yer Little Owie", "Ya Haven't been Bangin' on the Keyboard or Slappin' the Mouse Around or Kickin' the CPU (Central Processin' Unit) Have Ya???" and Other Such Nonsense.

The Users Would Look at Me Like I Had Crash Landed in Roswell (But it Seemed to Take All of the Steam That They Had Built Up, to Vent on Me, Right Out of Them and Defused a Potentially Hazardous-to-My-Health Situation), BUTT I Would Jest Ask Them the Standard Questions that ANY Really GOOD Computer Tech Would Ask, As I Kept Gently Typing Away on the Keyboard and Jigglin' the Mouse. This Kept Them Off-Balance and Diverted Their Attention While I Fixed the "Problem" (Which Was Oft Times a "Loose NUT" Behind the Keyboard and Mouse). Once Fixed, I Would Ask Them ta Sit Down and See if'n the Problem was "Fixed" (Which I KNEW it WAS, BUTT They Didn't), AND Once They (Amazedly) Verified that the "Problem" was Resolved, I Cautioned Them Once Again that Computers Were People TOO and Deserved the SAME "RKC" for the Soul (Reference Chapter 7) that Anyone ELSE Did, and I Excused MySelf to Serve My Other Customers (Amid GREATFUL Cheers of Praise).

Now that I Have "Vetted" My Credentials, I Can Tell Y'all About Them Thar Computer Beasties and Y'all Jest MIGHT Believe What I Have t' SAY About 'em. Computers ARE Like People: They have Hearts (Power Supplies) that Pump Vital Elements (Electrons=Blood) to All Parts of the Body via Veins and Arteries (Blue and Red Wires). They Breathe via Cooling Fans. They Have Arms and Fingers (on Their Hard Drives). They have Legs (to Stand on the Floor or Desk). They Have Brains With a Frontal Lobe (Central Processor), Short Term Memory (RAM), and Long Term Memory (Hard Drive). They Even Practice Social Networking via a Network Interface Card/Adapter (NIC) and Hook Up via Cat5(E) EtherNet or Fiber Optic Cables with "Male" and "Female" Connectors. Whenever the PC Builders (Companies OR Private Individuals) Put These Beasties Together (If'n They Want a TRUELY "TOP QUALITY" Product) They Test EVERY Part Before They Put Their Stamp of Approval ON it. Most Folks Don't Even Realize How TRULY HUMAN Most PCs Really Are, BUTT With ALL of that.......a PC is Just a Collection of Mechanical and Electronic Parts that Are Good for NUTHIN' Without a Soul (Operating System). Without a Fully Booted UP Operating System, the Whole Mess is Just SO Much Trash, and ONLY Good for Spare Parts.......Do Y'all SEE Where I'm a Goin' With This.....SOME of Y'all DO..... Some of Y'all Don't.....BUTT..... MOST of Y'all Hadn't Got a "CLUE".........

Let's Talk About Somethin' ELSE fer a While.......I Heard the Other Day that Back in the 60's and 70's There Was These Folks that Put on Some Kindly a Rubber Suits with Their Eyes Covered, Their Nose and Ears Plugged, AND Would Lay Down and Float in Tepid Water in Them Thar Things Called "Isolation Tanks" ta Do Somethin' Called "Sensory Deprivation Therapy". I Had NEVER Heard as Such Before, BUTT They was SUPPOSED t' be Simulatin' the Conditions of the Womb and Gittin' Back ta Their "Inner Child" or Some Such. Had Y'all EVER Heard of Such Nonsense?? I Also Heard Tell that After a Few Hours of that Crap They Couldn't TAKE it Anymore and Would Holler t' Be Let OUT, and When They DID Git Out (After Bein' SOOOO Sensory Deprived for SOOOO Long), They Would "Cry Like a Baby" or "Scream Bloody Murder". Do Y'all SEE Where I'm Goin' With This.....SOME of Y'all DO..... Some of Y'all Don't.....BUTT MOST of Y'all STILL Hadn't Got a "CLUE".........BUTT Yer JEST About Ready for that BIG Ole "Brain Slap" I Promised Y'all.......

Remember WAYYYY Back Before We Talked About Computers and Sensory Deprivation Therapy, That I Said Y'all Wasn't READY to Believe that We NIPers KNOW When Human Life Begins?? Well, NOW Yer JEST About Ready. Let's Tie This ALL Together with a Big Pink and Blue Ribbon....... There is NO HUMAN LIFE in the WOMB.........Like a Computer Without a Booted UP Operating System is JUST a Bunch of Electrical and "MECHANICAL" Parts, a Human Fetus is JUST a Collection of Electrical and "BIOLOGICAL" Parts......JUST Like Each Individual Part of a Computer is TESTED During the Assembly Process, SO Each Individual Muscle Group in a Human Fetus is TESTED During Assembly as the Nerve Fiber is Connected to the Muscle Tissue.....a Wrist Muscle Being TESTED is a Small Twitch, a Bicep Muscle is a Larger Twitch, and a Hamstring an Even LARGER Twitch, etc. We NIPers can Cause the Exact SAME "Twitchy" Reaction in a Dead Frog With a Little Electrical Current.

Yer Probably Not Convinced Yet, SO Let's Dig a Little Deeper in the Well (Womb).......Have ANY of Y'all Ever Seen the Distortions that a Human Fetus Goes Through as it is SQUEEZED Through That Thar TINY Little Birth Canal Between Y'alls Gals Legs?? Do Y'all ACTUALLY Think a Lovin' GOD Would Put ANY Living Thing (Let Alone a Human Being Created in HIS Own Image) Though THAT Kind of Torture?? Has ANY Fetus EVER Made a Sound (and Ya KNOW How Vocal We Human Beings ARE When We're in PAIN) as it is Contorted Beyond Endurance AND Spit Out Like a Mellon Seed??

("As a Lamb before the Shearers, He Uttered NOT a Word"......I'll Git ta This Later On) Can Y'all Even IMAGINE How Y'all Would FEEL if'n Y'all Had to ENDURE That Kind of Torture??? (Well, Y'all WON'T Have t' IMAGINE it, Y'all Will Be LIVIN' it for the NEXT FOUR YEARS .....Thanks to "MASSA" President Obamma Ramma and HIS "Antics").

Yer JEST About Ready fer the "Brain Slap", So Here it Comes.......After the Fetus is Removed from the Mother's Body, GOD Installs the Human Soul (Boots Up the Human Operating System) and All of a SUDDEN Things Begin ta Happen in an INSTANT of Time. JUST Like When a Computer Boots Up and the Processor Begins to Function and Starts Accepting Input from the Keyboard and Mouse, AND ta Display Results on the Monitor, So TOO With a Human Fetus.......When GOD Installs the Soul AND Boots it Up, All of the Nerve Endings Begin to Provide Input to the Human Brain and it is "Overloaded" with SIGHTS (Red, Green, Blue, Bright, Dark, etc.), SOUNDS (Loud, Soft, Sharp, Dull, Voices, Bangs, Pops, Whistles, etc.), SMELLS (Alcohol, Ammonia, Bleach, Sweet, Pungent, Blood, Feces, Starch, Perfume, etc.), TASTES (Sweet, Bitter, Salty, Sour, etc.), TOUCHES (Smooth, Rough, Sharp, Dull, Hot, Cold, Hard, Soft, etc.), AND Them Thar TOUGH ta Describe and DEAL With (EVEN fer Us ADULTS) Human "EMOTIONAL" Fellin's......AND the ONLY Thing that Poor Brand NEW "Human Being" (NOT a "Fetus" Any MORE) WITH the Consciousness of a Booted Up Soul CAN Do is "SCREAM BLOODY MURDER" !!! AND JUST Like Those IDIOTs Emerging from the Isolation Tanks After a FEW Hours of Sensory Deprivation "THEY" Let the World Know that They are ALIVE (with "Human LIFE") with That First "PRIMAL SCREAM" !!!

Let Me Speak NOW ta ALL of Y'all Pissed OFF Catholics Out There.......Are Y'all BORN AGAIN CHRISTians OR Are Y'all CONCEIVED AGAIN CHRISTians?? (OR Do Ya EVEN Consider Yer Poor Cofused Selves ta Be "Born Again" at ALL??)??? Even YOU Silly Idiot's Know that a Human SPIRIT Begins Life at BIRTH and NOT "CONEPTION", So WHY the HECK Would Y'all Think that a Human SOUL Would Be ANY Different?? According to the NIPer Handbook, the Life of an Animal is in the Blood (Body), BUTT the Life of a Human Being is in the SOUL, and the SOUL is Installed JUST Before that First PRIMAL SCREAM, and THAT Dear Readers is the EXACT Moment that We NIPers Perform the FAMOUS NIPer "BassAkerds" Magic Trick and Switch180 Degrees from PRO-Choice to Pro-LIFE AND We STAY That Way Forever MORE (Since, UNLIKE a Fragile Human BODY, the Human SOUL and SPIRIT Endure Eternally). We NIPers Believe that the Human BODY DOES Have a Beginning (at Conception) And an Ending (at Body/Physical Death), BUTT the SOUL Has a Beginning (at Birth) and NO Ending (Everlasting Life), AND the Human SPIRIT Has a Beginning at the SECOND Birth (Born Again) and NO Ending (Everlasting Life). Some "Religions" (Remember Dear Readers, CHRISTianity is NOT a Religion, BUTT it IS a Personal and Private Relationship Between Each Individual Human Being and the LORD Jesus CHRIST) Believe that NOT All Human Beings (Souls) Have Everlasting Life, BUTT We NIPers Believe that EVERY HUMAN SOUL Has EVERLASTING LIFE (It's Just a Matter of WHERE Ya SPEND that Everlasting Life.....in HEAVEN or that "OTHER" Place).

Now that We Have Y'all GOOD and PISSED OFF.......Let's Add ANOTHER Log ta the FIRE And Take it ONE Step Further......We Need to LET the Scientists Use the INHUMAN Parts of Aborted Fetuses, AND Still Born Fetuses for Research to Treat LIVING Bodies of Human Beings Who HAVE a Booted Up SOUL. Y'all CHRISTans that PROFESS to Believe that Yer God is Omniscient (ALL Knowing) and Yet Y'all Don't BELIEVE that Yer God KNEW Billions and Billions of Years Before HE Created the Universe in a BIG BANG, the Identity of Each and Every Woman Who Would Abort a Fetus and Did NOT Bother to Create a SOUL ta Go inta it?? How Stupid IS Your God?? OUR NIPer GOD (Accordin' to Our NIPer Handbook) IS Omniscient and IS "Efficient and Effective" Enough to KNOW Exactly HOW MANY Human Souls to Create to Have ONE for Each and Every Fetus that is Viable (has a Brain Capable of Containing a SOUL) And Brought to Term (NOT Aborted). Y'all Folks Out There that are STILL Undecided About Whether Y'all Believe in a God (and If So, Which One)……PLEASE Consider Being a NEW Independence Party (NIPer) Thinker and Accept the OMNISCIENCE (ALL Knowing), OMNIPOTENCE (ALL Powerful), and OMNIPRESENCE (Able to be Everywhere in the Universe at Once) of OUR "BIG 3" GOD Family (GOD the FATHER, GOD the SON, AND….. GOD the FATHER's Significant "OTHER", Reference Chapter 24).

We in the NEW Independence Party Always Try t' Remember t' Give Credit Where Credit is Due, SOOOOO in Keepin' With That TIME HONORED Tradition, We NIPers Give a BIG Ole Tip o' the Hat to OUR "CORRECT" Pastor Teacher (Who Will Remain Nameless at This Time, BUTT You KNOW WHO Ya are……. "Junior"…..) for Providin' Me (AND the NIPers) the Foundation Upon Which ta Build THIS Chapter and MANY More Throughout This Little "Baby" of Mine.

Did THAT Crap Make ANY Sense to Y'all on Pages 21-24, or Am I JEST Funnin' Ya…..YOU Decide!!!

Chapter 5

How CAN We NIPers Git Prayer BACK inta the Schools ???

WOW, We Lost a LOT of Folks with that LAST Topic. Is Anyone Left Out THERE???.... There??....there? Well, Let's Jest HOPE They Needed ta Go t' the Bathroom or Git Somethin' ta Eat or Drink (Like a Dr Pepper and an RKC) and WILL Come Back When They Get Over Sulkin'. Those of Y'all CHRISTians (the Ones Who Emphasize CHRIST in CHRISTmas instead of Lettin' those Atheists Steal the "Xmas" Spirit from Ya) that are STILL With Me are Probably Wondering What Unusual and Unique Way We NIPers are Gonna Come UP with ta Git Prayer BACK inta the Schools (Like it Was When I was a "Little" NIPer Back in District 38 School in Hall County Nebraska). WHAT!?! Y'all Didn't Think I Was BORN in the "South" Did Ya?? Can't Y'all Even Tell the "DIFFERENCE" Between a TRUELY "Southern" DRAWL and One that Has Been "Perverted" by a STRONG Nebraska TWANG?? Dig the Tater Dirt Outta Yer Ears and Listen UP!!!......

Gittin' Prayer BACK inta the Schools AIN'T No Great Shakes, BUTT it WILL Take a Little Doin', BUTT Here's a Little Way ta Git Y'all Started.......First, Y'all Have t' Understand that There is Safety in Numbers; Second, Y'all Have t' Be Ready ta "STAND UP" fer Yer Rights as CHRISTians (Remember That Thar "Bill of Rights" in the GOOD Ole US Constitution Guarantees US Freedom "OF" Religion and NOT Freedom "FROM" Religion, Reference Chapter 6 on Them Thar GOD DAMNED "godLESS" Atheists), and Third (to Fill Out Our Trinity), and MOST Importantly (in the Positionof HONOR), Y'all Have to be Ready to "SING OUT" Fer Prayer in the Schools. That's "CORRECT", I Said "SING OUT"!!! Because "They" SUPPOSEDLY Took Prayer Out of the Schools to Separate "Church" (Organized Religion) from the "State" ("BIG Government"), BUTT CHRISTianity (Upon the Values, Principles, and Standards (VPS) of Which This GREAT United States of America was Founded) is NOT an Organized Religion, Organized Religions are Things Like Baptists, Methodists, Lutherans, Mormons, Catholics, Islamists, Hindus, Buddhists, Presbyterians, Episcopalians, Pentecostals, Church of God, Church of Christ, Assembly of God, Seventh Day Adventists, etc, Ad Infinitum, Ad Nauseum....... BUTTT, CHRISTianity is NOT a Religion: It is an Individual, Personal, and Private Relationship Between Each Individual (Who Accepts it) and the LORD Jesus CHRIST (So Say We NIPers, So Say We ALL!!!).

SO Now that We Got THAT Straight, Let's Start SINGIN' (That's Correct, I Said SINGIN') Prayer Back inta the Schools. Don't Try ta Pander t' ANY Specific Religion (That Means: Dontcha Get NO Priest, Preacher, Chaplain, Minister, or Pastor t' Give NO Prayer or Invocation) , Jest Git Yer Little Pep Club Together at Yer Next Sportin' Event 'n Have 'em "Spontaneously" Shout a Little Ditty Like THIS:

> LORD GOD ALMIGHTY, Please BLESS This Game
>
> We're ALL So GLAD that These Folks CAME
>
> We're Gonna' Play FAIR, BUTT We're Out to WIN
>
> PLEASE See Us ALL Safely HOME Again, AMEN!!!

Or This:

HEAVENLY FATHER, We're Playin' ToNIGHT

FILL Our HEARTS with COURAGE and FIGHT

PUT the FEAR of GOD in Our FOES

And PROTECT Our Fans WHEREEVER They Goes, AMEN!!!

Or JEST Come Up with Yer OWN Danged Prayer Song. It Ain't THAT Hard. I'm Sure Y'all Can Come Up with Somethin' a Whole HEAP Better'n I Can. We NIPers Believe Y'all Can Do ANYTHING Ya Put Yer Mind to, and "SURELY" Y'all Youngsters in School Can (and Don't Y'all DARE Tell Me NOT t' Call Ya "Shirley") Come Up with Somethin' Better'n an Old Fart Like ME.

Now What ARE Those Dad Burned Atheists Gonna DO, TRY ta Put the Whole Pep Squad in Jail??? What IF Y'all CHRISTians in the Crowd "STAND UP" (Fer Prayer in the Schools) and JOIN in the Singin'?? Are "They" Gonna Try ta Put Ya ALL in Jail?? I Bet Those Goll Darned Atheists Will Hear All of Those Raised Voices Praisin' a GOD that They Can't Even IMAGINE (at the TOP of Yer Lungs) and Keep Their Heads DOWN and Their DAMN Mouths SHUT (IF They Know What's GOOD for 'em They WILL). AND, If Some JUDGE Tries to Side with Them Thar Heathens, Then It's About Time Y'all CHRISTians Banded Together and Voted That JUDGE Out of Office (If it's One of Them Thar "Elected" Judges) OR Vote OUT The Dad Gum Yahoo That Appointed 'em (If it's One of Them Thar "Appointed" Judges). After Y'all Clear OUT Some of the Riff Raff from Those JUDGES Benches and Their Political BUDDIES, I Bet the Ones That are "LEFT" (AND by THAT We Mean ta SAY "the Ones that REMAIN"….. We AIN'T Referrin' t' Them Thar LEFT-Leanin' Liberal Damn Democrats AND We ESPECIALLY DON'T Wanna Stir Up Them Thar Radically RELIGIOUS Right-Wing Republicans….. Cause They'd Jest Git "Otta Control" with Their Radical "Religiousity" And "Srcew" the Whole Damn Thing UP) Will Be a Might Kindlier to Y'all CHRISTians and THEN Y'all Can REALLY Start ta Git Them Prayers BACK into the Hearts and Minds of Our School Kids (Cause They Really NEED 'em ta Pass ALL o' Them Thar STUPID Tests They Have t' Take These Days).

Now That Us NIPers Have Given Y'all a Little Inspirational "Booster Shot" in the Arm (or Maybe a Bit Farther "South"), Y'all SHOULD be Able ta Brainstorm a Few MORE Ways to Get Some Good Ole Timey Religion BACK inta the Schools. Current Events FORCE Us NIPers ta Ask OurSelves if'n We Have Done ENOUGH ta Git Prayer BACK inta the Hearts and Minds…..SOULS and SPIRITS of Our School Kids AND Whether it Would Have Made ANY Difference at ALL in the Columbine or More Recent Shooting in Newtown, Connecticut.

Ya KNOW, a LOT o' Folks (CHRISTians MOSTLY) are Askin', "HOW in the WORLD Could a LOVIN' GOD "LET" This HAPPEN ta Them Thar INNOCENT Kids??", Well, I'm Here ta TELL Ya (I Don't KNOW About YOUR God) that MY GOD is Lookin' Down at Y'all and Askin', "HOW COULD "Y'ALL" ALLOW THAT ta HAPPEN TO THEM THAR INNOCENT LITTLE KIDS???"……After

HE's Given Ya the "User's Guide and Maintenance Manual for a Human Life (UGMMHL)", and Sent HIS ONLY Begotten SON ta SHOW Ya HOW ta Treat Each Other with Respect, Kindness, and Courtesy (RKC), AND Given Ya TOTAL FREE WILL with Which Y'all Can CHOOSE ta KILL Each Other OFF (Like a Bunch of Heathen godLESS Atheists) OR LIVE According to the VALUES, PRINCIPLES, and STANDARDS that HE Gave Y'all in the UGMMHL. BUTT……Don't Ya Worry About Them Thar INNOCENT Little Kids……YOU Showed HIM that Y'all Couldn't Take ANY Better Care o' THEM Than Ya Did HIS ONLY SON….. SOOOOOO Them Thar Innocent Little Kids is With HIM…….HE "CAN" Take Care of 'em a WHOLE HEEP Better'n YOU Could……BUTT If'n Ya EVER Wanna "SEE" 'em Again……Ya'd Better Git OFF'n Yer DEAD ASSES and FIX That Thar SCREWED UP "JUSTICE" System a Yours and Start LIVIN' The Way HE (AND HIS ONLY Begotten SON) Taught Ya.

We NIPers Heard the Other Day on the GOD Damned Babble Box (TV) Somebody Sayin' the SAME as We (NIPers) Said "UP ABOVE" ……That Folks Was Wonderin' WHY a Lovin' GOD Would "LET" Somethin' Like THAT Thar Massacre in Sandy Hook School HAPPEN……And They HAD a "GREAT Comeback" ANSWER That Made US NIPers VERY ASHAMED That WE Didn't Think of it FIRST ….. "GOD's Not ALLOWED in Schools These Days"………….ALL of US "NEW" Independence Party Thinkers/Members (NIPers) Want to CHANGE THAT, And Nigh onta IMMEDIATELY at THAT !!!

Did THAT Crap Make ANY Sense to Y'all on Pages 25-27, or Am I JEST Funnin' Ya…..YOU Decide!!!

Chapter 6

WHAT Do We DO About Them Thar GOD DAMNED godLESS Atheists ???

Well, I'm GLAD Y'all Asked That. This Here GREAT GOD-Fearin' Country of Ours was Founded by GOD-Fearin' People Who JUST Wanted ta Worship Their OWN GOD in Their OWN Way. They NEVER Even "Considered" Not HAVIN' a GOD. That's Why the Famous "Bill of Rights" from Our US Constitution Guarantees Freedom "OF" Religion and NOT Freedom "FROM" Religion, And it's HIGH TIME that We GOD-Fearin' Folks Make That "Point" (Right UP Their Anal Orifices) VERY CLEAR ta Them Thar godLESS Atheist Folks. Atheists Have NO god, and Therefore They Have NO "POWER", Except that Which We GOD-Fearin' Folks GIVE 'em. YOU (Ya Sorry As..ed, Mealy Mouthed, Excuse for christIANS) are VOLUNTARILLY Given' Away the POWER of YOUR GOD ta Them Thar godLESS, powerLESS Heathen ATHEISTS!!!

Now If Y'all Atheists Out There Will KEEP Yer Heads DOWN and Yer DAMN Mouths SHUT, We NIPers Will Let Y'all STAY in This GREAT GOD-Fearin' NATION of OURS, BUTT If'n Y'all Want ta TRY ta "X" CHRIST Out of CHRISTmas (MAYBE Y'all Haven't Noticed BUTT We NIPers Like ta Really REALLY "EMPHASIZE" CHRIST in CHRISTmas, and Leave the Little "mas" for ALL o' Y'all Mutherfu.....Asshol.....Son-of-a-bit..... ATHEISTS), or Crosses Outta the Churches, and Prayer Outta the Schools, Then WE NIPers Have a Little Bit of Advice fer Ya: This Here GREAT GOD-Fearin' NATION of OURS is Just SURROUNDED by BOARDERS....PLEASE Don't Let 'em Hit Y'all in the ASSes on Yer Way OUT 'Cause We Don't NEED Ya HERE!!!

And That's ALL We Have to Say About THAT!!! Thanks, "Forrrrest, Forest Gump" (Tom Hanks) and Whoever First Thunk That Line Up.

Did THAT Crap Make ANY Sense to Y'all on Page 28, or Am I JEST Funnin' Ya......YOU Decide!!!

Chapter 7

What IS Rice Krispies Candy (RKC) fer the SOUL ???

Well, I Guess We SHOULD Start by Askin', "What IS Rice Krispies Candy?". We in the NEW Independence Party (NIPers) Don't Like to AssUMe Anything, Because that JEST Makes an Ass Out o' yoU and Me (and We DON'T Want ta Do THAT, Now DO We!?!). SOME Folks Git REALLY Upset When Ya Try ta Tell 'em Things that They Already THINK They Know (and Yet Sometimes Find Out by Listenin' that They Didn't Know as MUCH or as WELL as They THOUGHT They Did), SO We NIPers Like ta Ensure that "Everyone" is On the SAME Page by Explainin' Things that "Everybody Knows".....

Rice Krispies Candy (or RKC as We NIPers Call it), is a Little Concoction Made from Puffed Whole Grain Rice (fer Good Nutrition), and a Little Oil (to Make it Slide Down Yer Gullet Easier), and a Little Sweetness (Sugar or Honey, ta Make it Taste Better). Rice Krispies Candy (RKC), It's Chewy, It's Gooey, It's SOOOOO Delicious. There Ain't MANY Folks I Know Who Don't LIKE a Little RKC Once in a While. RKC Will Give Yer Body a Little "Jump Start" AND Yer Pleasure Center a Little Satisfaction, BUTT WHAT is RKC fer the SOUL??.......

RKC fer the SOUL is Respect, Kindness, and Courtesy (RKC). Rice Krispies Candy (RKC) Does fer the BODY What Respect, Kindness, and Courtesy (RKC) Does fer the SOUL. As I Said Earlier, We NIPers Haven't Found TOO Many Folks that Don't Like Rice Krispies Candy (RKC) fer Their Bodies, and in the SAME Manner, We NIPers Haven't Found TOO Many Folks that Don't Respond WELL ta Respect, Kindness, and Courtesy fer Their SOULS. Try it Sometime (If Ya Haven't Lately). Give Some (or Even ALL If'n Ya GOTS Enough) of Yer Friends, Family, and Co-Workers (or Even the Next Stranger Ya Meet on the Street) a Little Respect, Kindness, and Courtesy (RKC) fer Their SOULS, AND a Little Rice Krispies Candy (RKC) fer Their Body at the SAME Time Wouldn't Hurt a Bit Either.

Our NIPer Handbook (the "Users Guide and Maintenance Manual for a Human Life") Says to "Cast Yer "Bread" Upon the Waters and it Will Come Back t' Ya 10 Fold." Now I was Jest Thinkin' the Other Day: Back When Our Handbook was Written (Quite a Few Years Back), Them Folks Didn't Pound Their Grain (ta "Smitherines") Quite as FINE as We Do Today; it was More of a Whole Grain (Do Y'all SEE Where I'm a Goin' with This...SOME of Y'all DO....Some of Y'all Don't.....and MOST of Y'all Hadn't Got a "CLUE"....), SOOOO that When Combined with Oil and Honey (the Way They Liked ta DO in Them Days), It MAY Have Formed a Concoction Very Similar to RKC. SO We NIPers Would Like ta Give Y'all a Little Tiny "Brain Slap" to Knock Some Sense inta Ya: "Cast Yer RKC (Respect, Kindness, and Courtesy) Upon the Waters (the Waters of Yer Life, the Waters of Yer Neighbors' Lives, the Waters of This GREAT GOD-Fearin' NATION of OURS) and it Will Return to Ya 10 Fold."

I HOPE that We NIPers Have Convinced Y'all t' Spread Yer RKC Around and Not Just Keep it ta YerSelf. It Will Make Yer BODY And Yer SOUL a Bit "Heavy" (ta KEEP it ta YerSelves) AND in These Hard Times, We NIPers Feel that We Need ta Keep Our Minds/SOULS "Lean and Mean" (BUTT If'n Ya've EVER Seen ME, then Ya KNOW I Don't "Practice What I Preach" as Far as the BODY is Concerned, I Give Away PLENTY of RKC fer the SOUL, BUTT I Been a Keepin' TOO Much a the RKC fer the BODY t' MySelf). SO..... Y'all MAY Be the SAME Way and That's "OK" (Ya Know......

Like that Little Book "I'm OK, You're OK"??......or is it "I'm OK, You're So- So"??......I Forgit JEST Which......It's Been a LONG Time Since I Read it.....BUTT it's a Pretty GOOD Little Read.......Jest Like "Games People Play".....and There's a Pretty Goodn' on Non-Verbal Communication that I Can't Remember the Title of.......My Fergetter's Been Workin' Overtime Lately.......WHOA........WHAT the HELL Are Ya Doin' Lettin' Me Ramble ON Like This???.....Now Where was I......Oh Yeah, I 'Member Now.....).

We NIPers Understand if'n Y'all Have a Bit of a "Weight" Problem, So Do MOST of Us (and We're Gittin' a Little "AGE" on Us TOO...NO, I Meant ta Say a Little "Maturity"), BUUTTT... (That's a BIG BUUTTT by the Way) We Like ta Keep Our SOULS "Lean and Mean" by Givin' Away ALL of Our RKC fer the SOUL, BUUTT (There's that BIG BUUTTT Again), Every Time We Think We've Lost a Pound or Two We JEST Look Behind Us and There it is (That BIG BUUTTT). That RKC fer the SOUL Jest KEEPS Comin' Back t' Us 10 Fold (There Jest Ain't No Winnin' fer Losin'). We NIPers Really HOPE Y'all Have the SAME Kindly a "Problem". We Think that AMERICA is Critically "Hug Deficient" and a Whole HEEP a RKC fer the SOUL Would HELP Jest a Mite. PLEASE Help Us Out by GIVIN' a Little RKC fer the SOUL ta Yer "Neighbor" Today (Reference Chapter 33).

There's Jest One LAST Thing I'd Like t' Tell Y'all About RKC fer the SOUL, BUTT Before I DO, I Need t' Let Y'all KNOW that I'm a "Big Bull Shooter" (BBS), and as ANY GOOD Bull Shooter (GBS) Would Tell Ya: a BIG Helpin' a "BS" Slathered on TOP of That RKC fer the "SOUL" Will Give it an ENTIRELY "DIFFERENT" (And Even BETTER....."BEST"??) Flavor. Now I Caution Y'all NOT ta Try This at HOME with RKC fer Yer "BODY". If'n Y'all Slather a Heapin' Helpin' of REAL "BS" on Yer Rice Krispies Candy, We're Pretty SURE Yer NOT Gonna Like it. A Word t' the Wise SHOULD Be Sufficient (BUTT We're HOPIN' That it's Enough Fer Y'all "IDIOTS" as WELL)...... 'Nuff Said .... Movin' ON.....

Did THAT Crap Make ANY Sense to Y'all on Pages 29-30, or Am I JEST Funnin' Ya.....YOU Decide!!!

Chapter 8

WHO the Heck AM I, and WHY the HELL Should YOU Care ???

Ya'd Better Kick Yer Shoes OFF, Put Yer Feet UP, AND (If'n Yer a "Southerner") Grab YerSelf a RC Cola and a Moon Pie, or (If'n Yer a NIPer) Grab YerSelf a Dr Pepper And an RKC, 'Cause I'm Gonna TELL Y'all the Sad Tail (Waggin' the Dog) About the ONLY Subject that I Know ALMOST EVERYTHING There is to Know, And EVERYTHING that Y'all NEVER Wanted to Know About….. My OWN DAMN SELF!!! …..SOOOOO, Hold onta Yer Derrieres 'Cause'n Hyar We GOOO!!!….

I was BORN Runnin' Late and I AIN'T Caught Up YET; My Mom Went ta the Hospital in Labor One Night and I Didn't Pop Out Until 3 o'clock the NEXT Afternoon. I was Born in a Little Hospital in Grand Island, Nebraska (I Ain't Gonna Tell Y'all WHEN 'Cause I'm a Bit Sensitive About My Age), and I Gradiated Second Highest from the Eighth Grade in Hall County from the District 38 School. In THEM Days (of "Yester Year" When We Had ta WALK 3 Miles t' School, AGAINST the Wind, UP Hill….BOTH Ways….in ALL Kinds o' Weather), the District 38 School Covered Kindergarten through Eighth Grade. I Wasn't NO Great Shakes at Larnin' Nuthin' Until Third Grade When the School Nurse (Remember Them, Y'all Baby Boomers??) Who Came Around Once a Year Said the "3 Magic Words"(a Trinity) that Changed My Life FerEVER……."Check His Eyes." And from Then On, It was Straight "A"s fer Me (Along with the "4 Eyes" Moniker/Nickname).

I Gradiated Valedictorian (That's TOP o' the Class fer Those of Y'all from Them Thar High Schools Where They Expect Y'all ta Be "Equally" Mediocre) from High School with a Straight "1" Average. Now BEFORE Y'all Think LESS of My High School or Git the Idea that I was "Dumb as They Come" or "Stupid as the Day is Long" , Y'all NEED ta Know that in THEM Days a "1" Was an "A", and a "1.0" Average Was an Extremely GOOD Thing and a "4.0" Average was "Bottom of the Barrel" (Unlike the BassAkerds Way Them Thar Educated IDIOTS Grade NOW). I Don't Remember a LOT from Those Days Other than I Played Trumpet in the Band and I Studied an Awful Lot, BUTT I DO Remember Goin' ta Somethin' Called "Boy's State" Where We Went ta the Capital City of Nebraksa (Lincoln) and Played Like We KNEW What Our State Government Was ALL About: We Elected a Governor, and Legislators, and Judges (as I Remember it I was a Lawyer, BUTT I Didn't Find Out About it Until My Court Date Had Come and Gone…...Ya Know, Kindly a Like a LOT o' Lawyers Today…….So I Guess it WAS Pretty Realistic), BUTT The ONLY Thing I Remember REALLY Well Was that One Night There was This Fella that Had This Piece of Paper that Had These "Fart" Sayin's on it…….Ya Know, Things Like: An Honest Person Farts Fair, A Dishonest Person Farts and Blames it on the Dog, A Vain Person Loves the Smell of His Own Farts, A Devious Person Farts and Then Says, "Who the Hell Shit??", And……. Well Y'all Git the General Idea…….. I SHORE Wish I Knew Where I Could Git a COPY o' That Thar Piece a Paper…….Ya Know…..JEST Fer "Old Times" Sake……Movin' On…..

After High School, I Went inta the US Air Force fer About 24 Years. I Spent the First 4 Years in Hawaii, and Then a Year in Key West, Florida Before I Decided that There Warn't No "Future" fer Me in Ground Radio Repair, So I Re-Trained inta Computer Programmin' fer the $10,000.00 Re-Enlistment Bonus (Not ta Mention that I Seemed ta Take t' "IT" Like a Duck Takes t' Water….Y'all Know, Cool and Calm on the Surface and Paddlin' Like HELL Beneath it), Then it Was On ta Montgomery, Alabama

Fer Me, Where I Got Involved in the Square Dance/Round Dance/Clog Dance Community and Met the "LOVE of My Life"…..My Dear Lovely Wife. We've Been Together a Little Over 27 Years , SOOOOO I Guess I'll Keep Her (Especially Since Nobody ELSE Would Be Able ta Put Up with EITHER of US Except'n Each Other…or So SHE Says…And "Yes Dear…..I Believe Ya…Yes Dear…YES DEAR!!!").

After a Little Over 7 Years in Montgomery, the Air Force Sent Me and My Sweetheart (Yes, I'm Talkin' About My Lovely Wife…….Git Yer Mind Outta the Gutter…) fer a Little 4 Year Vacation ta Ramstein (That's "Correctly" Pronounced "Ramshtine") Air Base in (at THAT Time)" West" Germany. Before We Left, the Berlin Wall Came Down and We Were Jest in Plain Old "Germany". I was There Durin' rhe "Desert Storm" and Even Helped Write the Programs that Tracked the "Bomb" Damage Assessments (BDAs) that Were Later Changed ta the More "Politically Correct" Term:" Battle" Damage Assessments. And SPEAKIN' a "Damage", I Was ALSO at Ramstein AB When the "Italian" Version of the US Air Force "Thunderbirds", the "TriColorie" (Named After the "Three Colored" Flag of Italy) Sort a "Blew the Socks" OFF'n the Croud (Along with ALL a Their OTHER Clothes) When They "Crashed and Burned" INTO the Croud at the FLUGTAG (Flyin' Day) Airshow on 28 Aug 1988. I Had ta QUICK Peddle My Bike 10K/6 Miles Home ta Call My Wife (Who was Back in the US of A Takin' College Courses that She Couldn't Git in Germany Fer Her Medical Technologist Biology Degree), BEFORE the News Hit "The States", So's She Wouldn't Worry, BUTT She Said, "WHAT Air Disaster?!?" (Until it "Finally" HIT the News and THEN She Appreciated My "Thoughtfulness". When My 4 Year Vacation was Up, We Returned ta Montgomery, Alabama (My Wife's Home Stompin' Ground) Were I Served About 6 More Years Before Retirin'. Now If'n the Figures Don't Seem to Add Up ta 24 Years, It's Because I "Left" OUT the Time I "Rightly" Spent in Basic Training and Tech Schools Larnin' All that I Needed ta Know t' Do My Job in the Most "Efficient and Effective" Manner.

There WAS One Thing I Fergot t' Tell Ya and That WAS……When I Was Stationed in Key West, Florida, (ACTUALLY We Was a "Tennant" US Air Force Unit on the "Key West" Naval Air Station (NAS) Which Was ACTUALLY on Boca Raton Key, AND We Had Another US Air Force Buildin' on Boca Chika Key, AND Our Headquarters was ACTUALLY at Homestead AFB on the Florida Mainland, BUTT….. Fer the Sake a NOT Havin' ta Go inta ALL a This "Explainin'" CRAP, We JEST Said That We Was Stationed at Key West, Florida…..) My Supervisor Introduced Me (via Bible Study Tapes) ta My "Correct" Pastor Teacher (the Father of Robert B. Thieme, III, Who's Name I Cain't TELL Ya, And Who I Jest Call, "Junior"). I Cain't Tell Y'all His Name Because His Son (Robert B. Thieme, III) Said that I Couldn't and I Respect the Man (Even Though HE Don't Care MUCH Fer ME), BUTT, He Didn't Say that I Couldn't Mention HIS Name, SOOOO I'll NEVER Tell Y'all the Name of Robert B. Thieme the Third's Father. Wild Horses Couldn't Drag the Name of Robert B. Thieme, III's Father from My Mouth. No Amount of Torture Could EVER Make Me Utter the Name of Robert B. Thieme the Third's Father (Without Permission). I Jest Call Him "Junior", BUTT My Dear Wife Calls Him "Old LOUD Mouth" on Account of the Fact that I Have a Bit of a Hearin' Problem ("Tinnitus", "Tin Ear", or "Ringin' in the Ears") and When I'm Down at the Barn Cleanin' Horse Stalls (a Very GOOD Place ta Listen t' Bible Study Tapes with the Ammonia Fumes Comin' Up from the Pee Wholes to Clear Yer Sinuses and the CobWebs from Yer Brain), I Crank Them Thar Bible Study Tapes Up SOOOO LOUD that the Whole Dad Blamed Neighborhood Got a GOOD Dose of Bible Teachin'.

Jest Before I Retired from the US Air Force, I Decided that I Had a BUTT (and That's a BIG BUTT) Load of Computer Programmin' and Decided that Computer Networkin' Was the Thing fer Me, BUTT the Air Force Said that Us Old Farts Had ta Keep the Old Main Frame COBOL Programs Runnin' Until the Young Sprouts Could Learn Networkin' AND the New Client/Server Technology. I Did Like Always and Said, "Yes Sir, Yes Sir, Three Bags Full Sir" and Carried On Like a GOOD Trooper, BUTT Jest as SOON as I Retired, I Started Lookin' t' Git Me Some o' That Thar Windows Networkin' Experience. It Took Me a Couple a Years And I Had SEVERAL Jobs in the Meantime: When I Was with a "Temp" Agency, I Would be Inspectin', Stackin', and Packin' Little Plastic Pint and Quart Containers (and Lids) ONE Day and Workin' a Powder Coat Paint Line the NEXT. I Made the Silicon Rubber Molds They Use ta Create Them Thar Lightweight Designer Flower Pots fer a While, and Even Assembled, Repaired, and Delivered Business Copier Machines. I Worked a 90 Day Probation with the United States Postal Service (USPS) Before We BOTH Decided ta "Mutually" Part Ways. I Learned 3 (Y'all Know How We NIPers LOVE ta Deal in Trinity's) Things from My Time with the USPS: 1) That Our Values, Principles, and Standards (VPS) Differ GREATLY, 2) Why Yer Cards, Letters, and Packages Arrive in the Very SAD Condition They DO Sometimes, AND 3) Why Them Thar USPS Folks "Periodically" Go After Each Other with Automatic Weapons (Where Do Y'all Think "They" Came UP with the Term "Goin' Postal" Anyway?!?).

About the Time that I was Gonna GIVE Up on EVER Findin' a Computer Networkin' Job, My Wife Pointed Out an MIS (Management Information Systems) Assistant Job t' Me in the Classifieds and When I Interviewed fer it, I Found that the Guy Needin' an Assistant was One of the Guys on the US Air Force Help Desk Who Used ta Call Me at 0330 (That's "ZERO'Dark 30" fer Y'all Military Types) in the Morning t' Help Korea Resolve Their Little Computer Program Problems, and He Decided ta Give Me a Chance. I Learned Enough About Computer Networkin' from Him that (Along with My Little 30% VA Disability fer My Hearin' Loss and Bum Knee) I Qualified fer the Computer Networkin' Job I Hold Today with a "BIG Government" Organization.

My Lovely Wife and I Ain't Got NO Kids (and it's Probably a GOOD Thing, Since Every Time Some Friends of Ours Visit with THEIR Heathens, My Wife Says, "We Don't NEED Kids……If'n Ours Acted Like THAT We'd KILL 'em.", BUTT (Just Can't Loose That BIG BUTT) We DO Have 2 Cute Mixed Breed Chihuahuas (Daisy May and Hershey Poo), One White German Shepard (Cindy Sue), One House Cat (Mamma Kitty), 4 Barn Cats (Spotty Kitty, Taby Kitty, Blacky Kitty, and Yeller Kitty)…..We're REAL Inventive With'n Our "Kitty" Names, 'Cause a Kitty is Like a Dog with No Legs…..It Don't Matter WHAT Ya Call 'em…….They AIN'T a Gonna Come ta Ya ANYWAY, One Box Turtle….No That's Right, She Turned the Turtle Loose at the Lake…..., a Sweet Double Yeller Head Parrott (JR), a "Obnoxious" Ring Necked Yeller Parakeet, (Yella Bird) a Chinchilla (Chi-Chi), Some Tropical Salt Water Fish (with NO Names Causin' They Don't LAST Too Long), AND 5 Horses (Sam, Beauty, Missy, John Boy, and Dallas), So it Ain't Like We're All By Ourselves. Our "Family" Keeps Us Quite Busy. I KEEP the Neighborhood Guessin' About My Sanity by Cyclin' with Not Enough Wheels (Unicycle) or Too Many Seats (Tandem, Bicycle Built fer Two….with the GOOD LORD Peddlin' in the Rear, Who "They" Cain't Seem ta SEE). Neither Me NOR My Lovely Wife are Very Good at ALL at "Keepin' House" (WELLLLL….That's Not EXACTLY Accurate……We CAN Do a Fair Job a Keepin' the Place Clean When We Put Our Backs inta it, BUTT Our Jobs Wear Us OUT So Much that We Don't Have a LOT a Time and Effort Remainin' at the End of the Day), SOOOO Our Place is ALWAYS in a State of Disaster (We Usually Keep the Horse Barn Cleaner), BUTT I Jest Cain't Stand the Danged "Antiseptic" Atmosphere of Them Thar "Southern Living" and "Good Housekeeping" Kinds of Places. I Like to Put My Feet UP "Muddy" After a HARD Day at the Barn Cleanin' Stalls.

I Really LOVE My Big Baby, She's a Bit Hefty and Has a Pretty BIG BUTT, BUUTTT She's Sweet as All Outdoors……Wait a Minute……Did Y'all THINK Fer a MINUTE That I was Referrin' ta My Lovely Wife,,!?!....I Was Talkin' about My Big 1900 Pound Percheron Draft Horse/Quarter Horse Cross. Are Y'all Sayin' Ya Think My Wife is FAT and Has a BIG BUTT?!?........I'm Gonna TELL Her THAT, And THEN Ya'll WILL Be in TROUBLE. My Wife Can Manhandle (And I DON't Mean That She Can "WomanHandle" OR "PersonHandle"…….. I Mean "MAN Handle"ANY Horse in the Barn (Includin' MINE), SOOOO….. If'n I Was Y'ALL, I Wouldn't Git on THAT Little Lady's "Bad Side" (And I ALREADY Told Ya WAYYYYY TOO Much About Her "BAD" Side Back in Chapter 3). All a Her Horses are Rackin' and Tennessee Walkin' Horses with Sort a "High Spirits" Whereas MY Big Baby is Calm, Cool, and "Collected" (Equitation Wise).

My Wife is the Equestrian and I'm the "Ground Man" (I Haul Hay and Grain, Clean Stalls, Tack and Horse Trailers, Fix Fences, and Groom Horses). ALMOST Every Time I Git UP onta the Back of One a Them Thar Beasties of "My Wife's", I Feel Like I'm Sittin' on a Girder of a HIGH RISE Buildin' and in "Short Order" They Remind Me in a Very "Forceful Way" – Yer a "Ground" Man, Except fer My Sweet Baby. When I Get on Dallas' Back it Feels Like I'm a Sittin' on a Loadin' Dock and We Git Along Jest FINE. She's a Little Bit "Lazy" and SO Am I, So My Wife Says that We Were Jest MADE Fer Each Other…….

There's Not Much ELSE ta Tell Ya Except that Since I Started the NEW Independence Party (NIPers) AND Am Tryin' ta Git Sarah Palin and Herman Cain Elected President and Vice-President (Respectively) of These Here GREAT United States, My Family and Friends Think I'm "Crazy as a Loon" or "Loony as a Bed Bug". Ta Put It in the Words of My Favorite Father-Out-Law, "WHY Don't Ya Just CUT OUT This CRAP !!??!!!", AND "Yer Jest Makin' a DAMN FOOL Outta YerSelf", SOOOO I "Laughed" My Way Outta the Door Sayin', "I Hear There's GOOD Money in Makin' a DAMN FOOL Outta YerSelf These Days…..Jest Look at "MASSA President Obamma Ramma" Fer Instance!!!" I Cain't Seem t' Convince ANYONE That I DO HAVE a Plan that WILL WORK with the "Correct" Backers (Which I DO HAVE………the "BIG 3"…..…GOD the FATHER, GOD the SON, AND……GOD the FATHER's Significant "OTHER"), And Have the "Correct" CORE Constituency (Which I've Called ta "Service", Reference Chapter 3), And Base the NIPers on the Values, Principles, and Standards (VPS) of Our Handbook the "Holy Bible" Version of the "User's Guide and Maintenance Manual for a Human Life", AND Have the Support of EVERY SINGLE AMERICAN VOTER (Which I'm Workin' On via This Book). Oh Well…. Time Will Tell……. Waiting IS….(Just Like Valentine Michael Smith from Robert A. Heinlein's Book, "Stranger in a Strange Land"……a Pretty GOOD Little Read…..See If'n Ya Notice ANY Similarities…..BUTT If'n My Life Parallels "His"….Then I'm a Little "Apprehensive" About That Thar "ENDIN'"…..

IF (by Some MIRACLE) I Can "Git This Party Started…Git This Party STARTED…..GIT THIS PARTY STARTED!!!", Then, Gentle Reader (And Future NIPer??), I Ask Just ONE Favor: If Y'all EVER Want and/or "Choose" ta HONOR ME, Please DON'T Yell and Cheer Like the "Tea Party" Folks ……Please HONOR Me with ABSOLUTE SILENCE!!! Unlike John F. Kennedy, I Want ta HEAR the Sound of the SHOT that Takes My LIFE…..Because "THEY" are Gonna Have ta KILL Me t' STOP Me or SHUT Me UP……..."Long Live the NIPers"…….. "Long Live the NEW Independence Party", And …….. GOD BLESS AMERICA !!!

Jest One LAST Thing Before We Move On ta the Next Chapter: My Wife is Convinced that I Don't LOVE Her Anymore, SOOOOO When I'm "Gone" She Probably Won't Miss This "Old Fart" from Beauregard, AL, BUTT I Love HER More'n LIFE Itself, And ALMOST as MUCH as I LOVE My GOD. When I Proposed ta Her at the National Square Dance Convention in Birmingham, ALabama WAAYYY Back in 1985, She Made it VERRY Clear ta Me that Her HORSES Came First and I Came Second, And I Told Her That I Had "NO Problem" with That as Long as SHE Understood That "My GOD" Comes First and She is a VERRY Close Second. At THAT Time (While My GOD was ONLY Trainin' Me Up and Fillin' Me with Memories ta Relate to Y'all via This Book AND via My www.YouTube.com Videos, Along with Makin' Me a Sadder But Wiser Fella), She was FINE with That, BUTT Now That the "Check has Come Due" and My GOOD LORD Has Tasked Me with Larnin' the AMERICAN PUBLIC (Them's Y"ALL Idiots) Up a Bit…..She MIGHT Be Regrettin' That Decision a Mite.

SSSOOOOOOOO…… Whether Y'all Manage ta Make it t' "The End" of This Little "Baby" (Book) of Mine or NOT….. Please Skip ta the "Last" Page and Send Her a Little Somethin' from Me ta the P.O. Box Ya Find There. I Have PLENTY of Life Insurance SO She SHOULD Be OK, BUTT Times Bein' What They ARE (FOUR MORE YEARS, Jest LIKE the LAST 4, with "MASSA" President Obamma Ramma EnSlavein' the NATION with the Vile Addictive Drug Called "WELFAIR" via That Thar "BIG Government NANNY State"….. JEST Because "HE CAN" …. By STEALIN' the HARD –EARNED TRILLIONS o' Dollars from the Wallets and Pocketbooks of US HARD-Workin' AMERICAN Citizens ta GIVE it OUT Like "Candy" or "Ice Cream" ta BUY the VOTES o' SOME a the LAZY NO-Accounts that SUCK OFF'n the Government "TIT"….AND When HE Said "CHANGE", I Didn't KNOW That He Meant STEALIN' My "LAST DIME" ……Now I've SAID it Before AND I'll "SAY" it Again……..I Really DO Have "GREAT RESPECT" fer the "OFFICE" of the President of the GREAT GOD-Fearin' UNITED STATES of AMERICA….. BUUTTTT…..And THAT'S a REALLY BIG BUTT……I Have ABSOLUTELY NO "respect" FOR the Dad Gummed "TIT-TURD" Who "CURRENTLY" Occupies….. Like the "OCCUPIED" Sign on a Toilet…..the "OFFICE" of the Presidency TODAY……AND Fer the NEXT FOUR YEARS........... UNLESS We Can "Figger" a Way ta Git the "N-Word" Outta There a LOT EARILER…. Hint…Hint…HINT!!!

If'n Me and the NIPers Cain't Git This GREAT GOD-Fearin' Country Turned Back Around in Time, My Darlin' Wife MIGHT Need a Little "Extra" ta Keep OUR "Family" Together (Reference Chapter 8). SO If'n Anything "UNUSUAL" Happens ta ME, Dear Readers, I'm Leavin' My Dear Wife in Yer Tender Care, SOOOO I HOPE Y'all DON'T Let Me Down…….. 'Cause If'n Ya DO……..Whether Ya Believe in HIM or NOT……. MY GOD's GONNA GIT YA FER THAT !!!!!.........Y'all HAVE Been WARNED!!!

Did THAT Crap Make ANY Sense to Y'all on Pages 31-35, or Am I JEST Funnin' Ya…..YOU Decide!!!

Chapter 9

How the HECK Can We NIPers SOLVE AMERICA's Immigration Problem ???

That's Another One a Them Thar Questions that We NIPers are SOOO GLAD Y'all Asked. We've Heard All KINDS of Ridiculous Answers t' That Question, SOOO We Figure That ONE More Wouldn't Hurt a Bit. We in the NEW Independence Party (NIPers) Think that EVERYONE Livin' in the Good Ole US of A Should Pull their Own Weight (and a Tiny Bit More), And That Illegal Aliens (Foreigners and NOT Outer Space Folks......We Have a Whole "DIFFERENT" Plan Fer Them Thar Outer Space Types) Ain't No Different. We NIPers Have a Plan that Will Cover ALL of the Bases. It Will Deal with the Illegals Already in This Country, the Backlog In-Processing the Ones Wantin' to Git in "Legally", AND Ensure that We Can Git Rid of All of This Damn Bilingual Crap. Does That Sound Like a Plan ta Y'all?? Then Listen UP!!!.....

I Bet Ya Never Heard of an Immigration Plan Like THIS Before (Because We NIPers Have Jest a Little Bit "Different" Way of Lookin' at Things Than ANYONE Else):

1. Round Up ALL of the Illegal Foreigners (Especially the Construction Workers) in This GREAT GOD-Fearin' Country of Ours and Take 'em ta the Point of Entry into This Nation that is Closest to Where They Crossed Illegally. There are Probably a LOT of Illegal Canadians in the USA, BUTT We Don't Seem ta Mind That, SOOOOO...fer the Sake of THIS Example We Will Concentrate on Our Southern Border with Mexico.

2. Once We Have Them ALL Collected at the Mexican Border, We Put 'em ta Work Buildin' Immigrant Processin' Stations. ALL Along the Border We Will Have These Processin' Stations Built to a Standard Configuration: We NIPers Like t' Deal in 3s (Trinity's), So These Processing Stations Will Be Built with 3 Distinct Sections with 3 Distinct Purposes. The Northern (USA) Section Will Contain Border Guard Quarters and a Ground Transportation Office (Staffed by a Combination of Immigration Service and Bilingual Illegal Immigrants). The Southern (Mexico) Section Will Contain a School that Will Teach American English and American Citizenship (Staffed by Bilingual Illegal Immigrants). In the Center of the Facility Will Be the Third Section that will be Equally Split Between USA and Mexico (with the Border Runnin' Exactly Down the Middle).

3. This Third Section is the MOST Important Because This is Where the Backlog of Temporary and Permanent VISAs Will be Processed. We NIPers Figure that the Illegal Immigrants in This Country (USA) Would Be the BEST (Since They Came from Mexico, and the Mexican Culture) ta Determine Who Were the "BAD Guys" (ta "Keep OUT" of the USA) AND Who Were the "GOOD Guys" (ta Be "Let IN" ta the USA with All Official Paperwork Completed Correctly). There Will Be an ENTER Door on the Mexico Side of the Border and an EXIT Door on the USA Side. A Line of Desks Will Go Straight Down the Center in Line with the Border. The Mexicans Seekin' Entry into the USA (Who have Graduated from the Language/Civics School) Will be Processed Efficiently and Effectively into This Country by the Illegal Immigrants. Once Those

Illegal Immigrants Have "Served" at Least 3 Years (We NIPers LOVE Them Thar Trinity's) Processin' LEGAL Immigrants Paperwork (AND Have Graduated from the Language/Civics School), They Will be Eligible ta Step from Behind the Desk ta the Front of the Desk and be Processed into This Country as LEGAL Immigrants.

4. When the LEGAL Immigrants EXIT the Processin' Station (with Their Band NEW Social Security Numbers) on the USA Side, They Will Proceed to the Transportation Office Where They Will be Taken ta the Nearest US City, AND They Will be Taken to Another Processing Station Where They Will be Put in Contact with Relatives They May Have in the US or an Employment Agency that Will Help Them Find Appropriate Employment to Their Education Level and Skill Set.

We NIPers Think That This Process Would Be MUCH More Respectful, Kind, and Courteous to BOTH Our LEGAL and ILLEGAL Mexican Immigrants, and MUCH More Productive (as Opposed to Destructive) to the US Labor Force. Try Runnin' This Past Those Lousy LEFT-Leanin' Liberal Damn Democrats OR Those Rascally Radically Religious RIGHT-Wing Republicans and See if it Flies as High, Far, and Fast as it Does With Us NEW Independence Party (NIPer) Thinkers/Members.

Did THAT Crap Make ANY Sense to Y'all on Pages 36-37, or Am I JEST Funnin' Ya.....YOU Decide!!!

Chapter 10

What IS the "User's Guide and Maintenance Manual for a Human Life" ???

We've Mentioned the Answer ta This Question (in Part) in Previous Chapters, BUTT Intend t' Cover it "in Depth" in This Chapter. Since Religion and Politics are Such Volatile Subjects ta MANY (if'n Not MOST) Americans, We Have ta Tread "Lightly" on This Here Subject ta Avoid Offending Any of Y'alls "Sensitive Sensibilites"........LIKE HELL WE DO!!! If'n Ya Cain't Stand the HEAT, Then Why the HELL Did Ya Start Readin' This Little NIPer Cook Book in the First Place?? We NIPers are Tryin' t' Git This Here GREAT GOD-Fearin' Nation of Ours Back on the Road to GREATNESS, and That Don't Mean Pussyfootin' Around with No Namby-Pamby, Mealy Mouthed "Politically Correct" BullShootin'...

The Title "The Holy Bible" Has Been Used (and Abused) by Too MANY "So Called" CHRISTians Over the Years. The "Koran" Has ALSO Gotten Its Share of "Bad Press" from Those Who "Distort" Its Contents as Well. The "Traditional" Titles of These Works (and Others) Cause Controversy and Conflict which is "Detrimental" ta the NIPer Goal of Cooperation and Coordination, So We CHOOSE t' Resolve Those Conflicts Through a Currently Popular Process Called "Re-Branding". HOWEVER, Re-Branding Only Works if'n Y'all Have a QUALITY Product That Has Gotten a "Bad Rep" or "Bad Rap" That is TOTALLY Undeserved. Re-Branding is NOT Designed ta Turn a "Pig's Ear" inta a "Silk Purse" by Slappin' a PRADA Logo on it.

Not Long Ago, I Heard of This Organization Who's Employees Was NOT Takin' Very GOOD Care o' Customers and They Figured ta Improve Their Customer Relationship by ReBrandin' TheirSelves (BEFORE They Had Earned BACK Their Customer's Trust and Respect Through TOP Quality Customer Service). We NIPers NIPed That Crap in the Buds with One Simple Statement: "A Rose by Any Other Name Will Smell as Sweet, BUTT the SAME Goes fer a TURD!!!". Needless t' Say, the "Re-Branding" Project Died on the Vine. HOWEVER, Due to a Recent Change in Leadership (Not Management...I Said LEADERSHIP.....There's a BIG Difference.......Reference Chapter 14) That SAME Organization is Well on the Road ta Recovery, and RE-EARNING the Trust, Respect, and Sometimes Even PRAISE of Their Customer Base.......SOOOOOO....of Course, Now There is No NEED ta "ReBrand" Because the Employees Raised Their Quality of Service Under the SAME Name and Restored its HONOR.

Now That Y'all Know How and Why NOT t' Re-Brand, Let's Talk about How t' Do it Correctly: To Avoid All of This "One-Upsmanship" About WHO is "Right" and WHO is "Wrong", and Which Version is "Right" ("CORRECT".....So's We DON'T Associate Our NIPer Selves with Them Thar Radically Religious RIGHT-Wing Republicans) and Which Version is "Wrong" (AND We Don't Want Them Thar LEFT-Leanin' Liberal DAMN Democrats ta Be "LEFT" OUT EITHER), We NIPers Avoid This Conflict All Together By Lumping'ALL Versions of GOD's "Word" Under the "Content" Category of the "User's Guide and Maintenance Manual for a Human Life". We NIPers Endorse the "Holy Bible" Version, BUTT We're Flexible And at the SAME Time Confident Enough in Our Beliefs to Tolerate and Even Embrace the Beliefs of Others (as LONG as We AGREE to AGREE on Our "Similarities" and AGREE to DISAGREE on Our "Differences".....Like Me and My Lovely Wife DO). We NIPers Think That is Why the "CURRENT" Administration is So INEFFECTIVE......They Are Always.......ALWAYS Concentratin' on DIFFERENCES (Which Make Us Unique, BUTT CAN Cause Conflict) instead of a

Concentratin' on SIMILARITIES (That Give Us Cause fer Agreement Which DOES Facilitate Effective and Efficient Goal Accomplishment).

We NIPers Also Believe that the "User's Guide and Maintenance Manual for a Human Life" Title Describes the Content and Usage of the GOOD Book Better than a Title that "Seems" ta Insinuate that Our GOD's Plan has a Bunch of "Holes" in it. We Believe that Our GOD's Plan is a Perfect Plan, Even Though it CAN Be a Bit "Difficult" ta Understand in Places and at Times. That is the Reason We NIPers Believe that We NEED a FULL TIME Spiritual Advisor Who Knows the Original Languages of the Scriptures (Hebrew and Aramaic in the OLD Testament and Koine or "Common" Greek in the NEW Testament) to Ensure that We are NOT Missing Something in the Translation Although That STILL Leaves the Complications of MisInterpretation, and MisApplication ta Deal with…..(See Chapter 35).

There MAY Be "Other" Versions of the "User's Guide and Maintenance Manual for a Human Life" than the 3 We Mentioned, and ALL are Welcome in the NEW Independence Party, as Long as They Don't Violate the 3 Foundation Principles of the NIPers: 1) Respect for All People, Property, and Beliefs; 2) Kindness to Self and to Others; and 3) Courtesy EVEN in the Face of DIS-Courtesy. We Believe that the "User's Guide and Maintenance Manual for a Human Life" Lives Up to Its Name by Teachin' Us How to Live Our Lives "Efficiently and Effectively", and MOST Important, How to Fix 'em When They're Broke.

Chapter 11

WHAT's the "DIFFERENCE" Between a "Hoe" and a "Culler" ???

We NIPers Have a Little TEST fer ALL a Y'all AMERICANS Out There to See if'n Ya "Have What it Takes" ta BE a Member of the NEW Independence Party (NIPer). If'n You Cain't PASS This Simple Little TEST, Then There is VERRY Little Chance of Changing the Political Landscape of This Country:

We NIPers Have Found that There is a VERRY FINE Piece of Agricultural Equipment Whose Name Has been "Defamed" by a Small, Uncouth Sect of the Population. This Fine Agricultural Tool is Usually Called a "Hoe" Which Sounds Very Similar to A Vile, Degrading Term for Women Used by a Small, Degenerate Portion of the Music Industry. We NIPers Feel that This FINE Agricultural Tool is Gettin' a "Bad Rap" Because of This Association. Therefore, We NIPers Propose to "Re-Brand" This VERRY FINE Agricultural Tool as a "Culler" Because it is Normally Used to Cull Weeds from Yer Garden. We Chose This Name Because it "Sounds" Like the Word "Color" and Instead of Reminding Us of a Vile, Degradin' Word for Women, it Would Serve to Remind Us of the Contributions of ALL of the Fine PEOPLE of "Color" Who Have Contributed SOOOO Much ta the "Rich History" of This GREAT GOD-Fearin' NATION of OURS.

The Next Time Y'all Go t' Cull the Weeds from Yer Vegetable Garden or Flower Bed with Yer "Culler", Y'all Will be Reminded of the Contributions of Folks Like Martin Luther King, Medgar Evers, Malcolm X, George Washington Carver, Rosa Parks, The Tuskegee Airmen, Wing Luke, Phil Hayasaka, Rev Mineo Katigiri, Carlos Santana, Desi Arnaz, Jose Canseco, Sacagawea, Pocahontas, Will Rogers, etc., BUTT ta Accomplish This Re-Brandin', Ya'll Will Have t' "Convince" Local Businesses Who SELL This FINE Agricultural Tool ta "Re-Brand" it from a "Hoe" to a "Culler". This May Require a "Boycott" of the Businesses ta Git Their Attention, and Letters ta the "Corporate Office", and Board of Directors. If Y'all Ain't Got the Cahones t' Even Get a "Hoe" Re-Branded to a "Culler", Then Startin' a Brand NEW Independence Party Chapter in Yer Area's Gonna Be Nigh onta Impossible.

Of COURSE, Y'all CEOs of Them Thar Businesses COULD Take the Initiative ta Make This NAME CHANGE on Yer OWN (Jest Because it is the "CORRECT" Thing ta DO) WITHOUT Yer Customers Havin' ta Hit Ya "Where it HURTS" (in the Wallet or Pocketbook......Like the DAMN THEIVIN' FEDERAL, STATE. And LOCAL "BIG Governments" Likes ta DO) by Boycottin' Yer Business Until Ya "Git the MESSAGE" and Re-BRAND That VERRY FINE Agricultural Tool from a "Hoe" to a "Culler".......BUTT.....That's ENTIRELY Up ta Y'ALL (WELLLL......Not REALLY Up ta Y'all.... It's Up ta US NIPers and the ENTIRE AMERICAN POPULATION Customer Base)...... POWER TO the PEOPLE!!!......

BUTT.....ONLY If'n Y'ALL Are Willin' Ta Make the SACRIFICES REQUIRED (Like This "Other" Fella a Couple Thousand Years Ago Who Got Hung on a Cross) ta SIEZE the POWER from "BIG Business", "BIG Government", "BIG Churches", AND "BIG BROTHER" (Satan, the WORLD, And Our OWN Sinful Selves) in General.......the Choice is YOURS (And ALWAYS Has Been)......The "BALL's in YOUR COURT".......Make it a "Three Pointer" (a Trinity) fer the NIPers (the "NEW" Independence Party)!!!.......GOOD LUCK Passin' This Little "TEST"...We NIPers Will Be WATCHIN'

Ya ta SEE If'n Y'all Have the Initiative, Determination, Commitment, Inventiveness, Perseverance, Dedication, AND "Intestinal Fortitude" Required ta PASS This TEST (And "Qualify" as NIPer Material), Because from What We NEW Independence Party Members (NIPers) Have "SEEN" a Yer Few Piddlin' "ATTEMPTS" at Changin' Things Fer the "Better" in OUR GREAT AMERICAN Society…..Yer NOT Doin' a Very GOOD Job of it………….SOOOOO We NIPers Feel That We Have a VERRY TOUGH Job Ahead a US ta Git Y'all "Larned UP" ta PASS That Little Multiple-Choice Test Comin' Up in Nov 2016, AND ta Start Makin' a REAL "Difference"(Fer the "BEST") in the Socio-Political "Landscape".

Did THAT Crap Make ANY Sense to Y'all on Pages 40-41, or Am I JEST Funnin' Ya…..YOU Decide!!!

Chapter 12

What's the "DIFFERENCE" Between an AFRICAN-American And an AMERICAN-African ???

We NIPers Would Be HAPPY and "Pleased as Punch" ta Clear Up this Little Misconception Fer Y'all TRUE AMERICANS Readin' This Here Little Book (BUTT We Was Kindly a HOPIN' That Thar Little "Difference" Would be Intuitively Obvious t' Ya). The SHORT Answer is: An AMERICAN-African is a NEW Independence Party (NIPer) Thinker (That's THINKER......Not STINKER...... snif.... Snif.... SNIF..... Well, I KNOW I Remembered t' Put On My RIGHT Guard This Mornin' for Protection Agaist the Stink o' Them Thar Radically Religious RIGHT-Wing Republicans, BUTT I MAY Have Fergot My LEFT Guard to Protect Against the Stink o' Them Thar LEFT-Leanin' Liberal Damn Democrats, BUTT That's Jest Because We NIPers Seem t' Have MORE in Common with Those Radically Religious Right-Wing Republicans....as BAD as They Seem....that We Do Them Thar Left-Leanin' Liberal Damn Democrats, BUTT I'm Here t' Tell Ya, It's Good, Honest, Hard-Workin' Sweat that Yer Smellin' and NOT the Fact that I Ain't Bathed in a Few Days.....snif.....Snif.....SNIF.....As Best I Remember it Anyways......I TOLD Ya BEFORE that My Fergitter's Been Workin' Overtime Lately.... Maybe That's Where All the Sweat Came from......I'll Have t' Check on That......DAMN....Y'all Let Me Ramble ON AGIN' and This Here SHORT Answer is Strechin' Nigh onta Half a Page.....Why Didn't Y'all STOP Me When Ya Saw I Had Got OFF Topic???......Oh Well.....It's OK.....I Fergive Ya.....Now Where Was I... Oh Yeah......Now I Remember.....) and an AFRICAN-American is NOT.

Well, Since Y'all Managed t' Wade Thru That Thar SHORT Answer Without TOO Much Trouble, This Here LONG Answer Should be a Piece a Cake: There Are an Awful LOT of MINORITIES Out There in AMERICA these days (e.g,, AFRICAN-Americans, ORIENTAL-Americans, LATINO-Americans and LATINA- Americans, ASIAN-Americans , MIDDEL EASTERN-Americans, etc.) Who THINK They are Gittin' the Short End a the Stick from Us "Silent Majority" Unhyphenated, Plain Ole AMERICANS. And We NIPers Would Like t' CHANGE That (But Probably NOT in the Way That Y'all are Thinkin'.....SOME a Y'all SEE Where I'm a Goin' with This ....Some a Y'all Don't...and MOST a Y'all Haven't Got a "CLUE".....as USUAL.....).

Before We Git ta Y'all "Hyphenated" Americans Out There, We'd Like t' Say a Word or Two t' Y'all Dad Blamed "Silent Majority" AMERICANS Out There: It's HIGH TIME That Ya Git OFF'n Yer Dead ASSES and Quit Lettin' All These Goll Darned HYPHENATED-American Minorities Push Y'all Around (Especially with Them "EQUAL Opportunity" Regulations that Make it Where a Poor Ole Caucasian "Unhyphenated" AMERICAN Man Like ME Cain't Hardly Git Hired No More, Even Though My Work Ethics Follow the Values, Principles, and Standards (VPS) of the NIPer Handbook of Doin' My Job as Unto MY LORD... and Believe You ME Folks, HIS Standards Are WAAAYYYYYY Above the Standards of My Current "BIG Government" Organization). Lately I've Been Overloaded at Work Pullin' 2 and a Half Workloads with Little 5 Day Suspense's that They Should KNOW Dang Well are Gonna Take 7 Days t' Do Correctly from 4 "Different" BIG Wigs that ALL Think that THEIR Suspense is the ONLY One I Need t' Be Workin' On AND I'm AFRAID That Their Gonna FIRE Me Any DAY Now Fer "Unsatisfactory Performance".....Well Y'all Git the IDEA......That's MY Problem and NOT

YOURS…..UNLESS Yer One a Them Thar "MOOCHIN'" Folks Who Will READ a Fella's "Baby" (Book) Fer FREE and Git a Whole HEEP a GOOD Advice Fer Gittin' Yer LIFE and This GREAT GOD-Fearin' NATION of OURS Back "On Track", AND Ya DON'T Send a Little "VALUE" ta P.O. Box 2149, Tuskegee, AL 36083 …..BUTT I HOPE Y'all See What I'm a Talkin' About. My Lovely Wife Jest GAVE Me the Solution……..She Said that If'n I Don't Want t' Be Fired or I Wanna Be Able t' Git a Job with NO PROBLEMO……I Jest Need t' be a 99% Disabled AFRICAN-American (or LATINA-American) WOMAN…….SORRY, BUTT I Don't Think I Wanna GO There…..at THIS Time…..

OK, I've Ranted and Raved Enough……Let's Git BACK On Topic: In the NEW Independence Party (NIPers), We Like ta Put This GREAT GOD-Fearin' Country of AMERICA "FIRST". SOOO Therefore, Any of Y'all "Hyphenated" American "Minorities" Out There, We'd Just Like Y'all t' Do a Little "Re-Brandin'" on YerSelves (Like YOU Mr Herman Cain) as AMERICAN- Africans, AMERICAN- Asians, AMERICAN-Orientals, AMERICAN-Latinos and AMERICAN- Latinas, etc. Do Y'all See the Subtle "Difference"??? It's Subtle, BUTT it Makes ALL of the Difference in the WORLD (And TO the WORLD) When Y'all JUST Put AMERICA "FIRST" fer a Change. We NIPers Think That If MORE AMERICANS Would Put AMERICA "FIRST", Then This Here GREAT GOD-Fearin' COUNTRY of'n OURS Would Be in SOOOO Much Better Shape than it is Today (Under the CURRENT "AFRICAN-American" Administration). PLEASE Tell Me YOU Wouldn't Folla HIS Example Mr Cain…

I Don't KNOW If Any of Y'all Remember or NOT, BUTT There Was This Little Feller a Few Years Back Who Got Us t' the Moon (Now MOST of Y'all Think We Got t' the Moon on Rocket Ships, BUTT We Didn't) With This Little Phrase: "Ask NOT What YOU can DO fer Yer Country, BUTT Jest HOW MUCH Your COUNTRY Can DO fer YOU"……NO, That's Not "Correct"…….That's the Way We DO it TODAY Under the CURRENT "AFRICAN-American" Administration….. Back THEN It Went, "Ask NOT What Your COUNTRY Can DO for YOU, BUTT Rather Ask What YOU Can DO for Your COUNTRY" (That's What REALLY Got Us t' the Moon). What Ever Happened t' That Little Fella….. Oh, Yeah, I Remember Now……He Got SHOT in the HEAD!!! So I Guess THAT Principle Died with Him (Along with the President's Council on Physical Fitness, and a LOT of Other GOOD Things in This Here GREAT UNITED STATES of OURS). WELLLL, We NIPers THINK that We Have the "BEST" PLAN Fer Gittn' Us BACK t' Them Thar "GOOD Ole Days", and Especially the Values, Principles, and Standards (VPS) That This GREAT GOD-Fearin' NATION of OURS was FOUNDED Upon.

Now, There Was ALSO This "Other" Fella (Who ALSO Got SHOT) a Few Years Ago And (as I Remember it) HE Was an AFRICAN-American (BUTT We NIPers Would Be Willin' ta Bet ANY Amount That If'n He Was ALIVE Today….He'd BE an AMERICAN-African NIPer….) Who Made This Little Speech About NOT Payin' Attention t' the Color of a Person's Skin, BUTT Instead a That Payin' Attention ta the "Content of Their Character". Perhaps Y'all Have Heard of Him and Perhaps NOT, BUTT His Name was Martin Luther King, And HE Had a Lot of Things ta Say About Bein' "FREE at LAST !!!", AND We NIPers Kindly a Think He MIGHT a Been Talkin' About Bein' "FREE" From That Vile Adictive Drug Called "WELFAIR" that the "Nanny State" of MASSA President has Been Peddlin' Lately (Reference Chapters 3, 8, 17, 26). If'n Ya Got the Guts….. READ ON……

Did THAT Crap Make ANY Sense to Y'all on Pages 42-43, or Am I JEST Funnin' Ya…..YOU Decide!!!

Chapter 13

WHO's Tryin' ta START a "NEW" AMERICAN Revolution in This GREAT GOD-Fearin" NATION of OURS (One Voter at a Time) ???

In Case Y'all Don't KNOW (or Haven't NOTICED), 13 is My (and the NIPers)" LUCKy" (and That Means Good LUCK, Reference Chapter 57) Number. It Stands for "1" GOD in "3" Persons (a "Family") …....GOD the FATHER…....GOD the SON…….AND GOD the FATHER's Significant "OTHER" (Reference Chapter 24). SOOOOOO…..This Chapter 13 (Thirteen) is the FOUNDATION Chapter of My Little "Baby" (Book). We NIPers Are Gonna (Y'all KNOW How We NEW Independence Party Folks Like ta Deal in "THREE's" or "TRINITY's"): 1) REVOLUTIONIZE the Executive Branch of the Federal Government; 2) REVOLUTIONIZE the Political Process; AND 3) REVOLUTIONIZE Your "Relationship" with Your God (Exceptin' for Y'all godLESS DAMN Atheists Out There) !!!

In Case I Fergot t' Mention it Earlier (Ya KNOW My Fergitter's Been Workin' Overtime Lately….. SO I HOPE…..Like Earnest T. Bass from Mayberry….That I'm NOT a Chewin' My Cabbage Twicet), MY and the NIPers' LUCKy Number (Y'all KNOW About LUCK Don't Ya??....."Good" LUCK = The LORD's UNlimited CARIN' KINDness, and "Bad" LUCK = Lucifer's UNcarin' Counterfeit Knock-OFF……I Figured Y'all DID, BUTT I Jest Wanted t' Be SURE) is Thirteen (Which Reminds US NIPers of Our "BIG 3" Backers…..Y'all Know….One GOD in Three Personalities…..1+3=13…..or No, Maybe That's 1+3=4…..Oh Heck, Y'all KNOW What I Mean……Movin' ON…..).

Thirteen ALSO Reminds US NIPers of the 13 Original Colonies and Tryin' t' Git BACK t' the Values, Principles, and Standards (VPS) That GREW Them (with a Few Trials, Tribulations, and Civil War) into The GREAT 50 UNITED STAES that We Are "Runnin' inta the Ground" Today. That Seems SUCH a Shame to US NIPers that We Just HAD t' Try and DO Somethin' About it. Throughout This Here Little Book We're Tryin' REAL HARD t' Convince Y'all that We KNOW What the HELL We're Doin' and that We DO Have a "GOOD" Plan t' Make it All "BETTER" (No…..That's Wrong…..Them Left-Leanin' Liberal Damn Democrats are "GOOD"….and Them Radically Religious Right-Wing Republicans are "BETTER", BUTT We NIPers Are The "BEST" There EVER WAS….), So, I Meant ta Say "BEST", and We're Kindly a HOPIN' that a Few of Y'all GREAT GOD-Fearin' AMERICANS Out There Can See Some SENSE in it and Want ta JOIN Us (Cause There Ain't NO Way Y'all Can BEAT Us with the "BIG 3" Backin' Us, Reference Chapter 56).

I Don't Know if'n Y'all Couch 'Taters Have Gotten Up OFF'n Yer DEAD ASSes Lately and Looked Outside, BUTT This Here GREAT GOD-Fearin' NATION of OURS is in a HEEP o' TROUBLE. We Got Leeches Suckin' Off 'n the Government Tit, We're Spemdin' Money Like There's No Tomorrow, Our Senators and Congressmen are Makin' Their "Points" by Showin' Each Other Pictures of Pigs in Lipstick Instead o' Usin' Their Word's…….If'n They KNOW Any Longer than 4 Letters…..and the Problem Runs ALL the Way Up ta the HIGHEST OFFICE in the LAND ("The BUCK Stops HERE"….. NO it DON'T…..It Continues on t' CHINA). Am I Getting' THROUGH ta ANY o' Y'all Out There??? LISTEN UP PEOPLE!!! There IS a "BEST" (There, I Got it "Correctly" This Time) WAY and If'n Y'all Will Just LISTEN t' Us NIPers, We Can TEACH it to Ya.

"WE THE NIPers…." Have Decided That This GREAT GOD-Fearin' NATION of OURS Needs a "NEW" AMERICAN Revolution (One Voter at a Time). We're NOT Gonna Use Bombs or Guns (Although I DO Have This Little Green Ribbon with a Bronze Star on it from the US Air Force that Indicates I AM an EXPERT Marksman in BOTH the M-16 Gas-Powered Automatic Rifle AND the .38 Caliber Police Special Revolver…..No I Wasn't a Security Policeman…..I Was the Non-Commissioned Officer (NCO) in Charge of the Maxwell AFB – Gunter Annex Honor Guard Team, Who Give HONORS to Our Departed Military Veterans, and For Every 5 Fire Team Blank Firin' M-16 Rifles Ya Take from the Armory, Ya Hafta Carry ONE Loaded (with Real LIVE Bullets) .38 Caliber Revolver t' Protect it from Those Nere-Do-Wells Out There Who Would Try ta Steal it from Ya and Take OFF the Flash Suppressor and Use it Nefariously (with LIVE Ammunition)…..and Since There are 7 Rifles on an Honor Guard Fire Team, Ya Hafta Have 2 Folks Carryin' Loaded .38s……And Before Y'all Ask, NO……I Never Had t' Shoot ANY One…..BUTT, I'm Here t' Tell Y'all…..If'n ANY of Y'all Out There HAD Tried t' TAKE One o' Them Thar M-16 Rifles……I'd a SHOT Ya Dead in a Heartbeat and NOT Lost a Wink a Sleep Over it…… That's How We WON WWII, AND That's Why We Ain't WON Another'n Since……And DON'T Try t' Bring Up "DESERT STORM", Cause We STOPPED Short of the Goal and Had to Go BACK and Clean Up the MESS…..and We STILL Ain't Done Yet……..Oh, DAMN……Now What am I Gonna Tell Y'all in Chapter 42…WEELLLLL…I'll Think of Somethin'….I Got Time Yet….Now Where Was I??.....

Oh Yeah, I Remember Now…..I Think Today Them Honor Guard Fire Teams Use Them Old WWII (or Was it WWI) M-1 Breach Loader (Meanin' Ya Have t' Maually Chamber a New Round After Each Shot) Rifles Which Don't Require the Same Protection as the M-16s. BUTT (I Jest Cain't Seem t' Loose that BIG BUTT, Maybe a Little Time on the Treadmill Wouldn't Hurt Whenever I Git Done Writin' Y'all This Little Book) We was Sayin' (WAAAYYY Back Up Yonder) That This Here "NEW" AMERICAN Revolution Won't Be Fought on the Battlefield with Bombs and Guns (That's OLD Timey Thinkin' and WE Are "NEW" Independence Party (NIPer) Thinkers)……It Will be Fought in the Pollin' Booths with a Word Processor, and We'll DO it from CyberSpace (That's How We 21st Century High-Tech RedNecks Do it)…..And If'n Y'all Don't KNOW the POWER of a Word Processor, Jest Check Out Chapter 15 Comin' Up Shortly……

BUTT Let's Git Back t' That Little "NEW" AMERICAN Revolution We NIPers Plan t' Start, and See If'n We Can Explain it in a Way that We Can CALM Yer Fears (If'n Ya was Considerin' Becomin' One o' OUR Little NIPers)……or Maybe We'll Jest SCARE Y'all t' DEATH (If'n Yer One o' Them Thar LEFT-Leanin' Liberal Damn Democrats OR One o' Them Thar Radically Religious RIGHT-Wing Republicans….)…..BUTT….. Whichever……..Hold onta Yer Derriere's 'Cause Here We GOOOO……. "Back in the Days" When We Still HAD a Few FREEDOMs in This Country (You Know…..Like in the Days of Good Ole Teddy "Bully" Roosevelt , One of Our NIPer Heroes We Admire and Love) We AMERICANS Had a Little Different "Mind Set" and We NEW Independence Party Members (NIPers) Would Like t' Get BACK t' That…….Wouldn't YOU??

Throughout This Little Book (If'n Y'all Read it Cover t' Cover OR TOP t' BOTTOM) Y'all Will Find That We NIPers Have Laid Out ALMOST Our Entire Tactical and Strategic Plans for the "NEW" Revolution (NO…When it Comes t' the REALLY "Super-Secret" Stuff…..We Ain't Gonna Tell Ya …..WE AIN'T GONNA TELL YA!!!....BUTT We WILL Tell Y'all…. Ms Palin and Mr Cain… If'n Y'all EVER Decide t' Come On Board the NIPer Train…..I Meant the NIPer 13 Bomb-Bustin' Bus

CONVOYYYYY), Along with the NEW Independence Party (NIPer) Platform, Our Values, Principles, and Standards (VPS) Found in Our Handbook (Reference Chapter 10……DAMN, Y'all Fergit as Fast as I Do….That was ONLY a Couple a Chapters Ago) and Other Such Nonsense.

If'n Y'all Ever Need a BREAK from This Dry Borin' Stuff in My Little Book, or Y'all Jest Wanna Hear (from My Own Virtual CyberSpace Lips) What Y'all Will Be Missin' If'n Ya DON'T Buy This Book on CD (Where I Never CAN Manage t' Read Word-fer-Word and ALWAYS Have ta "Embellish" a Bit), Then Jest Go Out to That Little www.YouTube.com Site and Check Out the Collected Wit, Wisdom, and Outlandish Opinions of A. L. "BIG AL" Nolram. I Got a Couple a Videos Out There that I Tried ta Git t' Go Viral Last Year, BUTT There Ain't None a Y'all Seem t' Be Interested in Listen'n to 'em Because MOST of 'em are About 13-14 Minutes Long and I KNOW There Aren't Hardly ANY of Y'all Out There with an Attention Span THAT Long……a 7-10 Minute "Sound Byte" is About Y'alls Limit….and USUALLY it's Jest a Minute or Two t' Watch Them Thar ChipyMonks Water Skiin' or Squirrels Humpin' or Some Other Such Nonsense, While This GREAT GOD-Fearin' NATION of OURS Goes t' HELL in a HandBaskett…. BUTT…..I Figured I'd be NICE and Give Y'all an ALTERNATIVE (Ya Know….. Kindly a Like the NEW Independence Party (NIPers) is an ALTERNATIVE t' Them Thar Lousy LEFT-Leanin' Liberal Damn Democrats AND Them Thar Rascally Radically Religious RIGHT-Wing Republicans That Y'all Have Been Electin' fer the Last Few Years). I Probably Have Said This BEFORE (And Y'all KNOW I Don't Like t' Chew My Cabbage Twicet…..BUTT Y'all ALSO Know that My Fergitter's Been Workin' Overtime, BUTT SOME Things Really are WORTH Repeatin'…..). Which Reminds Me….Back When I was Larnin' t' Be a Trainer in the Good Ole United States Air Force, I Was Taught the "Rules of Learning" and Good Ole RULE #3 Applies Here:

1. The FIRST Thing Learned is the BEST Remembered

2. The LAST Thing Learned is the BEST Remembered

3. The Thing Most Often REPEATED is the BEST Remembered

4. The Thing Learned in a TRAUMATIC Situation is the BEST Remembered

For More on RULE #4 and it's Application, Reference Chapter 29.

Now There Y'all Go AGAIN, Lettin' Me Ramble On Like that …..the LACK of Ability ta Keep Me On Track and "ON Point" (Kindly a Like the NPR Radio Program) on YOUR Part, Does NOT Indicate a LACK Of Intent t' Confuse Ya and KEEP Y'all OFF Balance on MY Part. As I Have Told My Current "Leaders" Many Times: The WARNING About US Non-Commissioned Officers (NCOs), That Was Removed from the "US Army Officers Handbook" (ed 1898) for "Politically Correct" Reasons, About Us NCOs Being "enlisted men, although stupid and oftentimes lazy, can be incredibly sly and cunning and bear considerable watching", SHOULD Have Been Left IN There Because I EXEMPLIFY That Thar Statement. Now WHAT Was My "Original" Thought Before Y'all Got Me Talkin' All This TRASH…. Oh Yeah….I Remember Now…..

The Main "THRUST" (I Saw Ya Flinch….and Don't Say Ya Didn't 'Cause I SAW Ya) of the NEW Independence Party (NIPers) is ta Git Sarah Palin and Herman Cain Elected President and Vice-President (Respectively) on the NIPer Ticket in the Nov 2016 Elections, SO We Can Git This Country in GOOD Enough Shape that I Can Safely and Privately Work on a Few MORE Little Book Projects I Have in

Mind (See the Very End of This Here Little Book for a Preview of Comin' Attractions to a Book Store Near You…..OR. If'n Yer a Readin' This Here "Electronic" Version, Jest "Peek" Back Up ta the "Letter ta the Editors" Between the "Table of…Contents" and "Chapter One"). ALSO, We Want t' Try ta Convince Ms Palin and Mr Cain t' JOIN Us fer That Little 50 State Bus Tour, Because (I Don't Know about Y'all….. BUTT) I Ain't Never BEEN t' ALL 50 UNITED STATES of AMERICA and I'd Kindly a Like t' DO That on AMERICA's Dime (…..WHAT!?!.....Y'all Didn't Realize That We NIPers Was Plannin' on Y'all…."The AMERICAN Publc"….Footin' the Bill???......I Ain't Got THAT Kind of MONEY….Who the Heck Do Y'all Think I AM…..Donald Trump or Warren Buffett???). Them Thar Left-Leanin' Liberal Damn Democrats and Those Radically Religious Right-Wing Republicans Have Been Soakin' Y'all fer "Their" Campaign Funds fer Years and All that Y'all Git fer it is a Couple o' 3-5 Day "Ringling Bros. and Barnum and Bailey" Style Circuses Called the "Democratic" Convention And the"Republican" Convention. If'n Y'all Wanna Know What We NIPers Plan t' Do with the HARD-EARNED Money (and NOT MUCH of it) that Y'all Give Us, Check Out Chapter 22, BUTT Fer Now, I'm DONE Here… Movin' ON…….

Did THAT Crap Make ANY Sense to Y'all on Pages 44-47, or Am I JEST Funnin' Ya.....YOU Decide!!!

Chapter 14

WHAT's the "DIFFERENCE" Between "Leadership" and "Management" ???

Many Folks Think that These 2 Terms are Interchangeable, But We NIPers are Gonna Try t' Explain the "Difference" in a Way that Jest MIGHT Make Sense t' Y'all:

The SHORT Answer is: "Managers" Manage THINGS (Time, Money, Supplies, etc.) and They Ain't Very Concerned About Their People (They TRY ta Treat Their "People" Like "Things" TOO), Whereas "Leaders" Lead PEOPLE (Inspire Confidence, Encourage Initiative, Provide Training and Motivation, etc.) and "People" DO the Work, BUTT REALLY "Effective" Leaders of People are Also Pretty GREAT Managers of the Time, Money, and Supplies that Their People NEED to Do the Job "CORRECTLY" the VERY First Time.

Ready or Not, Here Comes the LONG Answer: There's This "Friend" of Mine (in This Really "BIG Government" Organization) Who's Been Tryin' fer YEARS ta Convince His Coworkers and Supervisors (Since He's in a One Deep Position with Nobody t' Supervise , and Because of a Recent Restructure is Doin' the Work of TWO Folks While ONLY Gittin' the Pay and Recognition of ONE) that There's a BIG "Difference" Between Jest Gittin' the Job Done ("Git 'er Done") and "Takin' the Time t' Do the Job CORRECTLY the Very First Time", BUTT He Ain't Havin' MUCH Success at it (Reference Chapter 16, Comin' Up in a Bit). So I Tried t' Help Him Out by Explainin' that There's a BIG "Difference" Between the 2 Concepts of "Leadership" and "Management"……..

"Managers" Manage THINGS (Time, Money, Supplies, etc.) and They Ain't Very Concerned about Their PEOPLE,Because They Treat Their PEOPLE (Subordinates) Like THINGS (Objects)…..Like Them Thar Interchangeable "Cogs" in the Corporate Machine (Kindly a Like That There Manager Mr Cogswell of Cogswell Cogs on that Little Cartoon Show "The Jetsons" Always Treated George Jetson Like a Cog Whenever He Would Try t' Do Somethin' for the Improvement of the Company). I Told My "Good Buddy" (and My Part-Time Executive Assistant) Not t' Worry TOO Much About Them Thar Tit-Turd Managers….. Because He Told Me that There was a Recent Personnel Change that Brought a REAL LEADER into His "Chain of Command". I Advised My Good Buddy t' WORK with This New Leader (Who was Willin' t' ACTUALLY "LISTEN", And Respond Favorably, to What He Had t' Say). Now Y'all HAVE t' Understand a Little Somethin' About My Friend (and Part-Time Executive Assistant)….. He's One a Those Types Who Keep Their Eye's and Ears OPEN and Their Mouths Shut MOST of the Time, BUTT He's ALSO One a Those Types that On Those RARE Occasions When He DOES Speak UP, Y'all Had DAMN Well Better Listen t' Him Because He HAS Somethin' t' SAY that's WORTH Listenin' To (And Usually NEEDS ta Be ACTED Upon Fer the GOOD of the Company in General AND His CUSTOMERS in Particular…Needless ta SAY, He LIVES "Customer Service"…So I Won't Say it).

I Told Him t' Do a "Core Dump" o' His "Corporate Knowledge" to This NEW LEADER, and Maybe Try and Convince that NEW LEADER of His VALUE ta the Company and t' Demonstrate (Through the Actions of His BODY) that the Decisions (of His Mind/SOUL) Were a DIRECT Result of the BELIEFS of His Heart/SPIRIT (and, of Course, of His GOD). He Tells Me that He Believes that the Process is Progessin' Well, Since That NEW LEADER Keeps Tellin' Him that, "I'm WITH Ya When Yer RIGHT". Now I Tried t' Caution My Little Part-Time Executive Assistant, to be VERY WARY of that Statement, Because That Thar NEW LEADER Might NOT Be WITH Ya When Yer WRONG. A Really GOOD Leader Will Be WITH Ya Even When Yer WRONG (and ESPECIALLY When Yer WRONG and Ya NEED the SUPORT of Yer Leader the MOST) And Try His BEST t' Protect Ya (EVEN If Ya Do Silly Things Like Call Yer Managers a Bunch a "Tit-Turds"). My Good Little "Buddy" Said that He Felt PRETTY Confident That Thar NEW LEADER Fella Would Help t' Protect Him (as BEST He Could), BUTT I Told Him the BEST Way t' Handle Someone Who's "WITH Ya When Yer RIGHT" is t' Never NEVER Be WRONG, and He Said that He Could See the SENSE in that, and I Used the Opportunity t' Remind Him that We in the NEW Independence Party (NIPers) Like t' Make SENSE, and He Was Kindly a Embarrassed that He Had Forgotten that VERY Important Fact About the NIPers (BUTT, Jest Like ME, He's Been So STRESSED Lately that His Fergitter Has Been Workin' Overtime TOO and His Brain Has Been Crampin' Up) .

The "Friend" I've Been Talkin' About (My Little Part-Time Executive Assistant) Has Been Takin' a Few Chances with His Career Lately and His WIFE Has Been Worried About Him Loosin' His "BIG Government" Organization Job (Until He Can Come Up with ANOTHER Source of Income), BUTT HE Feels that His "Current" Value t' the Company (and Especially t' His CUSTOMERS) is So GREAT (Since He's Doin' TWO Jobs fer the Price of ONE) that They Cain't POSSIBLY Consider Bootin' Him Out the Door (Especially with ALL of the Organizational "Dead Wood" Layin' Around that's About t' Burn the Company Down If'n That There NEW LEADER Don't Figure Out a Way t' "Light a Fire" Under it or Throw it Out with the TRASH).

HOWEVER, I Tried t' TEACH My Good "Buddy" a Thing or 3 (We Like t' Deal in Trinity's in the NIPers, Reference Chapter 24) that I Larned Whilst I was in the US Air Force About CYOA (Cover Your OWN Ass), BUTT He Said That He was WAYYY Ahead of Me. He Said That He Had Several OFF-Site Copies of His PERSONAL Home Directory with Trusted Friends, Who Had Instructions to Release 'em t' Them Thar EXPOSE' Media Types Like John Stossel and That Thar Geraldo Rivera Fella If'n Anything "Unusual" Was t' Happen t' Him (or If'n He Didn't "Check-in" with Them Every 30 Days), AND That If'n He Couldn't Manage t' Git THIS Little Book o' Mine Published (He's Doin' His VERY BEST in His OFF-Duty Time t' HELP Me with Getting' My Little "Baby" Published), Then He Had This OTHER Book Idea Called "One MAN's EXPOSE' of the _____ ___" (Now Y'all Can Fill-in the Blanks Anyway Y'all Want, BUTT We Want t' KEEP the FULL Title a "Secret" fer a While Due to Copyright Protection, BUTT I'll Give Y'all a Little Hint: The First Blank is an Acronym that Sort of Rhymes with "TRAVISty", and the Second Blank is an Abbreviation That Kindly a "Perfectly" Rhymes with "VA").

I Asked Him If'n That Warn't a Bit "Risky", BUTT He Assured Me That There Was This Thing Caled a "Whistle Blower Protection Act" That Should Give Him ALL a the Protection He Would EVER Need. Since Them Thar EXPOSE's Seem t' Be a Sellin' Pretty GOOD These Days, I Told Him that I Would be VERRRY Interested in Discussin' His Thoughts on the Matter, BUTT He Said That If'n We Can Git the Proper Encouragement and Support that We NEED t' Git THIS Little "Baby' o' Mine Published then There'd Probably Be No NEED ta EVER Discuss that Little EXPOSE' Book Deal. HOWEVER, I Told

Him That the NEXT Chapter Would Feed "Right" (or "Left") Inta that EXPOSE' Idea, If'n He Decided t' Go That Way……

Now I Told Y'all THAT t' Tell Ya THIS: Whether Y'all Have "Tit-Turd" Managers or INSPIRIN' LEADERS in YOUR Organization of Choice, ALWAYS Do Your "Job" as Unto Your God. I Don't KNOW About YOUR God, BUTT MY GOD Expects MORE of Me (Higher Standards of Excellence, Higher Standards of Quality, Higher Standards of Timeliness, Higher Standards of Customer Service, AND NOT Jest "LIP" Service) Every Day than My Supervisors Can POSSIBLY Imagine (BECAUSE If'n Ya REALLY Want ta KNOW My "VALUE" ta That Thar "BIG Government" Organization…. DON'T Ask My "Supervisor's" Because "They" Don't Know a "Hoot and a Holler: About Me…..They EVEN Ask ME Fer a "SELF Evaluation" So's They Know WHAT ta Write in My "Performance Eval" ……NO……..If'n Ya REALLY Want ta KNOW My "VALUE" ta the Organization…….Then Y'all JUST Ask My "CUSTOMERS" Who REALLY Know My TOP Quality "Customer Service" Values, Principles, and Standards), AND the MOST Amazing Thing is: I FAIL ta Live Up t' the Standards of My GOD EVERY Single Day, BUTT at the End of Each Day (So Far), My GOD Has Given Me ANOTHER Day of Life ta Try t' Do "BETTER Today than I Did Yesterday" and "BETTER Tomorrow than I Did Today". Don't YOU Wish That YOUR God Treated YOU That Way???.....or Maybe HE DOES…….We MAY Have the SAME GOD!!!...........Wouldn't THAT Be AMAZING and WONDERFUL !?!!!

Before I "Wind UP" This Little Chapter Let Me "Wind Y'ALL UP" with a Little "Corollary" ta the Definition of "Leadership" That I Just Gave Ya: I Was Down at the Barn Cleanin' Horse Stalls Again This Weekend (My "BEST" Place Fer Getting' Inspirational Ideas) and I Heard Old MASSA President Obamma Ramma a Spoutin' Some CRAP About Bein' "EQUAL" ta Try ta "JUSTIFY" Stealin' My (AND Yer'ns) HARD-EARNED Money ta Let His "NANNY State", "BIGG Government" Git "Their" Filthy"Double-Stick Taped" Mitts on it So's They Can "GIVE" it (or What's "LEFT" of it After Them Thar LEFT-Leanin' Liberal DAMNED Democarats Git Through Takin' "Their" CUT)… SUPPOSEDLY ta Folks Who NEED it….. RATHER Than Let ME Make Up My OWN DAMNED Mind as ta WHAT I Wanna DO with My OWN HARD-EARNED Money And Decide ta Give it (of My OWN "FREE" Will) ta WHICHever a Them Thar "REPUTABLE" Charitys (NOT a Course ta Say That the "CURRENT Administration" AIN'T Very "REPUTABLE"…… .We NIPers WOULDN'T Want ta Say THAT……or WOULD WE!!???!!......YOU DECIDE !!!)

WE the NIPers of the UNITED STATES of AMERICA Do Agree that WE AMERICANS Were ALL "CREATED" ("BORN") "EQUAL" (as Little "Squallin' BRATS" Who Pee'd in Their Britches and Crapped in Their Pants), BUTT Y'all AMERICANS Have ALL Made "Different" LIFE Choices from THAT Time Onward (And SOME a US Have Made "BETTER" or "BEST" Life "CHOICES") That "EVOLVED" Ya inta the "Successes" or "Failures" That Y'all Are Today, And It's NOT ANY of Y'ALL's DUTY or RESPONSIBILITY ta Have ta UNWILLIN'LY DONATE Your "Success" ta Try and "COMPENSATE" Anyone ELSE Fer "Their" Failure ta "Succeed". As We NIPers Have Said ("Written") in "Other" Chapters, Especially Chapter 54, We ALL Have ta "SUFFER the Consequenses" of OUR "BAD" Decisions (That's Called "TOUGH LOVE", or Maybe "TOUGH TIITY", Or MAYBE Even "Quit Yer DAMN Leech-Suckin' OFF'n the MASSA President Obamma Ramma BIG Government TITTY", or SUMTHIN' Like That)….AND Be Able ta "REAP the Benefits" of Our "GOOD" Decisions (WITHOUT Some "Robbin' HOODlum" Federal Government Trying ta "Steal Yer LAST Dime") !!!

AND While We're on the "Subject" of "EQUALITY".......Let Me Tell Ya a Little Story (ANOTHER One a Them Thar "Leadership" Corollarys) from My "Military" Career About Airman "Bag-a-Donuts" (a Dedicated WORKER) And Little Airman "Box-a-Rocks" (a Dedicated SHIRKER). In the "Military" We Didn't HAVE None a Them Thar Obnoxious LABOR UNIONS That FORCE Ya ta Treat "WORKERs" and "SHIRKERs" "EQUALLY", We MOSTLY Had "Leaders" (NOT Tit-Turd "Managers" That Don't Know NUTHIN' About "People" Exceptin' ta Treat 'em Like "Objects") Who Did NOT Treat Their Troops "EQUALLY", BUUTT They DID Treat Them "FAIRLY". Let's Throw One MORE Troop inta the Mix Fer GOOD Measure (And ta Give Us a "Trinity" ta Work with): Little Airman "3-Bags-Full-of-it", Who is NEW to the Unit And is STILL Decidin' (Fer GOOD or BAD) Whether ta Be a WORKER Like Airman Bag-a-Donuts OR a SHIRKER Like Airman Box-a-Rocks. Before We Git TOO Far inta This EXITIN' Story, Let's Take a 'short' Paragraph Break ta Talk About "Performance Evaluation Systems" While Airman 3-Bags-Full-of-it Has Time ta "Observe" How Unit "Leadership" Deals with Them "Other" Two Airmen......

My "Performance" Has Been "Evaluated" by Several Different "Systems" in My Various "Careers Over the Years", BUTT Even Though I Was NEVER in the ARMY, I Hear That "THEIRS" was the "BEST" (MOST Efficient and Effective)......It ONLY Had Three (a "Trinity") Ratings (Because That is ALL Ya REALLY Need): 1) GOOD, 2) FAIR, and 3) POOR. The GOOD'ns Ya Promoted, the FAIR Ones Ya "LEFT" "RIGHT" Where They Was, AND The POOR Ones Ya Either "Kicked ASS" Until They Rated as FAIR or Ya "Kicked Their ASS OUT a the DOOR" (in ta The "CIVILIAN" World Where the Obnoxious LABOR UNIONS Would Ensure That They Were "EQUALLY", BUTT NOT "FAIRLY" Treated by Whichever "CIVILIAN" Company or Business They Chose ta "INFECT" with Their POOR "Attitude". OK.......BACK ta Our Excitin' Tale of the "Three Airmen".....

Little Airman 3-Bags-Full-of-it Has Been a Watchin' the "Other" Two Airmen Fer SOME Time Now, Under the 'Watchful Eye" of Master Sergeant "Objective-Management" (SOME a Ya Can SEE Where I'm a Goin' with This......Some a Ya Don't.......AND as ALWAYS......MOST a Ya Hadn't Got a "CLUE") AND She Has Noticed That MSgt Objective-Management Jest KEEPS a Pilin' the WORK onta the Plate of Airman Bag-a-Donuts Because He (Git THIS Now): Takes the TIME ta Do the Job/Task "Correctly" the Very First Time, And Does the "Correct" Job, in the "Correct" Way ALMOST Every Time, AND When He DOES Make a Mistake, He Admits it IMMEDIATELY, Apologises Fer it Dearly and Sincerely, "Corrects' the Mistake (And Any Negative Events "Caused" by the Mistake) And Moves ON ta His Next Task, BUTT Doesn't Seem ta Git Much Praise, Recognition, or Even "Attention" from MSgt Objective-Management (Exceptin' When the MSgt Comes by Once in a GREAT While ta Say, "Where's That Thar SUSPENCE That's Due by Close of Business (COB) Today???").

Little Airman 3-Bags-Full-of-it Has ALSO Noticed that Airman Box-a-Rocks Has Been Sittin' on His DEAD ASS Playin' Video Games This Whole Time And ONLY "Appears" t' Be "Productive" Whenever MSgt Objective-Management Comes Around (Which ISN'T Very Often) ta Git Airman Box-a-Rocks "Input" Fer the "Project Mangement Timeline", or the "SharePoint Calendar Updates", or the Bi-Weekly "Production Status Report", or the Semi-Annual "Self-Evaluation" (in Which Airman Box-a-Rocks is Very Sure ta ALWAYS Rate HisSelf as "OUTSTANDING" at Shirkin' His Duties and Gittin' MSgt Objective-Management ta PASS Them ta Airman Bag-a-Donuts), BUTT Airman Bag-a-Donuts Has SOO Much WORK ta Do That He Doesn't USUALLY Have the TIME ta Complete ALL a the BullShooin' Paperwork, SOOOOO His Performance Ratin' from MSgt Objective-Management Usually Suffers Fer it.

Little Airman 3-Bags-Full-of-it Had JEST About Decided WHICH of the "Other" Airmen ta "Emulate" When MY GOD Threw Her a Little "Curve Ball"......MSgt Objective-Management Had Reached His "High Year of Tenure" and Was "FORCED" ta Retire, And Was Replaced By Master Sergeant "Excellent-Leader" Who Practiced "Leadership" When Dealing with "People" and Practiced "Management" ONLY When Dealin' with "Objects", And NEVER Got the Two "Confused" (Like the "CURRENT" Tit-Turd Administration of the GREAT GOD-Fearin' UNITED STATES of AMERICA). SOOOOO Airman Bag-a-Donuts Got a "Promotion" ta "Team Leader", Airman Box-a-Rocks Got a BAD Conduct Discharge, And Airman 3-Bags-Full-of-it Learned a VALUABLE Lesson on the "Differences" Between "Leadership" and "Management"; "Equality" and "Fairness", AND the "NEW Independence Party (NIPers)" and EITHER Them Thar "Lousy LEFT-Leanin' Liberal DANM Democrats" OR Them Thar "Rascally Radically Religious RIGHT-Wing Republicans".......AND We NIPers HOPE That YOU (Gentle Readers) Learned a Little Sumthin' in This Chapter TOO.......Movin' ON.......

Did THAT Crap Make ANY Sense to Y'all on Pages 48-52, or Am I JEST Funnin' Ya.....YOU Decide!!!

Chapter 15

If the "Pen" is Mightier than the "Sword", is a "Word Processor" More Powerful than an "Atomic Bomb" ???

There is This Phrase that a LOT a Folks Use: "The Pen is Mightier than the Sword", BUTT We NEW Independence Party Members (NIPers) Feel that This Phrase is Out-Dated and SHOULD a Been Revised Several Years Ago to: "The TypeWriter is More Dangerous than a Sub-Machine Gun" (and it Kindly a Sounds Like One TOO, Especially Those Old Royal "Manual",as Opposed t' Them Thar Electric Model, TypeWriters (Bang…. Bang…. Bang, Bang, Bang…..Bang….Bang), HOWEVER in This Here Twenty-First Century, The Phrase SHOULD be VIRTUALIZED to "The Word Processor is MORE Powerful than an Atomic Bomb" (and CAN Be JEST as "Dangerous" in the Wrong Hands).

If Used with MALICE, a Word Processor Can Incite Violence…..Destroy Reputations…..AND Crumble the Very Foundation of Life, Liberty, and the Pursuit of Justice (No….That Should be Pursuit of HAPPINESS…..We Have "Legality" Instead of "Justice" These Days, Reference Chapter 53) that This GREAT GOD-Fearin' Country of Ours was BUILT Upon (Just Like an Atomic Bomb), BUTT, In the "Correct" Hands (As I Have Said Before, We NIPers AVOID the Use of the Word "RIGHT" t' Keep Us from Bein' Too Closely Associated with Them Thar Radically Religious RIGHT-Wing Republicans, NOT t' Mention Them Thar LEFT-Leanin' Liberal Damn Democrats…..So Let's PLEASE Not Mention Them Here, Reference Chapter 2), a Word Processor CAN EMPOWER an ENTIRE NATION (Like Our Sun, the Biggest Nuclear Reactor in Our Solar System). We NIPers TRY ta Emmulate that "Second" Use of the Word Processor Whenever Possible, BUTT We're Defintely NOT Adverse ta Usin' the "First" Use Either….. Whenever "Circumstances" Require it .

I May Be Wrong (I've Been Wrong Before and I'll Be Wrong Again……I Thought I WAS Wrong Once, However, I Found Out Later, t' My UTTER Chagrin, that I was Mistaken) and Totally "Psychotic", BUTT I Have the "Delusion of Grandeur" that I May ACTUALLY Be Usin' This Here Word Processor of Mine (And the NIPers) t' EMPOWER the AMERICAN Public t' Rise UP Off'n Their Dead ASSES and JOIN the "NEW" AMERICAN Revolution of the NEW Independence Party (NIPer) ta Take BACK This GREAT GOD-Fearin' NATION of OURS from Them Thar Heathen godLESS Atheists by Gittin' Ms Sarah Palin and Mr Herman Cain Elected President and Vice-President (Respectively) on the NEW Independence Party (NIPer) Ticket in Them Thar Nov 2016 Elections (Reference Chapter 18, Comin' Up Pretty Dog Gone Soon).

Now If'n Y'all Got's SUMTHIN' ta Say That's WORTH Sayin' AND Ya Wanna Say it in Writin'…. Jest See Ole Tim Murphy from AuthorHouse. SOME a Them Thar "Publishin' Folks" is Pretty "Pricey", BUTT…..I Got's MY "Baby" Out to Ya via eBook, AND Paperback, WITH Copyright Pertection on AuthorHouse's "LEGACY" Plan (And Like Ken Dorfman of "Animal House"……I Figger I Must Be a "Legacy" TOOOOO……Cause I Kindly a Looks Like Him……And Folks is Always a Callin' ME a "Dorf"…..or a "Doof"……or Maybe it's a "Dork"…….AHHH HELL……Y'all KNOW What I Mean …..Y'ALL's the Ones Who's a Been Callin' Me THAT……Movin' ON…) Fer About $950 Base Price, BUTT My GOOD LORD KNEW that was STILL a Bit Much Fer Me, SOOOOO Fer Jest THIS Month

(Jan 2013) Them Thar AuthorHouse Folks was a Runnin' a "SPECIAL" That ALL a Their Plans was a 25% OFF, AND Ya Got Some Kindly a "Press Release" Worth About $480 Fer FREE…..Now Ya CAIN'T Hardly Beat a Deal Like THAT with a Stick…..or a "Walkin' Stick"……Which Reminds Me …..I Need Ta Pass This ta My GOOD Buddy Calvin WalkingStick (Who's One a Them Thar "Native AMERICANS" That We "STOLE" This Here GREAT GOD-Fearin' NATION a OURS from…..I Don't Really BLAME Them Fer NOT Puttin' AMERICA "First" Like I Do Them Thar AFRICAN-Americans …..Them Thar "NATIVE AMERICANS" Can Call TheirSelves WHATEVER They WANT, on Account a THEY Was Here FIRST……BUTT….a Lot a Them Thar "NATIVE AMERICANS" Are a Gittin' Ya BACK Fer Buyin' This Country from 'em with a Few Strings a Beads……by Takin' it BACK "with INTEREST" through ALL a Them Thar Casinos They Own Now AIN'T They???

   AND If'n Ya THINK They ALL Worship Them "STRANGE Gods", Then Ya AIN'T Met Calvin WalkingStick, 'Cause HE Has the SAME GOD Family that I DO……And He was a Sayin' That His Grandad or Uncle or Sumthin' Had Written a Buncha POEMS That Was Purty Worth Listenin' to And That They was Collected inta This Little Book, And He was a Thinkin' a Gittin' 'em "Published"…. SOOOOO I Needs ta Inform Him ta Talk ta Ole Tim Murphy of AuthorHouse…….Now Tim Murphy SAID That He Didn't THINK That He was Related ta That "OTHER" Murphy Fella Who Had Sumthin' ta Do with "Murphy's LAW" (AND I SHORE "HOPE" That He's "CORRECT" About That 'Cause I Don't NEED "THAT" Kindly a HELP), BUTT Tim Murphy has Been SOOOOO Helpful (Although When I TOLD Him That My Little "Baby" was "PULITZER PRIZE" Winnin' Material, I Don't Think He Believed Me, BUTT He Hadn't Really READ it Yet) That I TOLD Him When I Make My FIRST 30 Million Dollars……He's Gonna Git 3 (10%) of it (BUTT I Don't THINK He Believed THAT Either, BUTT I'm a Man a My WORD…..And My WORD is My BOND)……SOOOOO I Imagine That HE'S Gonna Have the SAME Look on HIS Face That "Erin Brockovich" Had on HER Face When She Got HER Check from the Fella SHE Helped Out So Much…….I WISH I Could BE There ta SEE it…..

   BUTT Jest Like "Peter Sellers" in "BEING THERE"……I Got's a GREAT GOD-Fearin' NATION ta SAVE, And I Got's ta Git My Little NIPers a Rallied Together AND a Rollin' ON Down the Road in That Thar 13 Bomb-Bustin' Bus CONVOYYYYYY ta Meet EVERY SINGLE AMERICAN Voter (If'n THEY Decide ta Take the Time and Effort ta Come Out ta Meet US), And Start OUR NEW AMERICAN Revolution (One Voter at a Time), AND Git My Little NEW Independece Party Started (We Gotta Git This Party Started……We GOTTA Git This PARTY Started……WE GOTTA GIT THIS PARTY STARTED……YEAH !!!), AND Git Ms Sarah Palin And Mr Herman Cain Elected President and Vice-Presdient (Respectively) on the NIPer "WRITE-IN" Ballot Campaign in Them Thar Nov 2016 Elections …..WELLLLLL I Guess THAT's QUITE Enough ta Be Gittin' ON with…..Better Be a Movin' ON…..

Did THAT Crap Make ANY Sense to Y'all on Page 53-54, or Am I JEST Funnin' Ya……YOU Decide!!!

Chapter 16

Are Ya the "Git 'er Dun" Type, OR is There a "BETTER" ("BEST" ??) Way ???

Are You (Gentle Reader) One a Them Thar "Git 'er Done" Types (Like Them Thar LEFT-Leanin' Liberal Damn Democrats AND Them Thar Radically Religious RIGHT-Wing Republicans) or Do Y'all Subscribe t' the NEW Independence Party (NIPer) Philosophy of "Take the TIME ta Do Yer Damn Duty "CORRECTLY" the Very FIRST Time, AND Make Damn SURE that Ya Do the "Correct" JOB in the "Correct" WAY at the "Correct" TIME."??? My Little Part-Time Executive Assistant Tried ta Tell One o' His Co-Workers (in That "BIG Government" Organization He Works for) That Very Thing One Day and the Little Co-Worker Said, "What's the "Difference???". Is it Any WONDER Why Them There "BIG Government" FolksWaste SOOOO Much a Our TAX Dollars, and Operate SOOOO Inefficiently and SOOOO Ineffectually with THAT Kinda Attitude???

We NIPers Don't JEST Wanna "Git 'er Done", Because That Ain't Consistent with Our GOD's Policy of Constant Vigilence, Constant Improvement, and Constant Standard of Excellence. We Don't KNOW About YOUR God, BUTT OUR GOD Demand's MORE of Us NIPers on a Daily Basis than Y'all Can Possibly Imagine, AND We Continue ta Fail t' Meet That Standard of Perfection, BUTT We Don't Let THAT Discourage Us and We Try ALL the HARDER ta Learn MORE and ACHIEVE More (Quicker, Cheaper, and MORE Efficiently in the Use of Tools and Supplies). If'n THAT is YOUR Philosophy TOO, Then YOU Might Be a NEW Independence Party Thinker (NIPer) and NOT Even KNOW it, and We SHORE Could Use Yer Help in Getting' Ms Sarah Palin and Mr Herman Cain Elected President and Vice-President (Respectively) on the NEW Independence Party Ticket for Them Nov 2016 Elections.

HOWEVER, There's a LOT a Time (and a FEW Elections) Between Now and Then, and It'd Be Kinda NICE If'n Ms Palin and Mr Cain Had a Few Pre-Placed NIPer Thinkers in the Senate and House of Representatives ta Work WITH Them (as Opposed t' Against 'em) So that Ms "Future Madam President" Palin Wouldn't Have Such a HARD Time as the First "Lady" (and Remember There is a BIG Difference Between a "Woman" and a "Lady") President. AND While We're on the TOPIC of First "Lady"….. I Meant "First Lady", We NIPers Have an Idea that Will Save Mr Palin from Havin' ta Perform Duties as the 1st "First Husband"……Palin Family and Cain Family…..Listen UP !!!....'Cause Y'all are Gonna Have ta Work "Together" as a "TEAM" t' Make This WORK……..

The "Traditional" Role of the "Spouse of the President" Will NEED ta "Change" Due to the Precident of the President Bein' a Male Changin' ta a Female…….Have I Gotten Ya GOOD and Confused Yet???.. GOOD!!! Now Yer Ready for the NEW Precident……Mr Cain, While We Train Ya UP ta Take Ms Palin's Job as President in 2020, We NEED t' Train Yer WIFE (the "Second Lady", and We ALL Know that When Yer Number 2, Ya ALWAYS Try HARDER) ta Be the "First Lady" By Lettin' HER Take On the Duties of "First Lady" While She's Still ONLY the "Second Lady"……This Get's Mr Palin Outta That Onerous Duty of Bein' the 1st "First Husband"…..Does THAT Sound GOOD t' Ya Mr Palin??? Have We MAYBE Made a NEW Independence Party Thinker/Member (NIPer) Outta Ya YET???...... WEELLLLLLL…..We're Gonna Keep Workin' on Ya…….JEST Keep ON Readin'……

This Page Has Been "INTENTIONALLY" ("RIGHTly") "LEFT" BLANK.

(Exceptin' Fer the Chapter Trailer, And the Text Above, AND The Text Below This Line)

(ta HONOR the Makers of "Zork II", the SAME as Them Thar Makers of "Zork")

Did THAT Crap Make ANY Sense to Y'all on Pages 55-56, or Am I JEST Funnin' Ya.....YOU Decide!!!

Chapter 17

How CAN We REFORM the Tax System, AND, Pay Off the National Debt at the SAME TIME ???

I'm Tellin' Ya Right NOW that THIS Chapter Works in Conjunction with Chapter 47, So Don't Git Yer Panties in a Wad If'n I Tell Ya t' Refer ta Chapter 47 Fer an Explanation of What the "FREEDOM" Tax is. We NIPers TOTALLY Agree with Mr Herman Cain's 9-9-9 Flat Tax Plan, Because When We NIPers Git Done Parin' Down the Federal Government (And Turn the BULK o' That Power BACK ta the STATES) There Should be MORE'n Enough in the Treasury (Especially If'n Mr Warren "Money Man" Buffett is a Handlin' it) ta Do ALL of the REALLY Important Stuff : 1) Safety/Security from OTHERS by the Active Duty Military and CIA; 2) Safety/Security from OURSELVES by the National Guard and FBI; and Finally 3) Preservation/Maintenance of Our Pretty "Sadly" Neglected Transportation and Communication Infrastructures by Federal Agencies Specifically Created, Designed, and Equiped to "Preserve, Maintain, And ENHANCE" Them Thar VERRY Important InfraStuctures.

Let's Us Talk Fer a Minute About the NIPer Philosophy Regardin' TAXES and Especially in Regards ta INCOME Taxes: In the Days in Which Our NIPer Handbook (the "User's Guide and Maintenance Manual for a Human Life" or "UGMMHL", "Holy Bible" Version) was Written, There Weren't NO Such THING as Separation of "Church" (Organized Religion) and "State" (Government)..........The GOSH DARNED Hebrew Orthodxy WAS the "State" (That's Called a "Theocracy", with GOD in Charge, and NOT a "Democracy", Where the PEOPLE are SUPPOSED ta Be "in Charge" via a "Representative" form of Government). Since the "Church" (Organized Hebrew Religion) WAS the "State" (Theocratic Government), When The Hebrews Were Asked to "TITHE" (10%), Then That "INCOME TAX" Went Toward the Daily Runnin' of the "Government" and the Hebrews "Free Will Offerin's" ("Charity") Went Toward GOD's Work of Takin' Care of the Widows, Orphans, and Infirm ("Severely" Disabled).

HOWEVER, Today's "Benevolent" Churches Have "Perverted" GOD's Perfect Plan and DUPE Y'all Inta Thinkin' That Y'all Have ta Pay THEM That "TITHE" (10%) Which SHOULD (as "INCOME TAX") Be Goin' Toward the Runnin' of the "Government" , THUS Allowin' That DAMNed Faceless Federal Government ta BILK Ya Fer a WHOLE HEEP More'n GOD Authorized 'em to (ONLY 10%). Now Don't Get Me WRONG......I Ain't Sayin' That Ya Shouldn't Give Money t' Yer "Church" ......We NIPers are JUSTly Tellin' Ya That Ya Got it ALL BassAkerd's (and Therfore, Y'all Need ta Perform the FAMOUS NIPer "BassAkerds Magic Trick" ta Put it BACK t' the CORRECT Way): Ya SHOULD Be Givin' No MORE Than a Tithe (10%) t' the Runnin' of the Federal Government, and That SHOULD Give Ya Enough Left in Yer Pocketbook ta Give 5%, 10%, 30%, or MORE ta the "Churches" (and of Course OTHER "Charitable" Organizations) ta Take Care o' Them Thar Widows, Orphans, and Infirm ("Severely" Disabled). This MEANS That We Can Git RID o' That DAMNed Adictive Drug Called "WELFAIR" (Which is an ABOMINATION ta the SOUL, Because it Saps the Initiative and "Repect fer Self" Out of a Person), And Git BACK ta GOD's Plan of Usin' "Charity" (Which is ONLY Obnoxious t' the SOUL, and Causes a Person t' Wanna DO Somethin' ta Git OFF of Charity, And Even "Pay it FORWARD" to Another Needy Person, Once They are Able ta Git OFF'n it All Together).

Once Again, We NIPers TOTALLY Agree with Mr Herman Cain's Proposal of 9% PERSONAL Income Tax, 9% CORPORATE Income Tax, and 9% SALES (or "FREEDOM", Reference Chapter 47) Tax. This is WELL Under the 10% Limit Set by GOD (and Allows fer the States ta Git a Little from Ya Without Breakin' Yer Piggy Bank). ONCE We NIPers Institute This "FLAT" Tax Rate (and Git RID o' ALL o' Them Thar "Loopholes" and "Escape Clauses") Then EVERYONE Will Contribute EQUALLY (and THAT Means: If'n Yer Son or Daughter Mows Lawns or Babysits and Makes $10, Then They Owe $1.00 to the Federal Government for Keepin' ALQEADA from Attackin', and Fer Keepin' the Kid Down the Street from Stealin' the Other Nine Dollars (OR the Whole Danged Lawn Mower), and for the Roads, Bridges, and Underpasses They Used ta GIT ta Them Thar "Jobs" (in an Economy Where So FEW Folks HAVE One), Along with the Internet and Phones They Used ta "Advertize" Their Services and Make Contact with Their Customers, etc….Etc…..ETC…….I THINK Y'all Git the "BIG Picture" That We DON'T Need "BIG Government" in Our LIVES Any MORE Than Necessary……AND Remember NOT ta FERGIT ta Check OUT Chapter 47 on the FREEDOM Tax ta Pay OFF the "National DEBT"…..Fer the KIDs …..Ya KNOW…….We NIPers Cain't STAND ta Think a Them Thar KIDS Havin' ta Be "SADDLED" with THAT "Dead Horse" a Hangin' Around Their Necks…..Movin' ON…..

Did THAT Crap Make ANY Sense to Y'all on Pages 57-58, or Am I JEST Funnin' Ya…..YOU Decide!!!

Chapter 18

How CAN the NIPers "Convince" Ms Sarah Palin ta Be OUR Presidential Candidate and Mr Herman Cain ta Be OUR Vice-Presidential Candidate ???

WEELLLLLL…..We TOLD Ya Why We NIPers Want Ms Sarah Palin and Mr Herman Cain as OUR Presidential and Vice-Presidential Candidates in Chapter 3, BUTT We STILL Gotta "Convince" THEM:

Ms Palin….Dear Lady….And You ARE a LADY, And Don't Let ANYONE Tell Ya Any Differently, Because (as I'm SURE You Are Aware……There is a BIG "Difference" Between a "Woman" and a "Lady"……JUST as There is a BIG "Difference" Between a "Man" and a "Gentleman"……Take that as "Gospel" from Me……a "Gentleman" from the "Old School" Where "Manners" Were Beaten inta Us by Lovin' Parents AND Teachers, So's We Wouldn't Go Around Actin' Like a Buncha godLESS Heathens and Disruptin' Folks Conversations, and…….Oh, I'm VERRY SORRY….Dear Lady……I Seem ta Have Gotten OFF "Point" Somehow…..Again…..PLEASE Fergive This Old Fart……Now Where Was I…..

NOW I Remember…..I Was a Tryin' ta Convince Ya t' Be OUR Presidential Candidate fer the NEW Independence Party (NIPers) Fer Them Thar Nov 2016 Elections. We Woulda Been a WHOLE HEEP Better OFF (instead a FOUR MORE YEARS of the SAME Crap that We've Had ta Put UP with Fer the LAST Four) If'n We NIPers Coulda Gotten Yer (And Mr Cain's) Attention in Time Fer Them Thar 2012 Elections….BUTT…..It MAY Work Out "BEST" This Way…..We Don't LIKE ta RUSH Things TOO Much…. And According'ta Our NIPer Motto (ONE of MANY We Like ta Refer to), "Take the TIME ta Do the Job "CORRECTLY" the VERY First Time"…..We Figger that the Next Four (4) Years Will be "Sufficient" ta Git This Here NEW Independence Party Started ("We're Gonna Git This Party Started…. We're Gonna GIT This Party STARTED …..WE'RE GONNA GIT THIS PARTY STARTED !!!"….. YEAH !!!), And ta Complete Our Three….Count 'em, THREE….13 Bomb-Bustin' Bus 50 State NIPer Campaign Tours of the GREAT GOD-Fearin' GOOD Ole US of A, AND Git YOU and Mr Herman Cain Elected ta the HIGHEST Offices in the Land (in a "Landslide" by the TOTALLY Impossible Process of a "Write In" Campaign)…..WEELLLL….I Think ya Git the Idea that We NIPers Have Our Work Cut Out Fer Us Fer the Next 4 Years or So…..

Thoughout This Little "Baby" (Book) o' Mine We NIPers Are a Gonna TRY Our BEST ta Convince YOU and Mr Cain ta JOIN the NEW Independence Party, And JOIN Us Fer the Trinity of 13 Bomb-Bustin' Bus 50 State Campaigns, AND JOIN Us Fer Yer Jam Bang UP GREAT Inaugeration Party in Jan 2017 (See Chapter 49 Fer a Few Details), BUTT……in THIS Here Chapter We're Gonna Make JEST a Slightly "DIFFERENT" Appeal ta Yer Sensitive Sensabilities That We Feel Just MIGHT Git Ya ON-BOARD the NIPer Train (or 13 Bomb-Bustin; Bus CONVOYYYYY, See Chapter 22, If'n Ya Haven't Already)…..

We're Gonna TRY ta Convince Ya That We NIPers (and ME in Particular) Know a"Thing 'er 3 About a Thing 'er 3"…..Now I USED ta Know a "Thing 'er Two About a Thing 'er Two" (Which ACTUALLY "Sings" a Little Better t' Yer "Ear Bones"), BUTT (I'm a Showin' Ya My BIG BUTT Again….SOOOO Ya KNOW What's a Comin'…..), When MY "CORRECT" Pastor Teacher (Who I Cain't Name….. Fer

Reasons Explianed in OTHER Chapters of My Book) Convinced Me That I was a Triune (Trinity) Being (with a BODY, SOUL, and SPIRIT), Then I "Discovered" That I Knew a "Thing 'er Three About a Thing 'er Three".....Now That YOU and I Are on the SAME Page.......Let's Turn That Page, and Git ON with the Convincin'.......

   I'm Gonna Talk ta Ya About the NIPer Philosophy of the "FREE Pass" ta Heaven, Downs Syndrome Children in General, And YOUR Son "Trig" in Particular......We NIPers Just HAVE the Distinct Feelin' That When You Git Done Readin' This Here Chapter, You're Gonna Be BEGGIN' Us ta Git Ya Elected ta the Presidency of This Here GREAT GOD-Fearin' Nation of OURS....BUTT...We MAY Be WRONG (it Wouldn't Be the FIRST Time), We've Been WRONG Before and We'll Be WRONG Again, BUTT.... We Don't THINK We're Gonna Be WRONG.....THIS Time.....

   We NIPers Believe That We KNOW EXACTLY What Happened in the Garden of Eden When Adam and Eve Ate the "Poisonous" Forbidden Fruit from the "Tree of the Knowledge of GOOD and EVIL".....I KNOW......I KNOW.....Yer Sayin' ta YerSelf, "What the HELL Does This Have ta Do with a "FREE Pass" ta Heaven, Downs Syndrome Children in General, And MY SON "Trig" in Particular?!!?".....
WELLLLLL....If'n You'll UNWad Yer Panties and Hold onta Them Thar Horses a Yours Fer a Minute, I'm About ta TELL Ya.....And I'm a GONNA Tell Ya, According ta the NIPer "Handbook" Principle of "The FIRST Shall be LAST, And the LAST Shall be FIRST" By Startin' with Yer SON "Trig".....

   I KNOW That I DON'T Have ta Tell Ya That Yer SON "Trig" is "Special", BUTT I DO Havr ta Tell Ya Just HOW "Special" He IS....Your SON "Trig" (Along with ALL Downs Syndrome Children, AND Any "Normal" Child Who Has NOT Developed "Mentally" ta the Point o' Bein' Able ta Make a Logical, Reasonable, and Rational Decision ta Accept CHRIST as Their Savior).....Has a "FREE Pass" ta Heaven, AND I'm SORRY (Because it is a SIN), BUTT I Really "ENVY" Your SON......Because I ONLY Have 23 Chromosomes, And Therefore Do NOT Have a "FREE Pass" ta Heaven......I (Like YOU) Must Make a Conscious Descision ta Accept the LORD Jesus CHRIST as My Savior (.....According ta "MY" GOD's WORD... Now I Don't KNOW About YOUR God.....on Account a Ya Ain't TOLD Me About Yer God, I'm Just Talkin' About "MY GOD") in Order ta Have a CHANCE ta Git inta Heaven......

   Let's Back UP a Bit and Let Me Go inta a Little More Detail.....Once Upon a Time....in the Garden of Eden......GOD Created Adam and Eve with 24 Chromosomes (That 24th One Being a "Shield" Against the KNOWLEDGE of EVIL......And THAT's Why Downs Syndrome Kid's Are So Kind and Lovin' ALL of the Time......Because They are "Innocent" and Have NEVER KNOWN EVIL.....Because That 24th Chromosome KEEPS the KNOWLEDGE of EVIL "OUT" of Their Minds/SOULS)....AND the Serpent ("Possessed" by Satan/Lucifer/ "Son of the Morning"/Devil/Whatever) Beguiled Eve to EAT of the "Poisonous" Fruit of the "Tree of the Knowledge of GOOD and EVIL", and Her 24th Chromosone Was "KILLED" and She LOST Her "Shield" and IMMEDIATELY Knew EVIL......And Could Tell the "Difference" Between GOOD and EVIL, And KNEW That She Had DONE EVIL, And Convinced Her Damged Fool of a Husband ta EAT......WEELLLLL, Y'all KNOW the "Rest of the Story" (as the Late GREAT Paul Harvey Used ta Say.....And If'n Ya DON'T.....Ya Can Just Look it UP in the NIPer "Handbook" in "The First Book of Moses Called GENESIS").....

   I Don't KNOW About YOUR God (Cause Ya STILL Ain't TOLD Me About Him Yet), BUTT "MY" GOD Said, "Suffer the Little Children ta Come Unta ME, Because Their's is the Kingdom of Heaven", Which MEANS That ALL a Those Sandy Hook School Kids are in Heaven with HIM Right NOW....

AND (Yer Gonna LOVE THIS), Since Downs Syndrome Kids NEVER Quit Bein' Kids, AND NEVER Are Able ta Make a Descision For OR Against MY GOD…….They ALL Have "DOUBLE COUPON FREE PASSES ta HEAVEN"……Now I REALLY "ENVY" Yer SON "Trig"…..And I KNOW It's a "SIN", BUTT I Just Cain't HELP it, And I WANT ta MEET Him SOOOO Badly, Because Its Been a Coon's Age (Back When I Helped with a "Special Olympics" in My "Military" Career) Since I Got a Hug From Somebody with a "DOUBLE COUPON FREE Pass" ta Heaven……Do Ya THINK That Ya Just MIGHT Be Able ta Arrange That Fer Me…….If'n I Was ta Git Ya Elected as President of These Here GREAT GOD-Fearin' UNITED STATES of OURS???..........Pretty , PRETTY PLEEEEEEASE !!!

There is Just ONE LAST "Brain SLAP" I NEED ta Give Ya that Will Put Ya "Over the EDGE" (of the "Fiscal Cliff" Leadin' ta the "Landslide" that Will Put Ya in the White House Fer as LONNGGGG as Ya WANT ta Be….CONSIDER You THIS Ms Palin……the LORD Jesus CHRIST was a "PERFECT" Man (with a "Perfect" BODY), And Therefore MUST Have Had 24 Chomosomes (Provided by GOD the FATHER's SIGNIFICANT "OTHER" When He "Came" Upon the "Virgin" Mary), SOOOOO….. Isn't It Gonna Be a "SHOCK" ta Almost EVERYONE (Execept Maybe YOU, Your "Family", and ALL of The OTHER "Downs Syndrome Families") When "They" Git ta Heaven and Discover that the "Perfect" BODY of the LORD Jesus CHRIST is a "DOWNS SYNDROME" BODY…..WOW !!!!!

OK……You Go Dry Yer Eyes and Collect YerSelf Ms Palin…..Dear Lady……'Cause I Gots ta Try ta Git Mr Cain ON-BOARD the NIPer Train, BUTT I Ain't Got Nearly as GOOD a Ammunition ta Shoot Down HIS Objections as I Had ta Use Against YOU……SOOOOOO…..Mr Cain….Kind SIR…..Let's Jest SEE What This Old Fart from Beauregard, AL Has Up His Sleeve…..in His Bag o' Tricks…..Or Up His Anal Orifice…. That Could POSSIBLY Convince Ya ta Jump onta the NIPer Band Wagon (or the NIPer Train…. OR a NIPer13 Bomb-Bustin' Bus CONVOYYYYYY)……Let Me SEE…….

While I'm a Thinkin'a Somethin', I'd Be Willin' ta BET That YOU and Ms Palin are Kindly a Wonderin' "Who the Heck AM I, and WHY the HELL Should You CARE" Even AFTER Readin' Chapter 8….Ain't Ya??……Go ON…..You Can ADMIT IT…..Ain't Nobody Here BUTT Us Silly Chickens… I BET That YOU Can't Find Out ANYTHING About "BIG AL" Nolram, OTHER Than He's Got a Few www.YouTube.com Videos That Ain't Nobody a Lookin' at, And That He Tried ta Git a "Different" Book ("The Holy Bible Companion Series, from an Information Technology Perspective, The First Book of Moses Called GENESIS – How it ALL Began"…..ta Be "Immediately" Follerd by the "Second" Book in the Series, "The Holy Bible Companion Series, from an Information Technology Perspective, The Second Book of Moses Called Exodus – Let's Git the Flock Outta Here !!!") Published a Couple Years Ago AND Didn't Have NO Success at That Either.

Now Ya MIGHT be a Thinkin' That I'm ONE a Them Thar EX FBI or CIA Fellas Who Can Destroy ALL Evidence of Their PREVIOUS Nefarious Activities (BUTT, You'd Be WRONG), OR Ya MIGHT be a Thinkin' That I'm ONE a Them Thar Folks Under the "Witness Pertection" Program That Ya Cain't Find Unless'n They WANT Ya to (AND Ya'd Be WRONG Agin……And I'd Be a DAD Blamed FOOL ta Be a Writin' a Famous Masterpiece Like This and Tryin' ta Git a NEW Independence Party Started ta Take ON BOTH Them Thar LEFT-Leanin' Liberal DAMN Democrats AND Them Thar RADICALLY Religious RIGHT-Wing Republicans, AND Tryin' ta Git YOU and Ms Palin ON-BOARD the NIPer 13 Bomb-Bustin' Bus Campaign Tour for THREE Trips Around the 50 United States)…WHAT the HELL was Ya a Thinkin' SON……..Maybe We NIPers DON'T Need You as Our Vice-Presidential Candidate,

We THOUGHT You Was SMARTER Than THAT !!!!!.......Jest Funnin' Ya……And Ya Took it Pretty Well Too……..That Says a LOT Fer Yer "…..Content a Yer Character….."…..Thanks MLK…..

The Fact is QUITE a Bit Simpler than THAT Mess in the Last Paragraph…..A. L. "BIG AL" Nolram is a "Psudonym"…..It's My Pen Name, Like Samuel Langhorne Clemens Who Wrote All of His GREAT Works Under the Name "Mark Twain" . Ya SEE….. I SAW What Them Thar Penis-Suckin' Question Askin' "MEDIA" Types Did ta YOU and Ms Palin When Ya Stepped inta the Public Spotlight and I Said ta MySelf, "SELF…..Don't Ya DARE Let Somethin' Like THAT Happen ta YOU, Yer Friends and Family, Yer Co-Workers, Yer "Corporate Sponsors", Yer "Individual Sponsors" (MOST of Whom Fall inta the Previously Mentioned Categories), Yer "Mental Health Care Professionals" (MAYBE I Shouldn't Have Mentioned "Them"……Fregit I Said ANYTHING About That……Sorry About That Dr "B"…. We'll "TALK" About that the NEXT Time We Have One a Our Little "Sessions"…SHHHHH…Sorry..), BUTT It Don't Matter None……ALL a My Friends and Family Have Known Fer YEARS That I was a Bit "Different", and Jest a Bit OFF'n My NUTT, BUTT….Since I've Been a Writin' This Here "Baby" a Mine They're ALL Convinced That I'm "Crazy as a Loon", "Loony as a Bed Bug", And Jest ABOUT ta Drive THEM All Crazy……Go Figger…..ta Put It in the Words of My Favorite Father-Out-Law, "WHY Don't Ya Just CUT OUT This CRAP !!??!!!"…….

And THAT May Be Yer and Ms Palin's Opinion o' Things TOO…….in Which Case My GOOD LORD Will Put Me in Touch With Someone ELSE That HE Thinks Can Run This Here GREAT GOD-Fearin' NATION Better'n YOU TWO, BUTT That's Probably Gonna Take HIM a While……So's in the Meantime I'm a Gonna TRY ta Git Folks ta Read This Here Book, and Take a Gander at a FEW a My Little YouTube Videos, And MAYBE Donate Enough Money ta P.O. Box 2149 Tuskegee, AL 36083 (WELL Ya Didn't Think I'd Be STUPID Enough ta Use My HOME Address Did Ya??…….YOU Really AIN'T the BRIGHTEST Bulb on the CHRISTmas Tree ARE Ya??…..) ta Git the Roof Fixed and the Rest of the House Fixed UP a Bit, AND Git OUT a That DAD BLAMED "BIG Government" Job Where They'er Just Workin' Me ta DEATH …….BUTT……The GOOD LORD Willin' and the Creek Don't Rise….I'll Jest Keep Pkuggin' Away at That "BIG Government" Job and Start Learnin' Mandarin CHINESE, Fer When MY GOOD LORD "FINALLY" Gives UP on This Country and "Shifts" HIS BLESSIN' ta CHINA (Where ALL a OUR Money's Been "Shiftin'" These Days)…….Oh Well…JEST Fergit that I Said Anything About Gittin' Y'all Elected………(And IF'N Ya REALLY Believe THAT, Then Ya "ARE" PURTY DUMB)……..I'm Gonna KEEP Hammerin' at Them Dag Gummed LOCKED DOORS a Yours Until I Git Ya in the NEW Independence Party and MAKE Ya TWO of "My Little NIPers", AND Make Ya LIKE IT……SOOOOO THERE !!!!!!!!!……….

Yer GONNA Be SORRY…….DON'T Watch MY Little YouTube Videos Will Ya………DON'T Bother ta Read MY Little "Baby"……DON'T Take the Time ta Reply ta MY E-Mails HUH !?!……..I Think I'm Gonna Sich MY GOD On YA…..Dear GREAT GOD in HEAVEN, I Gots a Little PROBLEM That I'd LIKE YA Ta Handle Fer Me When Ya Git "Around to It" AND I Got Yer "Round TUIT" Right Here in My Pocket…….One Side Says "TUIT" o' Course…..And The "Flip" Side (Like That "Sign a the NIPers" That I'm About ta "Flip" ta Them Folks That AIN'T Watchin' My YouTube Videos So's They'll Go Viral, and NOT a HELPIN' Me Out By Commentin' On My Book, AND NOT Donatin' a DAMN Dime ta P.O. Box 2149, Tuskegee, AL 36083….) Says, "… A TIME TO EVERY PURPOSE UNDER THE HEAVEN… Eccl. 3:1"…..And NOW IS THE TIME Fer ALL GOOD GOD's ta COME ta the AID o' THEIR PROPHETS……Go GIT 'em "MATE(S)"!!! (Reference Chapter 55).

This Page Has Been "INTENTIONALLY" ("RIGHTly") "LEFT" BLANK.

(Exceptin' Fer the Chapter Trailer, And the Text Above, AND The Text Below This Line)

(ta HONOR the Makers of "Zork III", the SAME as Them Thar Makers of "Zork" and "Zork II")

Did THAT Crap Make ANY Sense to Y'all on Pages 59-63, or Am I JEST Funnin' Ya.....YOU Decide!!!

Chapter 19

Why WOULD Bill O'Reilly, Glen Beck, AND Rush Limbaugh Make GOOD SPIN Controllers ??

HOLLLLYYYYY CRAP, Folks…….I Been Flappin' My Gums and NOT Payin' Enough Attention ta My "BABY"…….I FINALLY Found a Highliter in This MESS of a House a Mine…..(Since My Lovely Wife FINALLY Got a FIRE Lit Under My Fat. Wide Buttox and Got Me ta Helpin'…..ALTHOUGH as a "Hoarder" I Tend ta "Hinder" More than I "HELP"…..and I FINALLY "Took the Time" ta Go Thru the "Table o' Contents" a My Little "Baby"…..AND I Found That I ONLY Gots 15 MORE Chapters t' Write Y'all Before I'm DONE (NO…….I'll NEVER Be "DONE"……If'n Ya AIN'T Figgered THAT Much Out about Me Yet, Then Ya REALLY Don't KNOW Me…..And Probably Never WILL)….., BUTT Due ta My OCDOF (That's "Obsessive-Complusive, DISPleasure ta Other Folks"…..Fer You INFURIATIN' Mental "Laymen" Out There)…..I'll Be NitPikin' My "Baby" ta DEATH (And a Pullin' Her "TEETH" And Puttin' in Even "Sharper, Deadlier, and More "VICIOUS" Teeth)……SSOOOOOO, "Theoretically" I COULD Be Ready Fer My Little "Baby's" Comin' OUT Party By NEW YEARS DAY of "BIG AL's" "LUCKy" YEAR…….YEEEEEHAWWWWWWWW !!!

OOPs…….I Guess I Kindly a Got Carried Away in the "HEAT" (BUTT It Shore is Chilly in Here….. Maybe I Needs ta Check the Thermostat) of the "Moment"…….I Was a SPOSED ta Be Tellin' Ya about WHY Bill O'Reilly, Glen Beck, and Rush Limbaugh Would Make Good SPIN Controllers…..Now Let's See……Why Was That Agin??.....Oh Yeah…..I Remember Now (I'm a Tellin' Ya Folks….When Ya Have Yer Fergitter in OverDrive……Now NOT Like "BTO" – "Bachman-Turner OVERDRIVE" Who's Music I Happen ta Like…..I Mean "OverDrive" Like on the Transmission a My 1997 Ford Explorer That Don't Work No More, and is "Dead in the Yard", And Several Folks've Come by Wantin' ta Buy, BUTT I Wouldn't Sell 'Cause I Said that I'd Jest Have ta Use the Money ta Buy Me a Storage Shed t' Hold ALL a the Crap I Gots Stuck in There, BUTT That My Lovely WIFE Convinced Me ta Clean OUT….in Her Dad Gummed "Cleanin' Frenzy" She's Been in Lately, and Give it Away Fer a Tax Write OFF, BUTT There Waren't as MUCH Stuff in There as I Thought, 'Cause it ONLY Took Us ONE Afternoon ta Clean it Out and There Was STILL a Little Room in My SHOP Buildin' ta SQUEEZE That Crap inta…..)…..

Sorry, BUTT I Jest LOST My Train a Thought (or it Ran OFF'n the Tracks…..Or My "Point" Again) …..That's "CORRECT"…..My Poor Ole Brain was a "SPINnin' Outa Control" Again and I Was a Gonna TELL Ya WHY Bill O'Reilly, Glen Beck, and Rush Limbaugh Would Make Pretty Damn Good SPIN Controllers…..SOOOOO…..Let's "Git 'er DONE" (NO……I THOUGHT I 'd Gotten That THORUGH Y're Thick Scull By NOW……"Ya TAKE the TIME ta Do the Job "CORRECTLY" the VERRY First TIME"…..MAN, Y'all Are DENSE…..I Ain't NEVER Gonna Git AMERICA Back on "TOP a the HEEP" with "Material" Like Y'ALL ta Have ta Work With…..GOOD LORD…..Give Me STRENGTH).

Bill O'Reilly (In SPITE a the Fact That He's a Ill Mannered BORE Who Likes ta Interrupt His "Guests"…..More Like Verbal "Punchin' Bags"….in the NAME o' "Movin' His Little Show Along"… When the MILITARY Came Up with a Little Way ta "Move Things Along" Efficiently and Effectively AGES Ago……"Break, Break….Unit ONE ta BASE, OVER":….".BASE ta Unit ONE Go Ahead,

OVER".…."Unit ONE ta BASE, That Bill O'Reilly Fella SURE is a "Inetrrupin' SumBeech" Ain't He, OVER".…."BASE ta Unit ONE, Yeah He SHORE IS, BUTT That Thar "BIG AL" Fella , Who's One a Them Thar Gentlemen o' the "Old School", Will Teach Him a Manner or Two, OVER".…."Unit ONE ta BASE, Yeah, That's the Way We Figger it Too..…HOW Ya Think He's a Gonna DO it??, OVER"…… "BASE ta Unit ONE..…We Figger He'll Use MANNERS Agin Him, OVER".…."Unit ONE ta BASE, How's He Gonna Use MANNERS Agin the Yahoo??, OVER".…."BASE ta Unit ONE..…Ya KNOW That Thar AIR TIME on National TV is MORE Precious than PLATINUM Dontcha??, OVER".…."Unit ONE ta BASE, YEAH.…So WHAT?!?, OVER".…."BASE ta Unit ONE, We Figger that the FIRST Time That Thar O'Reilley Fella Interrupts "BIG AL", Mr Nolram Will Count ta 10 on His Little Piddys.. ONE Little Piddy..…TWO Little Piddys..…THREE Little Piddys.…Until He Gits ta 10 Little Piddys .…And Then He'll Fold His Piddys Reverently and Ask If'n He May Be Allowed ta Speak NOW.…And If'n That O'Reilly Fella is SMART..…Which is DOUBTFUL.…He'll Say YES and "BIG AL" Will Take UP "RIGHT" Where He "LEFT" OFF and Finish His "Point" Concisely and Succinctly as He ALWAYS Does.…AND If'n He Says NO, Then "BIG AL" Will Likely as NOT Walk RIGHT (or LEFT) OFF'n the Set, OVER".…."Unit ONE ta BASE, Yeah, BUTT What If'n He Says YES, And THEN Interrupts "BIG AL" a SECOND Time, OVER".…."BASE ta Unit ONE, KNOWIN' "BIG AL" The Way We DO.… Since We're ALL Some a His "Little NIPers"..…He'll Count ta 20 on His Little Piddys……Now 10 Seconds a "DEAD AIR" Time on National TV is a "Lifetime", BUTT 20 Seconds is an "ETERNITY", OVER".…."Unit ONE ta BASE, Yeah, BUTT What If'n That Thar O'Reilly Fella STILL Don't Git the "MESSAGE" on Account a His Bein'a Hard-Headed, "Mulish" Kindly a STUBBORN Son-of-a-Gun, and Interrupts "BIG AL" a THIRD Time??, OVER"..…"BASE ta Unit ONE, Then Likely as NOT, "BIG AL" Would Jest Use His "THREE (a Trinity) Strikes and Yer OUT" Standard and Walk RIGHT (or LEFT) OFF'n the SET, 'Cause He KNOWS That Thar O'Reilly Fella Needs HIM, More'n HE Needs Bill O'Reilly Cause HE Can Put HIS "Message" Out on the INTERNET (CyberSpace) Fer FREE Anytime HE WANTS to, OVER".…."Unit ONE ta BASE. Yeah, That's The Way We Figger it TOO: LONGGG LIVE "BIG AL" and the NIPers.……I SAY it THREE (a Trinity) TIMES, OVER".… "BASE ta Unit ONE, WE HEAR it THREE (a Trinity) TIMES, OVER and OUT"..…"Unit ONE ta BASE, Roger.… Acknowledged.…5 By 5..…OVER and OUT"..……) IS a Fair ta Middlin' SPIN Controller, So We NIPers Figger If'n "BIG AL" Can Teach Him a Few Manners, Then Mr O'Reilly Will HELP SAVE NIPer Funds By Keepin' That EX (Thank GOoDness) MASSA President Obamma Ramma from Gittin' ANY o' Them Thar $100,000.00 Bonuses Like We Mentioned WAYYYY Back UP in Chapter 3.

   Now Mr Glenn Beck, On the Other Hand is NOT an Ill Mannered BORE Like Mr O'Reilly (And as a Matter o' Fact He MUST Be Purrty FOND a Ill Mannered BORES, "Cause He Seems ta Git Along Purrty Damn GOOD with the Old Coot), BUTT Mr Beck CAN Git a MIGHT "Excited" When He "Gits on a Roll" Explainin' Them Thar Charts & Graphs He Uses SO Effectively and Efficiently ta PROVE His "Points", AND If'n Ya Make the Mistake a Givin' Him a Little Head Knod ta Let'm Know That Ya "Heard" What He Said and He Mistakes it Fer "Agreement" The He REALLY Gits "WOUND UP" and Takes OFF Like One o' Them Thar "SOP Whipped Camels" Doing Loop-d-Loops, and Flyin' a Bit Sideways, and Upside Down, and EVERY Which Way……Needless ta Say, He CAN Git a Little Carried Away with HisSelf Sometimes, BUTT There Ain't Hardly Nobody Better About Layin' the Facts on the Table and Gittin' Ya Informed on Stuff that SHOULD Be Important ta Ya and that Ya SHOULD Be INFORMED About So's Ya Can Make a BETTER Discision and a BETTER (No, "BEST") Choice on that Little Multiple-Choice Test in Nov 2016 than That DISSASTEROUS FIASCO of a FAILURE That

Ya Chose on the Nov 2012 Version of that Test. Mr BECK……PLEEEEASSE Sir HELP Me and the NIPers Git Our Facts Straight and Convince These Danged FOOL AMERICANS Out There that There IS a "BEST" Choice Fer That Nov 2016 Re-Take Test AND That Ms Sarah Palin and Mr Herman Cain on the NEW Independence Party (NIPer) "Write-IN" (Or "RIGHT ON!!!") Ballot is the ABSOLUTELY THE "BEST" Choice……PLEEEEASE………Kind SIR…… WE NEED Ya!!!

And THEN We Have Mr "RUSH" (Ta Let Yer Mouth Over-Power Yer Brain) Limbaugh…..I DON'T CARE……I STILL "LOVE" ta Hear Ya "GIVE IT" t' ALL of Those Folks Who NEED ta Be "GOTTEN TO". Yer MY Kind a "LOOSE CANNON" (and As ALL o' US "LOOSE CANNONS" KNOW…..The ONLY "SAFE" Place ta Be When Ya Have a "LOOSE CANNON" is ta Be Firmly BEHIND Them, Because If'n Yer ANYWHERE ELSE Than "Firmly Behind" a "LOOSE CANNON", Then Yer In "OUR LINE OF FIRE"…..And Believe You ME, Don't NONE a Y'all Wanna Be in THIS Old FARTS "LINE OF FIRE"…..And SOMETIMES it AIN'T Even "SAFE" Bein' "Firmly Behind" Me…..Especially If'n I Been Eatin' Beans….."Beans, Beans the Musucal Fruit…..the More Ya EAT the MORE Ya Toot….The MORE Ya TOOT the Better Ya FEEL, SOOOOOO Let's Have Beans Fer EVERY MEAL"……Now Where Was I Agin…….Oh Yeah Mr RUSH "LOOSE CANNON" Limbaugh. KEEP the "FAITH" And KEEP UP the GOOD Work Yer a Doin' AND PLEEEASE Help Us KEEP from Lettin' Old EX (Thank GOoDness) MASSA President Obamma Ramma (Oh, That's "Correct"….He's STILL in Office Fer the NEXT FOUR YEARS…..I Keep Fergittin'….I Guess I've Jest Been "Imaginin'" How GREAT it Could BE in This Here GREAT GOD-Fearin' Nation of OURS WITHOUT Him in Office Fer SOOOOOOO Long That I Fergot That it Was ONLY a WONDERFUL DREAM…..BUTT Then I ALWAYS "WAKE UP" ta the NIGHTMARE of REALITY (FOUR MORE YEARS…..Jest Like the LAST FOUR)…From Gittin' ANY of Those $100,000.00 Bonuses We Mentioned in Chapter 3, By Holdin' US NIPers "Accountable" Fer OUR Mistakes, Makin' DAMN Sure That We Follow Our OWN Values, Principles, and Standards (According t' the NIPer Handbook, the "User's Guide and Maintenance Manual for a Human Life, the "UGMMHL"), AND fer Handlin' Those Mistakes (Reference Chapter 49).

Between the Three (a Trinity) of Y'all, We NIPers Figger That Thar EX (Thank GOoDness) MASSA President Obamma Ramma (Now If'n Ya THINK I'm a Makin' FUN of the "CURRENT" President of the UNITED STATES, Then……..Yer ABSOLUTELY "CORRECT"…..We NIPers Have GREAT RESPECT Fer the "OFFICE" of the President of the GREATEST NATION on EARTH…..We Jest AIN'T Got NO "respect" Fer the YAHOO That "CURRENTLY" Occupies That GREAT "OFFICE" …….JEST So's We Are PERFECTLY CLEAR on That "Point"……I'd Like ta "Stick" that "Point" Someplace Where the "Sun Don't Shine"…..RUIN the GREAT Reputation o' This GREAT GOD-Fearin' NATION a OURS Will Ya……GIVE the MAGNIFICENT Queen a England a Bunch a DAMNed Cheap-ASS CDs Will Ya…….SNUB the LEADER of the COUNTRY Holdin' MOST o' OUR DEBTS Will Ya…….I HOPE I've Made My "POINT" Very CLEAR…..AND Where I'd Like ta "STICK it"…..knock….Knock…..KNOCK…. There's Them DAMN Kids a Knockin' at the DOOR Agin "CLAIMIN' ta be the FBI……JEST a Sec…

Did THAT Crap Make ANY Sense to Y'all on Pages 64-66, or Am I JEST Funnin' Ya…..YOU Decide!!!

Chapter 20

Why WOULD "The Fox and Her Friends" (Little Gretchen and the Boys) Make Really GREAT Media Consultants ???

AHHHHH…..Come ON Now "Guys" and "Gal" (OOPS….I Meant ta Say "Gentlemen" and "Lady"), If'n Ya Cain't Take a Little Ribbin' Now and Then……Switch ta BBQed Chicken or Beef Instead o' Them Thar Tender Little "Baby Back's"……JEST Joshin' Ya…..BUTT….(Thers's That BIG BUTT a Mine Jest Hagnin' Out There All By ItSelf Agin)…..I WAS a Bit "Peved" When Ya Failed ta Reply ta the E-Mails I Sent Ya a Couple a Years Ago When I was a Tryin' ta Git My FIRST Book "The Holy Bible Companion Series, from an Information Technology Perspective, The First Book of Moses Called GENESIS – HOW it ALL Began" Published (And I SHORE Coulda USED Some Good Consultin').

And I Was REALLY "Miffed" with Y'all AND the United States Postal System (USPS) ,When I PAID Good HARD-EARNED Money ta Have Copies o' My Book Sent ta Y'all, and Bill O'Reilly, and Glenn Beck, and Mike Huckabee, and Sarah Palin (via FOX Network Address on Account of I Had NO CLUE Where She Might be Livin' Since She Had ta Quit Being the Governor of Alaska, and Had That Little BAD Experience o' Runnin' Fer Vice-President Along Side a "Maverick??" John McCain, And Probably Had a WHOLE HEEP a Speakin' Engagement Invitations Due ta the Success of "Her" Little Book "Going Rogue", AND Had that Little "Family Problem" that Them There "Poopin'Ratsys"...or Maybe They're "PapaRottsees"... or Are They Called "Peekin'Nazies"…..OH HELL….. Y'ALL Know the Little TIT-TURDS I'm a Talkin' About), AND Several Other Folks Who Had Recently (at THAT Time) Had Books Published and That I THOUGHT May Have Been Able ta Give Me Some GOOD Advice or MAYBE Even a Little HELP in Gittin' Someone…..ANYONE ta Give it a Little Read and Maybe a Comment or Two……BY REGISTERED MAIL "WITH" RETURN "SIGNED" RECEIPT REQUIRED (Which I Figgered I MIGHT be Able ta SELL on eBay ta Folks Who Might WANT Those Famous Folks Signatures, and I MIGHT Be Able ta Git Caught UP on a Few Bills…..), BUTT NOOOOO ….. The USPS Let SOME Little TIT-TURD ADMIN Type "SIGN" Fer ALL o' Them Thar Book Packages that Were Sent REGISTERED MAIL "WITH" RETURN "SIGNED" RECEIPT and Addressed ta the Folks Mentioned Above and NOT That Little TIT-TURD ADMIN Type…….Ya Just CAIN'T Trust NOBODY These Days and ESPECIALLY The FEDERAL GOVERNMENT (No WONDER the USPS is in Financial Trouble These Days If'n They Operate Like THAT and Take Folks HARD-EARNED Money Under FALSE Pretences a Gittin' Stuff ta the "Correct" Folks and Then Lettin' Some Little TIT-TURD ADMIN Type Sign Fer it……….a COURSE I Shudda KNOWN That Was the Way They Operated After the Way They Treated ME Durin' My Little 90 Day Probation Period with 'em When I THOUGHT I Might Wanna Make a Career Outa Bein' a Clerk at the Opelika, AL Post Office….. BUTT That's One a Them Thar "OTHER" Stories Y'all Ain't Too Fond o' Hearin' About…….Now What Was I a Sayin'??…….

OH Yeah…….AND Y'all AIN'T Makin' No "Bownie" Points (I THINK That Has Somethin' ta Do with a Nose and a ASS and Somethin' ELSE…..I Fergit…..BUTT….It'll Come BACK ta Me….) By Ignorin' My E-Mails THIS Year (or LAST Year, Since THIS Year is About OVER and I Don't Know HOW Long it's Gonna Take Yer Sorry "Anal Orifices" ta Git Around ta Readin' This Here Book) as I am

Tryin' DESPERATELY ta Git SOMEONE, SOMEWHERE, SOMEHOW....Ta HELP This Poor Old CRAZY (and If'n Ya Don't BELIEVE That, Jest Ask ANY of My Friends, Family, Co-Workers, And Mental Health Professionsals) Old Reprobate, "Mouth-of-the-South", "Curmudgeon at Large". And General "Know-it-ALL", ADSD/COPD/OCDOF/AARP/AAA Anal-Retentive SOB, and Pain in the "Southern" End of the Human Digestive Tract t' Git My Little "Baby" Inta the Hands o' the AMERICAN PUBLIC (Whether They LIKE it or NOT !!!).....

   BUTT, Besides ALL a THAT.......I STILL Think that Y'all Would Make DAMN GOOD Media Consultants Fer Me and the NEW Independence Party (NIPers) in Our GOAL (of the Moment) ta Git Ms Sarah Palin and Mr Herman Cain Elected President and Vice-President (Respectively) on the NIPer Write-IN Ballot in the Nov 2016 Elections. AND Mr Doocy......I REALLY Have ta Compliment Ya On Yer Little Book "Tales from the DAD's Side" that I Listened to SEVERAL Times on CD, BUTT.....I Have ta Tell Ya that the ONLY Line that MY GOOD LORD Allowed Me ta Remember Outa ALL of the GREAT Stories that Ya Told in That WONDERFUL Little Book was THIS: "Coincedence is GOD's Way of Doin' Things Anonymously". It Made Me Look BACK Over ALL of the SUPPOSEDLY Random "Coincedences" in My Life and "SEE" That EVERYTHING My GOOD LORD Had Taught Me and Done FOR Me in My Nigh onta 60 Year Existance Had Been Focused Toward THIS "Pivot Point" in Time ta Give Me the "Leverage" I NEED ta Move an ENTIRE NATION (and Possilbly SOMEDAY the WORLD) Toward a "Better" (NO...."BEST") Way of LIFE (in the World That the LORD, MY GOD Has Provided US).

Did THAT Crap Make ANY Sense to Y'all on Pages 67-68, or Am I JEST Funnin' Ya.....YOU Decide!!!

Chapter 21

WHY Do We Hafta Call Them "Secretaries", And Can We Pleeease NOT ???

"Back in the Days", After the FIRST American Revolution, the Folks on the Cabinet Advisin' the President of the United States of America were Called "Secretaries" So's That the AMERICAN Public Would Know that the "Leader of the Free World" was Bein' Advised by Men (There Weren't NO Women "Secretaries" in Them Days……They was ALL Men) Who Could Read, Write, and Cipher. At THAT Time, Not EVERYONE Knew Their Readin', Writin', and 'Rithmetic, SOOOO……They Called the Leaders of the Cabinet Departments "Secretaries", BUTT Today, Even "Secretaries" Don't Wanna be Called "Secretaries"……They Wanna be Called "Administrative Assistants", or "Program Support Assistants", or "Executive Assistants", etc., Because the Term "Secretary" Got a Rather Negative Connotation Over the Years Since the Beginnin' Days o' This GREAT GOD-Fearin' NATION of OURS.

We NIPers Believe that (Since They are in the "Executive" Branch of the Federal Government and "Direct" the Actions of Their Departments) the Heads of the Cabinet Departments Should be Called "Executive Directors" instead of "Secretaries", Besides Since We NIPers Want Ms Sarah Palin as the President and Colin Powell as the Head of the Department of Defense, it Would Keep the VISION Out o' Our Heads of "Colin Powell in a MiniSkirt Bein' Chased Around the Oval Office Desk by Sarah Palin", OR (Since We Think Ms Oprah Winfrey Would Make a Mighty FINE Head of the Department of State) "Oprah Winfrey in a MiniSkirt Bein' Chased Around the Oval Office Desk by Sarah Palin". Those are JEST the Kind o' VISIONS That We NIPers Don't WANT in Our Heads……How about Y'ALL???

SOOOOO….One o' the MANY Changes We NIPers Would Like ta Make t' IMPROVE the Executive Branch (Besides Kickin' Out the "Current" Sorry-Assed Administration) of the Federal Government is t' Change the Titles of the Heads of the Various Departments. We NIPers are Kindly a HOPIN' Y'ALL "Common Sense" Thinkin' Folks (Even Though "Common Sense" Should "TECHNICALLY" be Called "UNCommon Sense" Since So FEW of Y'all Have it Out There Any More) Will Git Behind Us in This (And ALL of Our OTHER NIPer Ideas for FIXIN' This Country Back Up After the "Current" Tit-Turd Administration is Done Tryin' t' RUIN it……Like Makin' SURE that All THREE…..a "Trinity"…. Branches of the Federal Government Have "Term Limits" AND an "IMPEACHMENT Process" the SAME as the "EXECUTIVE" Branch Has NOW….hint…..Hint…..HINT!!!) and Help Us Git Ms Sarah Palin and Mr Herman Cain Elected as President and Vice-President (Respectively), Usin' a TOTALLY Unorthodox "WRITE-IN" Campaign (After Tourin' ALL 50 United States THREE Times on 13 Bomb-Bustin' Busses), on the NEW Independence Party (NIPer) Ticket for the Nov 2016 Elections (Along with Gittin' a Whole HEEP a NIPer Legislators Elected and Judges Appointed in the MEANTIME)……..If'n Yer Gonna DREAM………DREAM "BIG"…….And I AIN't a Talkin' About "BIG" Government….. (Fer MORE Info on ALL a the Topics in THIS Paragraph. Please Reference ALL of the "OTHER" Chapters in This Little "Baby" a Mine…..I AIN'T Tellin' Ya WHICH Ones…Yer Gonna HAVE ta Read 'em ALL…..Boo Hoo HOOOOO!!!)

Did THAT Crap Make ANY Sense to Y'all on Page 69, or Am I JEST Funnin' Ya…..YOU Decide!!!

Chapter 22

WHY Do the NIPers Want to Take 13 Bomb-Bustin' Buses Across ALL of the 50 GREAT GOD-Fearin' United States THREE Times ???

WEELLLLLL.....ta Start with, I Don't Think ANYBODY Has Ever Done it Before, And I'm Almost CERTAIN that Neither Them Thar Left-Leanin' Liberal Damn Democrats NOR Them Thar Radically Religious Right-Wing Republicans Would EVER Put ThemSelves "On the Line" by Goin' ta Each of the 50 United States and Actually MEETIN' the AMERICAN PUBLIC. They Already KNOW What Ya NEED, SOO There's No Use WHATSOEVER ta Confuse the Issue by Lettin' Any of Y'all Express an Opinion Contrary to the FACTS as "They" Know Them. HOWEVER, We NIPers Think "Differently".

We NIPers Feel that We Cain't Do a GOOD Job a Runnin' This Country, Without Goin' Around ta All 50 States and at LEAST Givin' EVERY AMERICAN Voter the Chance ta Meet Us in Person and Express Yer Views on How This GREAT GOD-Fearin' NATION of OURS Should be Run. We NIPers Cain't Please Everyone, BUTT We CAN Sure as HELL Try t' Please MOST of Ya. We Wanna Take 13 o'Them Thar Bomb-Bustin' Busses, Like the Ones Our Troops Use in Afganistan (Since a Few a You Left-Leanin' Liberal Damn Democrats AND Radically Religious Right-Wing Republicans are a Wee Bit OFF'n Yer NUT and a Bit WACO ta Boot, So We Figger If'n We Want ta Git Through the Whole Three Year Election Campaign Alive and UnMaimed, We Need ta Protect OurSelves a Bit). Besides, When Ya Park 'em RIGHT, 13 Busses Make a 4-Square Fortress (3 Busses on Each Side = 12) Around the 13th Command Post Bus (Kindly a Like That Thar "Green Zone" in Iraq).....Doesn't THAT "Sound" Like "SOUND" Military Strategy and Tactics ta YOU, Mr Colin Powell, from the "Point" of View that We NIPers Are a Goin' ta WAR Against Them Thar LEFT-Leanin' Liberal DAMN Democrats AND Them Thar Radically Religious RIGHT-Wing Republicans, AND We Was Wantin' YOU ta Be the NEW Executive Director of the Department of Defense?!?......Whatcha Think.....HMMMMM?!?.

Now We NIPers Want t' Stop in EACH of the 50 States at LEAST Once Each Year, BUTT SOME of Y'all (Like Texas and California) are a Bit Spread Out, So We'll Probably Have ta Stop 2 or 3 Times...... PLUS We Want t' Make This Little 50 State Campaign Tour ONCE Each Year for EACH of the 3 Years Prior ta Them Thar Nov 2016 Elections. Not ONLY is it in HONOR of Our Backers (the "BIG 3"..... TRINITY... GOD the FATHER, GOD the SON, ...AND GOD the FATHER's Significant "OTHER"), BUTT it ALSO Provides Us a Much Better ("BEST" ??) Oportunity t' Meet EVERY AMERICAN Voter (Since We'll Be a Stoppin' at Least 3 Times in Each State, and We'll Do Our Best NOT ta Stop in the SAME Place Twice). Now, If'n Ya Prefer t' Watch Them Thar Damn "Democaratic" AND Radical "Republican" Media Circuses (After the Fashon of "Ringling Bros. and Barnum and Bailey" that Are Misleadingly Called "Conventions") from the Comfort of Yer Tater Couch Rather than Come Out and Meet Us NIPers Toe-t-Toe and Face-t-Face, Then By ALL Means Don't Let Us Ruin Yer Plans. BUTT If'n Ya "CARE" Just a Little Bit MORE About the Future of This GREAT GOD-Fearin' NATION of OURS than the Average "Joe" (or "Josephine") and WANT ta Meet Us, We'll Be Available TO Ya.

This is Gonna Be a Logistical "NightMARE", BUTT We NIPers Feel That If'n ANYONE Can "Pull it OFF" Or "REIN it IN" (....Ya KNOW.....Like "Pullin' OFF a Saddle" or "Reinin' in a NightStallion" or a "NightMARE"......OH JEST Fergit it.....I'm JEST a Waistin' My "GOOD Stuff" on Ya....), It Would Be Oprah Winfrey (Our Pick fer Head of the Department of State, Especaially If'n the 3 EX-Governors We Have Called ta Service "ALL" Report fer Duty, Reference Chapter 3), And LISTEN UP FOLKS...... We NIPers Are Gonna Do Our Dog Gonedest Ta Bring the WHOLE NIPer "Family" (the Whole Danged CORE Constituency) Along WITH Us t' Meet Ya…That Means ALL of Them Thar Wealthy, Influential, and Famous Folks that We NIPers Called ta Service in Chapter 3 Will Be INVITED t' Join Us on This Little 13 Bomb-Bustin' Bus 50 State Campaign Tour. Now Remember, These are Wealthy, Influential, and Famous Folks SOOOO.....Even If We CAN Git 'em ta Come WITH Us, They'll Probably Have a Few "Other" Commitments that Will Prevent Them from Being With Us the WHOLE Way, BUTT Can Ya Jest "IMAGINE" How Much Ya'd Have ta PAY t' See These Folks If'n They Weren't Donatin' Their Valiable Time Just ta See Ya in the HOPE's that You'd Allow them t' Serve Ya as The Executive Branch of the Government of This GREAT GOD-Fearin' NATION for as LONG as They Do the BEST for Ya (So's Y'all Will Keep Electin' 'em BACK Again and AGAIN). AND Speakin' of PAY (Finances), We May Need a Little Spendin' Money Fer Them Thar Fuel Guzzlin' Busses, So Here's the Way We Intend ta Handle THAT Little Problem…….

Every Time We Stop, We're Gonna Put Out Some "Pickle Barels" (Big Green 55 Gallon Drums), and If'n Ya LIKE What Ya Hear from Us…..Just Toss a Dollar or Three (or the Change in Your Pocket) inta the "Pickle Barel". If'n Ya Reach in Yer Pocket and Pull Out a Quarter and 2 Dimes, and Ya Say ta YerSelf, "SELF….What I Heard Warn't WORTH No Quarter", Then Toss in the 2 Dimes and Be Done with it. If'n Enough Folks LIKE What We NIPers Have ta Say, and Give Us a Buck or 3 ta Speed Us on Our Journey to Our NEXT Stop, Then it Won't Be NO PROBLEM ta "Meet and Greet" Anyone Who's Interested Enough ta Come See Us. If'n We FILL UP a "Pickle Barel", We'll Just Roll Out Another One, and When We Git Done with Our Politicin' and We Take Out "Enough" ta Git Us t' the NEXT Stoppin' Place, We'll Just Have Mr Warren Buffett (OUR NIPer Financial "Wizard"…..Like That There "Harry Potter" Fella) Set Up an Account with a LOCAL Bank, and Donate the Rest o' the Cash to the LOCAL Branch of the NIPers fer LOCAL Campaign Expenses.

Our Inspiration for This 13 Bomb-Bustin' Bus 50 State Campaign, Came from a "Trucker" Song that a Little Fella by the Name of C. W. McCall Sang a Few Years Back Called "CONVOY":

"We Gotta Mighty CONVOY Rollin' Through the Night"

That Gave Us NIPers the Idea of 13 Bomb-Bustin' Busses ("Mighty" CONVOY) and Fer Doin' All a Our Politicin' in the Daytime (While Our Drivers are a Gittin' Some Shut-Eye), and Then When We are Done with Our Politicin', the Drivers Will be Well Rested and Ready ta Drive All Night ta the Next Destination (Rollin' Through the Night). The Busses Will be Equipped with Sleepin' Quarters, as Well as Some Full-Service Bathrooms, Kitchenette, and Conference Area (as Well as a Few Super-Dupper TOP Secret Security Enhancements that We're "NOT Gonna Tell Ya!!!" at This Time fer Personnal Safety Reasons).

"We Gotta Mighty CONVOY, Ain't She a Beautifull Sight"

We're Gonna Have Them Thar Busses ALL Gussied Up With Pictures of Our Candidates and Slogans and Logos and What All, AND in Keepin' with Our NIPer Handbook (the First Shall be Last and the Last Shall be First), Bus Number 13 Will ALWAYS Be a Leadin' the Way and Bus Number One Will be Protectin' Our Rear (Derriere).

"Come On and JOIN Our CONVOY, Ain't Nuthin' Gonna Git in Our Way"

If'n Y'all Have the Time, We NIPers Would LOVE ta Have Ya Join Us fer the Trip t' the NEXT Stop, AND (Once Again, Accordin' to the NIPer Handbook) We Heard Tell that When Our Backers (the "BIG 3") are On Yer Side, There Ain't NOTHIN' That Can Stand Against Ya……Not NUTHIN' !!!

"We're Gonna Roll This Truckin' (Bussin') CONVOY Across the USA……CONVOYYYYY !!!

This is Why We Decided ta Stop in ALL of the 50 United States, and We Figgered If'n Once was GOOD and Twice was BETTER, Then 3 Times Would be "BEST", and We NIPers Always Like t' Associate OurSelves with the "BEST" (of AMERICA). THAT's Why We Want t' Meet Each and Every Individual Voter Out There Instead of Them BIG Special Interest Groups. Y'all May NOT Be Aware of it, BUTT Outa ALL o'Them Thar "BIG" Special Interest Groups (BIG Business, BIG Oil, BIG Labor Unions, the "OTHER" BIGuns: NRA, Christian Coalition, NAACP, AARP, etc., Ad Infinitum, Ad Nauseum) Cain't NONE of 'em VOTE??? "YOU and I" Can Vote, BUTT All that Them Thar BIG "Special Interest" Groups Can Do is Try ta BULLY Ya inta Votin' Fer Whoever "THEY" Think Will Treat 'em BETTER'n Anybody ELSE…..And Y'all Have Been LETTIN' 'em BULLY Ya inta Votin' "THEIR" WAY…… AND by the Way……How's that Been Workin' Out fer Ya Lately……Are Ya Jest POSSIBLY Ready ta QUIT Lettin' Them Thar BIG "Special Interest" Groups PUSH Ya Around and THINK Fer "YerSelf" fer a Change???... Maybe????......or Maybe NOT…….We'll See……Movin' ON……

On a Side Note, If'n Any of Y'all Remember That Little Song "CONVOY", Then Ya Know that it is Sung "CON…VOOYYYYYYYY" ta Simulate the Tootin' of an 18 Wheeler Tractor Air Horn, When We was Kids ("Little" NIPers) and (Instead of Pushin' a Button) the Air Horn was Tooted by Pullin' a Cord on the Cab Ceilin', Whenever We was Travelin' ta Visit Grandpa in Western Nebraska and Passed an 18 Wheeler We'd Pump Our Arms Up and Down ta Simulate the Action of Pullin' the Air Horn Cord, and MOST a the Time the Tucker Would Oblige Us By Tootin' "CON…VOOYYYYYYY" with a Short Toot Follered by a LONNGGGG TOOOOTTTTTT. Okay, I Can See that I'm Borin' Ya with This Little Detour Down Memory Lane, So Let's Git BACK on Course and Move onta the Next Chapter…..

BUTT Before I DO……Y'all Should KNOW By Now that I Gotta Beat a Dead Horse After the Barn Door is Closed with the Cart Inside…… How's THAT Fer Some Mixed Metaphors???..... SOOOO….. Ms Palin….Dear Lady…..And Mr Cain….Kind Sir…..Have Ya EVER Heard the Phrase: "It's NOT the Destination…..It's the JOURNEY"??? Whether We WIN the Election (Which I AND the NIPers Think We WILL) or NOT, Wouldn't Y'all Come WITH Us on This 13 Bomb-Bustin' Bus 50 State Campaign JUST for the Experience of Meetin' HARD WORKIN' AMERICANS in ALL Parts of This GREAT GOD-Fearin' NATION of OURS??? If'n Ya LIKE the Touch a HUMOR I've Put inta This Little "Baby" (Book) a Mine, I PROMISE Y'all that I'll Do My BEST t' Keep Ya in Stitches (Mental, NOT Literal) the WHOLE WAY. AND If'n Yer Afraid That We Won't Pick Up No Votes Along the Way, Just Remember….If'n YOU Convince 2 Folks and THEY Convince 2 Folks……..Pretty Soon Those NIPer Molehills Will Stack UP inta a MOUNTAIN That Y'all Can "Landslide" Off 'n Right (or Left) inta the White House……Just LOOK What the "Tea Party" Has Done WITHOUT the Leadership, Direction, and Focus of the NEW Independence Party (NIPers)……It Can be Done……It WILL Be Done……It MUST BE DONE !!!

This Page Has Been "INTENTIONALLY" ("RIGHTly") "LEFT" BLANK.

(Exceptin' Fer the Chapter Trailer, And the Text Above, AND The Text Below This Line)

(To HONOR the Makers of ....Now WHICH "ZORK" Was it Again....I Fergit....Oh DAMN...)

Did THAT Crap Make ANY Sense to Y'all on Pages 70-73, or Am I JEST Funnin' Ya.....YOU Decide!!!

Chapter 23

How CAN Ya Make Over $10 Million in ONE Month ???

This Chapter is fer Y'all Math Wizards Out There, BUTT the Rest a You Dummies Can Listen in and Ya Jest MIGHT Larn Sumthin'about Hyperboles and WHY YouTube Videos Go "Viral". The Concept We'll be Dealin' with Ain't a Linear Progression, and it's Not EXACTLY a Geometric Progression; It's MORE of a Logrithmic Progression. Y'all Remember the Commercial that Went Somethin' Like "You Tell 2 Folks…..and They'll Tell 2 Folks…..and They'll Tell 2 Folks….and so on…..AND So ON…… AND SO ON !!!"??? Well, it's Kindly a Like THAT.

The Trick ta Makin' Over 10 Million Dollars (in a 31 Day Month) is ta Pay YerSelf One Penny on Day One, Two Pennies on Day 2, Four Pennies on Day 3, Eight Pennies on Day 4…..and So On….. Doublin' the Amount Each Day Until on Day 30 Ya Pay YerSelf a Little Over 5 Million Dollars, and On Day 31 Ya Pay YerSelf Nearly 11 Million Dollars ($10,737,418.24). Of Course, It's a Whole HEEP Better If'n Ya Can Git Somebody ELSE ta Pay Ya Instead o' Payin' YerSelf, And THAT'S What We NIPers Was Kindly a HOPIN' Y'all HARD WORKIN' AMERICANS Out There Would Do Fer Us NIPers. UNLike SOME Folks (and of Course We're Talkin' about Them Thar LEFT-Leanin' Liberal Damn Democrats and Them Thar Radically Religious RIGHT-Wing Republicans) Who Expect Y'all t' be Able ta Afford $100 a Plate Lunches and $1000 a Plate Dinners ta Be Allowed t' Chit Chat with'n "Their" Candidates, We NIPers Will ONLY Ask Ya Fer a Dollar or 3 or the Change in Yer Pockets, ta Chit Chat with US Around the "Pickle Barel". We'll Give Ya a Cup o' "JOE" (or "JOSEPHINE"…..Ya Can TELL the "Difference" Because "JOE" Has a "Black" Rim and Handle AND He's a Bit Obnoxious and Will Give Ya the "Shakes" and Keep Ya UP Nights, While "JOSEPHINE" Has a "Orange" Rim and Handle AND is a Bit LESS "Caffinated" and Respectfull Enough ta Let Ya Git Yer "Shut Eye"), and a Piece a Humble Pie (Along with a Piece of Our Mind). We'll Give Ya the Chance t' Let Yer Hair DOWN and Prop Yer Feet UP, and Tell Us Just HOW Y'all Think We Otta Run This Here GREAT GOD- Fearin' NATION of YOURS !!!

I AND the NIPers Have Been Told Time and Time Again that There Jest Ain't NO WAY We Can Start a Brand NEW Independence Party AND Git Ms Sarah Palin and Mr Herman Cain Elected President and Vice-President (Respectively) on the NEW Independence Party (NIPer) Ticket Thru a RIDICULOUS "Write-IN" Campaign fer the Nov 2016 Elections, BUTT My WHOLE Life, I've Been Doin' Things that Scoffers Said Could NOT Be Done (It Just Makes Me Work ALL the HARDER t' Prove Them Thar UNBelievin', "Gripin' and Complainin'", "NO Plan a Their OWN", "SORRY ASSed Snickerin' and Snearin' SNOBS"….WRONG….... and MOST of the Time I DID !!!). I've Been Told by My Grade School Teachers Thru My College Professors that I Could Do ANYTHING I Put My Mind to, AND Like a Dad Blamed FOOL……I "BELIEVED" 'em…..And THAT Has Made ALL of the DIFFERENCE….. "Two Roads Diverged in a Yellow Wood and I…..I Took the One Less Traveled by…."….NAHHHH….. That's a Whole "Different" Story (Poem)…….REALLY Movin' ON This Time…..

Did THAT Crap Make ANY Sense to Y'all on Page 74, or Am I JEST Funnin' Ya…..YOU Decide!!!

Chapter 24

Do Y'all Have Jest ONE God, or a "Family" of GODs Like MINE ???

I'm Terribly SORRY……."NOT"…….BUTT This Here Chapter is STILL Under Construction in My Confused and Addled Brain, So Ther Ain't Nuthin' Here ta SEE Yet……So, Move Along…….I SAID, "MOVE ALONG"….No LOITTERIN' HERE…..Now….GIT….Until I TELL Ya that Y'all Can Peek!!!

I'm so….So….SOOOOOO SORRY, BUTT My Wife Has Said Many, MANY Times That "MEN" (and She ALWAYS Says That With an "Exaspirated" Bellow), "Can NEVER, EVER Manage ta FINISH ANYHTING That They START…THEREFORE…..Since My Dear Lovely Wife is Always, ALWAYS "RIGHT" (One a Them Thar Radically Religious RIGHT-Wing Republicans…."Yes Dear, YES DEAR… THREE…a Trinity…Garbage Bags FULL DEAR !!!") AND Therefore "I" Am Always "WRONG"….. ta KEEP from Bustin' Her "RIGHTeous" Little Bubble (AND Keep My BUTT Outta the DOG HOUSE …..'Cause I MEAN it…..The DOG Really DON'T Like UNInvited "Gusets"…..And SHE's an EVEN "WORSE" MAN-Hater Than My Dear Lovely WIFE) I Have "LEFT" (ta KEEP Everything "Fair and Balanced", BUTT NOT ta Confuse Me with One a Them Thar LEFT-Leanin' Liberal DAMN Democrats) This Here Chapter UNFinished (Which Makes the Entire BOOK UNFinished), So's That My Dear Sweet Wife Will CONTINUE ta Be "RIGHT" Where I "LEFT" Her……Glarin' at Me with That "LOOK" a Hers……I THINK it's About Time Fer Me ta Be Movin' ON…Since I KNOW What's GOOD Fer Me……My Dear Lovely WIFE of Course……..Is THAT OK Dear???......I "LEFT" it UNFinished….. BUTT I HAD ta Make it That Long So's it Would Be LONGGGER Than Chapter 34 or it Would Jest COMPLETELY Ruin the Humorous Esthetic Ambiance……What Do Ya MEAN…."BIG WORDS"…. And "Don't Ya Use That Smart-ASS, KNOW-it-ALL MALE Computer Programmer "TONE" with ME !!!" …..I TOLD Ya I'm a Computer Local Area Network (LAN) Manager NOW….I Don't Even "LIKE" Computer Programmin'……"Tone"??.....WHAT "TONE"?!?……Sorry Gentle Readers……I REALLY Got's ta Be MOVIN' ON…..

Did THAT Crap Make ANY Sense to Y'all on Page 75, or Am I JEST Funnin' Ya.....YOU Decide!!!

Chapter 25

What Ever HAPPENED ta Noah's Ark, AND Why Cain't We FIND it ???

The SHORT Answer is: Bird Poop…..I SHOULD Jest Leave it There and Move ON and Let Ya Figger it Out Yer OWN Damn Self, ….BUTT…. Then This Chapter Would Be the Shortest One and it Would COMPLETELY Ruin the Concept of Chapter 34, AND Besides Y'all Are Gonna NEED This Chapter about Manure ta Educate Ya Fer the Comin' Disaster When Technology Gits Wiped OUT, and Ya Have ta Go BACK ta (OR Worse Yet "START") Growin' Yer Own Fruits and Vegetables and Cannin' Them in Glass Jars instead o' Buyin' 'em in Metal Cans at the Local Grocery Store.

Before We Git ta WHAT Happened ta Noah's Ark and WHY Nobody's EVER Gonna Find it….. We NIPers Need ta Educate a Few of Ya on the Topic of Manure: MOST Folks Think that Manure is What Comes Outta the South End of a North Bound Bovine or Equine, BUTT That is Jest ONE of THREE (a Trinity) of Components that Make Up "Manure". Some of Y'all Git Yer "Fertilizer" from Them Thar Garden Sections of Department or Home Improvement Stores in Bags that Have 3 (a Trinity) of Numbers on Them Like 8-8-8, 10-10-10, 15-20-10, etc. Them Numbers Tell Ya the Concentration of the 3 MAIN Components of Manure, BUTT Since They Are Man-Made Chemical Fertilizers (Instead of GOD-Made Manure) They Are Deficient in Several Areas.

The Three MAIN Components of Manure are: 1) Feces or Poop (that Contains the Potassium Component, Since Mammals Shed Potassium via Feces, and This is the Component Designed by GOD ta Be Beneficial ta Flowerin' Plants), 2) Urine or Pee (that Contains the Nitrogen or AnHydrous Amonia Component, Since Mammals Shed Nitrogen via Urine, and This is the Component Designed by GOD ta Be Beneficial to the Green Leafy Parts of Plants), and Finally (in the Position of HONOR) 3) Bedding or "Filler" that Can Be Wood Shavings, Peanut Hulls, Pine Straw, Wheat Straw, etc. (that Decomposes inta Potash When Combined with the Urine and Feces, and This is the Component Designed by GOD ta Be Beneficial to the Roots of Plants).

Now That Ya Know the 3 MAIN Components of Manure AND That They Correspond ta the SAME 3 Components in Yer "Store Bought" Man-Made Chemical Fertilizer….. What's the "Difference", AND What's the "BIG Deal", AND What's ALL That Got ta DO with NOT Bein' Able ta Find Noah's Ark ??? "DAMN" BUTT Yer a Curious and Impatient Bunch……..Don't Git Yer Panties in Setcha Wad…… Especially If'n Yer Like My WIFE Who Told Me the Other Day that We Needed ta Hurry UP and Git the CHRISTmas Shoppin' Done So's She Could Git Home and Git Outta Them "Crack-Crawlin' Panties" She was a Wearin'……She Said, "If'n I Had WANTED a Thong…..I Would a BOUGHT a Thong", So I KNEW that She was a NEEDIN' Some NEW Panties Fer CHRISTmas……Oh HELL…..I Got OFF'n the TOPIC Again……..And If'n Y'all TELL Her That I TOLD Ya That Story…….My GOD'll GIT Ya Fer That, SO Keep it TO YERSELF!!!........Now Where Was I??.......Oh Yeah…..I Remember Now…..

The Reason that GOD-Made Manure is So Much Better'n the MAN-Made "Store Bought" Stuff is the Vermin…….Yeah That's What I Said……Vermin. The GOD-Made Manure (When Ya Clean it Outta the Horse or Cow Stalls and Pile the Feces, Urine, and Bedding Combination at the Bottom of the Hill and Let the Rain and Sun Do it's Work of Composin' it Together, Ya Git Tiny Livestock Infestin' it (Like

Earthworms, Beneficial Bacteria, Certain Fungi in the Form of Mushrooms, and ALL Kinds of Bugs and Beetles that "ASSIST" with the Decomposition, Recombination, and Aeration of the Compost Pile into the Richest, Sweetest (YES….I Said "Sweetest") Smellin' Black Loam Like Plantin' Material Ya EVER Did See. As EVERY Farmboy KNOWS…..Feces ONLY Smells "Stinky" a Few Hours after it Comes Outta an Animal…..And Urine ONLY Smells "Arromatic" When Ya Break the "Crust" Off'n the Pee Hole When Ya Shovel it Out as Yer Cleanin' the Stall…….After ALL of That Mess Sits Down at the Bottom of the Pasture Under Mother Natures Lovin' Care fer a Few Weeks, It Looses the "Stink" for the "Sweet" Smell of Rich Compost.

Jest ONE More Thing Before Y'all Are "READY" ta Understand WHAT Happened ta Noah's Ark, and Why NOBODY is Ever Gonna Find it……There are Several Different "Kinds of Feces", Jest Like There Are Several Different "Concentrations" of "Store Bought" Fertilizer (e.g., 10-10-10, 20-20-20, 30-30-30, 10-30-10). If'n I Remember "Correctly" (Which I Probably DON'T, So Check it Out YerSelf) the First Number is the Potasium Component (So Ya Want This ta be HIGH Fer Flowerin' Plants), the Second Number is the Nitrogen Component (So Ya Want That ta be HIGH Fer Green and Leafy Plants), AND the Third Number is the Potash Component (And Ya Want That ta be HIGH Fer Yer ROOT Plants). SOOOOOO…..ta Make a LONNGGG Story Shrt "Bird POOP" Which is a Combination of Urine AND Feces (Since Birds Do BOTH at the SAME TIME Through the SAME Orifice) is the MOST HIGHLY Concentrated of GOD's Natural Fertilizers…..It'll "BURN" Yer Crops If'n Ya Ain't Careful.

NOW Yer Ready Fer the Tail (Waggin' the Dog) of WHAT Happened ta Noah's Ark……the Story Begins with the "ODD" Way that it Was Constructed…….ta Make a Ship Water-Tight, Ya ONLY Have ta "Pitch" it (with a "Tar-Like" Tree Sap) on the "Outside" (Because If'n Ya "Pich" it on the "Inside" Then the Water COULD Git Trapped in the WOOD Between the Layers of Pitch and Rot Out, BUTT GOD Told Noah ta "Pitch" the Ark "INSIDE and OUT" and We'll Git ta the REASON Fer That in a Bit….. Then He Loaded Up ALL of Them Thar Animals 2 by 2 (NO….He DIDN'T…..Go BACK and Read the Story Again, and Y'all Will Find that the "UNCLEAN" (Predators Like Lions, Tigers, and Bears….Oh MY……Lions, and Tigers, and Bears….OH MY !!!) Were Loaded Up 2 by 2, BUTT the "CLEAN" Animals (Used for FOOD ta Feed Noah, His Family, AND the Pedatory Animals) Were Loaded Up By Sevens (AND This Included the HIGHLY CONCENTRATED Bird POOPIN' Birds…… SOME of Ya See Where I'm a Goin' with This……Some a Ya DON'T…….And as USUAL….MOST of Ya Haven'y Got a "CLUE").

I May Have ONLY Rained for 40 Days and 40 Nights, BUTT it was Nigh onta a YEAR Before That Ark Settled on Dry Land…….AND As LONG as That Ark was a Floatin' on the Water, it Was Keepin' that Compostin' "Bird POOP Concentrated Manure" Nice and COOL, BUTT as Soon as That Thar Ark Was High and Dry, Noah and the Animals KNEW ta Git the HECK Outta Dodge, Because Trouble was a "Brewin'" Down in the Bottom of that Ark. Let's Jest Put a FEW Facts Together Fer Ya and Let Ya Draw Yer OWN Conclusions About WHAT MIGHT Have Happened ta Noah's Ark…..Pitch or Pine Sap is a VERRY GOOD Fire Starter and Combustable Substance…….Bird POOP is VERRY Caustic and Generates Tremendous HEAT When Decomposin'…..The Ark was "Pitched" WITHIN and Without (Right Next ta That Smolderin' Bird POOP that was NO LONGER Cooled By the Surrounding Water), AND The WHOLE Danged ARK was Constructed from Gopher Wood (That Burns Like the Dickens Under the "Correct" Circumstances) AND If'n THAT Ain't Enough Fer Ya, with ALL o' that Methane Produced from the Bovine, Equine, and OTHER Mammal Feces, it Would Jest Take a Little Old Tiny

"Lightnin' Strike from Heaven Above" ta Light the Thing Up in a "Blaze o' Glory"....SOOOOOO....
What Do "YOU" Think MIGHT Have Happened ta Noah's Ark and WHY Hasn't ANYONE Been Able
ta FIND it........MY GOD KNOWS How ta "Clean UP" After HISSELF and Make SURE That There is
NO EVIDENCE Fer Ya ta Base Yer "Faith" Upon......."Faith is the Evidence of Things NOT Seen".

Did THAT Crap Make ANY Sense to Y'all on Pages 76-78, or Am I JEST Funnin' Ya.....YOU Decide!!!

Chapter 26

WHY is the RAPTURE Due to Occur in the "Spring" of 2033 and ARMAGEDDON in 2040 ???

This is Gonna be the Hardest Chapter in My Little "Baby'" ta Write Fer 3 (a Trinity) Reasons:

1.   It is The MOST Important and "Pivotal" Chapter in the Book
2.   It is The MOST Far Reaching and "Global/Universal" Chapter
3.   AND, I'm SORRY ta Say (Write) It is The Chapter YOU Will Believe the LEAST

ALMOST ALL Joking Aside, Before I Get to the "MEAT" of This Chapter, Here is a Little Mental "Appetizer" ("Brain Snack") Fer Ya t' "Munch" On….. It's a "Word Association" Test:

GOD

GOOD vs EVIL

GOD's Angels vs Satan's Demons

Jesus CHRIST vs ANTI-christ

25 Dec -0000 vs 21 Dec 1999

25 Dec 0013 vs 21 Dec 2012

Springtime 0033 vs Springtime 2033

FREE Pass to Heaven vs Descision FOR CHRIST

NEW Independence Party vs NEW WORLD ORDER

US vs THEM

It Kindly a "Looks" Like a "CHRISTmas Tree" If'n Ya Stretch Yer Imagination a Might…..Don't it??? WEELLLLLL……Let's Jest SEE If'n I Can EXPLAIN This Little "Word Association" Test (And "Lite UP" that "Tree" with the "Shinin' Light" of Reason) in a Way that it Will Make SENSE t' Ya: "In the Beginning There Was GOD", Then ONE of His "Angels" Said 5 Statements, Ending with "And I WILL Be Like the MOST HIGH GOD", And One Third of the Angelic Host "Believed" Lucifer, BUTT Two Thirds Remained "Loyal" to the MOST HIGH GOD. Lucifer Tried Several Times to Start a "Breeding Program" to "Equalize" the Odds (ONE Third of the "Angelic Host" Against TWO Thirds):

Dinosaurs = VelociRapter

Man-Beasts = Cro-Magnon and Neanderthal

Homo Sapiens = "And the Sons of GOD Saw the Daughters of Men....."

On or About 25 Dec 0000 B.C. (Before CHRIST) AND/OR A.D. (After Death??......NAAHHHHH.....
"Anum Dominium" = Latin for "In the Year of OUR LORD"), A SAVIOR Was Born Who is CHRIST
the LORD.....and On or About 25 Dec 0013....HE Received HIS "Right of Passage" and Bar Mitzvah
into the Jewish Faith.......HE Lived Approximately 33 Years on This Planet, Was Crucified on a Cross in
the Spring of 0033 A.D., was Buried and Rose Again (from the Dead)......And Ascended into Heaven.

On or About 21 Dec 1999 an ANTI-Christ was Born......"He" Received His "Right of Passage" on or
About 21 Dec 2012.....He Will Live for About 33 Years Before "Assuming Complete Command" of the
Planet Called "Earth".....at This Time (Springtime of 2033) at the "Anniversary" of HIS Death...CHRIST
Will Return for HIS "Followers" and "RAPTURE" Them.....He Will Arrive in a "BLAZE of Glory" (the
LARGEST Solar Flare in Recorded History) Which Will Wipe OUT Information Technology as We
Know it (Which is Gonna KILL MOST Forms of "Artificial/Technological" Heatin', SOOOO Fer the
Sake a Them Folks "Left Behind".....Leave "Global Warmin'" Alone....GOD KNOWS What He's a
Doin'). Chaos and Anarchy Will Reign (Rain ??) on the Earth for 7 Years of "Tribulation" Until the Year
2040 (Fourty Days and Fourty Nights.....Fourty Years in the Desert.....Fourty Years is a Generation....
.....Fourty Days of Pentecost......Fourty....40.....40.....40.....).....at the END of Which Time Will Be a
GREAT WAR Called AMAGGEDON.......to END the 2000 Years that Satan Was Given to Prove That
His Plan of "Lies, Avarace, and WELFAIR" (LAW) Could "Rule the Earth" Better Than GOD's Plan of
"Truth, Love, and CHARITY" ("TLC".....To Be Used by CHRIST to "Rule the Earth" in the NEXT
1000 Year "Millenium"......It "Seems" Only "Fair" Since Satan is Outnumbered 2 to 1 in Angelic
Forces).

After 1000 Years of "HELL On EARTH" as an ABSOLUTE DICTATOR with ABSOLUTE
POWER, and ABSOLUTE Standards of JUSTICE and RIGHTEOUSNESS (Who KNOWS the Very
"Thoughts and Intents of Your Heart" Because of HIS OMNISCIENCE.....And Therefore KNEW Every
Sin You Would EVER Committ in ETERNITY PAST.....and PAID for Them with the DEATH of HIS
BODY on a CROSS) Rules the Earth for a "Millenium" to PROVE that GOD is JUST in Condemning
.......WEELLLLLLL......That's Jest a Bit TOO Far inta the Furture Fer OUR Purposes HERE......

GOOD MUST Oppose EVIL......Jesus CHRIST MUST Oppose Satan/Lucifer/Devil/ETC.....AND
The NEW Independence Party (My Little NIPers)......MUST Oppose The NEW WORLD ORDER.....
(Even With Our Very Lives)......Whenever and Where Ever it Rears its Ugly Head (of a Snake).....

We NOW Return Control of This Book to its Author "BIG AL" Nolram.....And Return Your Sanity to
YOU "Dear Readers" as Well......What YOU Have Jest Read was JEST a "Glimpse" Into One of the
"Possible" FUTURE Episodes (That Take You from the "Darkest Reaches of the INNER Mind" to the...)
..........of The Television Series..... "OUTER LIMITS" !!!

OH…..I Almost Forgot……There Was ONE Statement in That "CHRISTmas Tree" That Didn't Belong, AND That I Didn't Cover Here…..Ms Palin…..This One's For YOU…..Dear Lady…..See Chapter 18 (Since I Haven't Written THAT Chapter Yet) ta Find Out WHO Has a "FREE Pass" ta Heaven…….as a Matter of Fact…….I Believe That I am FINALLY Ready to Write That Chapter NOW.

Did THAT Crap Make ANY Sense to Y'all on Pages 79-81, or Am I JEST Funnin' Ya…..YOU Decide!!!

Chapter 27

Are YOU a "miss, Miss, MISS" Type or a "make it, Make It, MAKE IT" Type ???

The Answer ta THIS Question is a Game Called "HORSE" that We Used t' Play at Recess Time on the Playground of the District 38 Grade School. It's a Very Simple Game that's Played with a Basketball. The Shooter Stands at the Free Throw Line and Shoots at the Basket; If'n They Make the Shot, They Get a Letter and Another Shot, and If They Miss, They Pass the Ball to the Next Kid in Line, and the First to Spell "H-O-R-S-E" (i.e., 5 Baskets) WINS the Game.

I'm NOT Gonna Talk about the Game Nor Much about the Shooter......I Wanna Talk t' Ya about the Kids Standin' in Line BEHIND the Shooter (Waitin' for Their Turn ta Shoot). Since We NIPers Like t' Deal in Trinity's, There are 3 Types of Kids: 1) The "Silent Majority" Who Keep their Mouths Shut and Jest "Watch" (They're Borin' as HELL.....Let's Move ON...); 2) The Kids Who Say, "miss, Miss, MISS" Because They Want the Shooter ta MISS, So They Can Git t' the Front of the Line Quicker ta Have They're Turn t' MISS; and Finally 3) The Kids Who Say, "make it, Make It, MAKE IT" Because They Figger That If'n They Root Fer the Shooter and The Shooter "MAKEs IT", Then Maybe the Shooter Will Root Fer THEM When It's Their Turn, and They'll Have the Encouragement and Self-Confidence ta "MAKE IT" TOO.......The Question IS: Which Type of Kid (Adult) are YOU???.....

Are YOU One of the "SILENT MAJORITY" Who Sits by as This GREAT GOD-Fearin' NATION of OURS Continues it's Downward Spiral Without Speakin' OUT Against Injustice and Oppression. Are You ONE of the "miss, Miss, MISS" Type Who Beat Others Down and Crawl Over Their Brused and Battered Bodies as You Claw Your Way ta the TOP of the HEEP. Or Maybe.....JUST MAYBE, You're the NEW Independence Party Thinker/Member (NIPer) Type Who Figgers, "The MORE People that I Encourage, Motovate, and Inspire to GREATNESS, the MORE There Will BE ta Lift ME t' Greater, Loftier GOALS Through Their Encouragement, Motivation, and Inspiration".......So the Question IS: Which Type of Kid (Adult) are YOU???........Maybe You're a NIPer TOO.....or at LEAST..... a NIPer "WANNA BE"........Read On (Gentle Reader).......READ ON.......

Did THAT Crap Make ANY Sense to Y'all on Page 82, or Am I JEST Funnin' Ya.....YOU Decide!!!

Chapter 28

WHY Do the 4 Houses of Hogwarts School of Witchcraft and Wizardry Conform So PERFECTLY with the 4 Quadrant Leadership Model ???

We're Gonna Gently "Remind" Y'all of This When We Talk about Our Favorite Authors in Chapter 44, BUTT (Ya Jest NEVER KNOW When Yer Gonna See My BIG BUTT Poop....I Mean POP Up Now Do Ya???) We're Gonna Expaaaaaand Upon it Here. I Don't Know WHAT Ever Happened ta the 4 Quadrant Leardership Model that I Have Been Taught Over the Years (Maybe Whoever Thunk it Up Got Shot Like John F. Kennedy or Martin Luther King and The Concept Died with 'em Kindly a Like "Their" Concepts Died.... I WONDER If'n the Concept of the NEW Independence Party (NIPers) Will Die with Me....HMmmm), BUTT It Conforms Perfectly with the 4 Student Houses in the "Hogwarts School of Witchcraft and Wizardry" from Author J. K. Rowling's "Harry Potter" Book Series......

As BEST I Recollect (Which Ain't None Too Great These Days with My Dog Gone Fergitter Workin' Overtime), the Upper Left-Hand Quadrant was the "Directors" Who Took the "LEAD" (That's "LEAD" as in "LEADership" and NOT "Lead" as in "ta Go Over Like a Lead Balloon"), Grabbed the Bull by the Horns, Grabbed the Tiger by the Tail, And Jest Generally Took Charge of ANY Situation "Against ALL Odds" and Despite the Danger or Hardship ta ThemSelves. This PERFECTLY Describes the House of "Griffendor" in J. K. Rowling's "Harry Potter Series. The Griffendors was ALWAYS the First inta the Fray, And USUALLY the Ones Who Turned "Adversity" to "Advantage" and "Sacrifice" inta "Success".

Near as I Can Remember, the Upper Right-Hand Quadrant was the "Socializers" Who Always Seem ta Remember Yer Birthday and Anniversary, Who are Always Inquirin' About Yer Health and That a Yer Family and Friends, Who Plan the "BEST" Parties, Who'd Give Ya the Shirt Off'n Their Back (Even If it WAS the ONLY Shirt They Had), Who are Always Willin' ta Lend a Helpin' Hand Even IF They Don't Always Know Exactly What ta Do or How ta Do it. They're Jest Generally Good Friends ta Have When Ya Need Someone ta Talk to or a Shoulder t' Cry on. The House of HufflePuff was the Home Away from Home of the "Socializers". Compassion, Condolence, and Caring Where Their Watch Words and They Were Purty Darned GOOD at All Three (a Trinity).

I Believe (If'n I'm Not Mistaken) that the Lower Left-Hand Quadrant was Where the Super-Smart "Intelectuals/Technicians" Were Located. These Are the Folks Who Have a LOT of "Book Larnin'", BUTT Who's "Social" Skills Leave a Little Bit ta Be Desired. These are Yer "Geeks", "Dweebs", And "Know-it-ALLs". They are MORE Concerned with Propositions, Postulates, and Paradigms Than They Are with "Actual Applications" (Like Color Coordinatin' Their Outfits, or Rememberin' NOT ta Mix Their "Stripes" with Their "Plaids"). The RavenClaw House was the IDEAL Place ta Put the "Brainy" "Intelectual/Technicians" Who Would ALWAYS Seem ta Come Up with That Obscure Fact or Bit of Logical Reasonin' at Jest the "Correct" Time ta Save the Day.

And Lastly (And "Definitely" LEASTLY), in the Lower Right-Hand "Slime-Pit of HELL" Quadrant was the "Relationship" Folks......Y'all KNOW.....the "BAD Ole Boy" Network.....The "You Scratch My Back and I'll Stab Ya in Yours" Types.....the "I'm in it Fer Whatever's in it Fer ME" Types.....The Stuck UP, Sneerin', Snickerin', Slimy "Slitheryn" House Folks. These were Always the Bullies, and the

Ones Who Were Always Hatchin' Plots and Schemes ta Git What They Didn't Earn, Deserve, or Even Appreciate. They USUALLY Rat-Packed Together in "Groups" Because They Were Too Cowardly and Despised by "Others" ta Risk Bein' Caught Alone and Outnumbered. These Were the TRUE Dregs from the Bottom of the Barel, and Were Always Willin' t' Accept a "Hand UP", So's that They Could "Beat DOWN" Anyone Who Stood in Their Way.

I Would REALLY Like ta Meet J. K. Rowling One Day and Have a Little Chit-Chat (Over a Cup a Tea and Some Biscuits) About Her Little "Harry Potter" Book Series as One GREAT Author to Another, ta Discuss the Contents of THIS Chapter and Her "Part" of Chapter 44 (now…Now….NOW….DON'T Ya Be a Thinkin' By THAT I'm a Makin' ANY Connection Between J. K. Rowling and One a Them Thar "Sadomasochistic Dominatrix (with Very HIGH Moral Character) in Skin Tight Red Leather"….. Because THAT is a Refference ta Mr Terry Goodkind…..OOOPS….I Mean ta the "WORKS" a Mr Terry Goodkind……PHEW…..I Nearly Done Pissed OFF Two of My Favorite Authors at ONCE), BUTT Since Nobody'll Probably Bother ta Read MY Little "Baby" (Book), I Don't See THAT as Happenin' Anytime Soon……Oh Well……..Movin' ON……

NAAHHHHH…..Y'all Should KNOW By NOW That I CAIN'T Leave it THERE…..Ms Rowling …..DEAR "LADY"……Yer Government's "LEADERS" Have ta Work in Coordination with MY Government's "LEADERS" Fer the "Betterment" of the Entire WORLD……SOOOOOO YOU And EVERY Citizen of EVERY Country in the WORLD "SHOULD" Be "Concerned"…..AND Have a "Vested Interest" in the "LEADERSHIP" of This GREAT GOD-Fearin' NATION of OURS Called the UNITED STATES of AMERICA…….AND I "Dearly and Sincerely" Apologize Fer the SHABBY Way that OUR "LEADER" Treated Yer "Magnificent Monarach" When She Graciously Visited Us "Errant" Colonies by Givin' Her a Bunch a Crappy CDs……PLEEASE Know that If'n OUR NEW Independence (Now I Realize That May Be a "Insensitive" Word ta Use in Yer Presence) Party (NIPer) Presidential Candidate Ms Sarah Palin Had Been in the "Office of the President" of the GREAT UNITED STATES of AMERICA at That Time…..SHE Would Have Treated the Supreme "LADY" of Yer Land with the RESPECT, KINDNESS, and COURTESY (RKC Fer the SOUL, Reference Chapter 7) that She Deserved AND Would Have Given Her "GOOD Gifts" as OUR NIPer "Handbook" Teaches Us.

PLEEASE Don't Hold the AMERICAN PEOPLE Responsible (Other than the SORRY ASSed Folks Who Voted the TIT-TURD inta Office…..TWICE…..) Fer the Unconscionable Actions of the "Current" Yahoo Who "Occupies" the "Oval Office"……Like the "Occupied" Sign on a WC (Water Closet or Loo) …….We NIPers (with YOUR And the OTHER "Concerned Citizens" of ALL of the OTHER Countries on This Planet SUPPORT)………and a "Pound" 'er Three……or a "Mark" 'er Three…..or a "Yen" 'er Three….or a "Frank" 'er Three…..or a "Ruble" 'er Three…..or a ……WEELLLLL Ya Git the "IDEA" …..ta US Post Office Box…..P.O. Box 2149, Tuskegee, AL 36083……Wouldn't Hurt Yer Pocketbook TOO Much……AND It "SURELY" Would HELP Git the NEW Independence Party (NIPers) OFF ta a GOOD Start at Gittin' Ms Sarah Palin and Mr Herman Cain Elected as President and Vice-Persident (Respectively) on the NEW Independence Party (NIPer) "Write-IN" Ticket Fer Them Thar Nov 2016 Elections (And PLEEASE Dear Lady….Don't Ya Think Fer a Moment That I Was a Tryin' ta Call Ya "Shirley"……I Would NEVER Do THAT…….Maybe…..)…….REALLY Movin' ON……

Did THAT Crap Make ANY Sense to Y'all on Pages 83-84, or Am I JEST Funnin' Ya…..YOU Decide!!!

Chapter 29

HOW is SPANKING My Kids EVER Gonna SAVE THEIR LIVES ???

Now Ever Since Dr Benjamin Spook (er Maybe That's "Spock", or "Scotty", or "Chekov", or "Bones"…..He was a Doctor Warn't He??.....See I TOLD Ya I'd Seen a Star Trek 'er Two WAYYY Back in Chapter 2) Convinced a BUNCH a Ya Danged FOOL Parents ta STOP Spankin' Yer Kids, the REST a Us Law-Abidin' Citizens Have Had to Put UP with Yer Dad Burned Heathen Yougins Fer the LONGGGGEST Time…..And We NIPers Are JEST About as Tired of it as We Can BE, SOOOOO… We're Gonna See If'n We Can Do Sumthin' About THAT with the Contents a This Here Chapter.

Spankin' Yer Kids (OR Jest Givin' Them a Good Ole "THUMP" on the Noggin' with a Well Cocked Finger) is a GOOD Way ta Git Their "Attention" (Kindly a Like Hittin' a MULE Between the Eyes with a 2x4, Baseball Bat, or Axe Handle ta Git THEIR "Attention"…..And In the Case a SOME of Y'all's Little Obnoxious BRATS…….NO, I'd Better Not GO There…..) Before a Little "Trainin' Session" Where Ya IMPART ta Their Backside a Few "Words o' Wisdom". Now I AIN'T Takin' About Beatin' Yer Kids ta DEATH (Exceptin' in "EXTREME" Cases Where Ya Shouldn't a Had 'em in the First Place Because YOU Were Such an Obnoxious Heathen YerSelf, and Ya Passed on Yer Obnoxiousness "with Compound Interest" ta Boot), I'm Jest Talkin' About Givin' em a Little "Trauma" ta Their "Guteous Maximi" ta Enforce the "Lesson" that Yer Tryin' ta Learn 'em (Like the 4th "Principle of Trainin'" that I Mentioned t' Ya Back in Chapter 13…..".4. The Thing Learned in a TRAUMATIC Situation is the BEST Remembered"…..I Can SEE That I Ain't Got THOUGH ta Ya Yet, SOOOOO…..Let Me Tell Ya a Little "Story" About "Franky and Johnny"……

Now THIS "Franky and Johnny" Weren't Lovers…..They Was Two Little Obnoxious Heathens Who Lived on Opposite Sides of the Street and Jest LOVED ta Git Together and See JEST How MUCH Dad Balmed Mischief They Could Cause, BUTT They WASN'T Supoosed ta CROSS the Street Without Their Mothers' Assistance and Watchful Carefulness. HOWEVER, When the "Cat's Away" Obnoxious Little Heathen Boys Will PLAY (AND Try ta Cross the Busy Street On Their OWN), And SOOOO…. Franky Looked Across the Street at Johnny, and Johnny Looked Across the Street at Franky, AND They SIMULTANEOUSLY Started ta CROSS ta Each Other. LUCKily Both a Their Mothers (Usin' That Famous "Woman's Intuition" that ALL Mothers HAVE) IMMEDIATELY and SIMULTANEOUSLY Came Outa Their Houses and "Snatched" Those Obnoxious Little Heathen Boys from the "Jaws of Death" (…..Too Bad Fer the REST of Us Who're Gonna Have ta Put UP with Their Obnoxiousness Fer the Rest a Their Lives……Which MAY Not Be THAT Long as You Will SEE…..)…..

Let's Take a "Dramatic Pause" (and a Paragraph Break) in Our Little "Story" of "Franky and Johnny" Fer a Public Service Announcement from the NEW Independence Party (NIPers) on Our Intention ta Help IMPROVE the Intelligence of the AMERICAN PUBLIC by REPEALIN' a Few "Laws"……We NIPers Feel that ALL Motor Cycle Helmet "Requirement" Laws Should be REPEALLED…..It Would Give Them Thar "STUPID" Folks that SHOULD Know Better'n ta Ride a Motor Cycle without a Good Helmet the FREEDOM and Opportunuty ta KILL TheirSelves BEFORE They Can Breed UP Any MORE "STUPID IDIOTS" Like ThemSelves ta Decrease the "Average" Intelligence of the AMERICAN

PUBLIC......JEST a Thought.......This Has Been a PUBLIC SERVICE Announcement from the NEW Independence Party (NIPers)......We NOW Return Ya ta the "Excitin' Conclusion" of the "Story" of "Franky and Johnny"......the Suspence is Jest KILLIN' Me......I HOPE it Will LAST......

Franky's Mother Was One a "THEM" Thar Folks Who Follered the Teachin's a Dr Spook and Calmly Explained ta Her Little Heathen Franky that If'n He Went inta the Street He Might Git Hit by a "Carless Driver" and "Killed", And THEN Took Him inta the House for a Little "Time OUT" (Which He USED Efficiently and Effectively ta Think Up Even MORE Obnoxious Mischief ta Git His Little BUTT inta as He Was a "Contemplaitin'" About What WAS a "Careless Driver" and WHAT Did it MEAN ta Git "KILLED"). Little Johnny's Mother, on the Other Hand, Was a FIRM Believer (as Are We NIPers) in the Axiom of "Spare the ROD and Spoil the Child" And Didn't Think that Dr Spook Knew His Anal Orifice from a Whole in the Ground, And Tanned Little Johnny's Backside with the Flat of Her Hand, as She Said Three Times (a Trinity)....."Don't You Go inta the Street AGAIN Without Me WITH You" Which Incorporates ALL 4 "Princples of Training" inta ONE:

1. The FIRST Thing Learned is the BEST Remembered (When She Said it the 1st Time)
2. The LAST Thing Learned is the BEST Remembered (When She Said it the 3rd Time)
3. The Thing MOST Often REPEATED is the BEST Remembered (by Sayin' it 3 Times)
4. The Thing Learned in a TRAUMATIC Situation is BEST Remembered (by the Vigourous Application of a Little "Blunt Force" TRAUMA ta the Heathen's Posterior)

NOW We Git ta the Really EXCITIN' Part Later That SAME Day........

Later that SAME Day, While BOTH Mother's Brains (AND "Mother's Intuition") Were DISABLED by "Days of Our Lives"......Franky and Johnny Were BACK on the Sidewalks in Front a Their Houses a Lookin' Across the Street at Each Other and Franky Jest Couldn't WAIT ta Tell Johnny About ALL a the NEAT Obnoxious Mischief that He Had Thought Up Durin' His Little "TimeOUT" Session, And He Stepped Out inta the Street and Was Run Over by a "Careless Driver" and "KILLED", BUTT When Little Johnny's Mother Came Flyin' Out of the House ta See WHAT GOD Awful "CRUNCH" Had Broke THROUGH Her Concentration and Disrupted Her Reverie with "Days of Our Lives", She Found Little Johnny Standin' "Rooted" ta the Sidewalk, Because "HE Didn't Want ta Disobey His Mother By Crossin' the Street Alone" (AND Takin' the CHANCE a Gittin' ANOTHER Application of "Words of Wizdom" ta His Little Derriere).

The MORAL of This Little "Story" About "Franky and Johnny" is that (CONTRARY ta the Teachin' of Dr Spook) Spankin' Yer Obnoxious Heathen Youngins CAN Save Their Lives (When it is Efficiently and Effectively Accompanied by "Words of Wisdom" Imparted According ta ALL FOUR "Principles of Training"), AND That "Lack of Spanking Obnoxious Heathen Kids" is the REASON that There are MORE Kids Named Johnny than there ARE Named Franky......I Think.......Maybe.....Movin' ON....

Did THAT Crap Make ANY Sense to Y'all on Pages 85-86, or Am I JEST Funnin' Ya.....YOU Decide!!!

Chapter 30

I May NOT Be "76....AND TIRED" Like Bill Cosby, BUTT Why DO Kids Tattoo and Pierce TheirSelves ???

I JEST Heard the Other Day that Mr Bill Cosby (One a My FAVORITE Comedians a ALL TIME) May NOT Even Have Written the Article Upon Which This Chapter is Based, BUTT Since This Book is a Political and Religious Satire Fer Our TIME.....I'm JEST Gonna IGNORE That Little FACT and JEST Proceed as If I Didn't KNOW Any BETTER (Which is the WAY I USUALLY Proceed Anyway, So's Y'all Probably Wouldn't Have EVEN Known the "Difference" If I Hadn't a TOLD Ya)...Anyhow Now...

It is NOT a SHOCK ta Us NIPers that Kids These Days are a Piercin' and a Tattooin' (Or Jest Tatin', BUTT....NOT Like Gramma's Tatin' that was a LOT Like Crochetin' Only "Finer".....I'm a Talkin' About "Tatin'" Like in Tattooin'......JEST So's We is All CLEAR on That) Their BODYs Because That's About ALL That This Here Society TODAY Has Left 'em ta Express Their "Individuallity" and "Uniqueness"......Let Me Explain a Little MORE than "Skin Deep".....

Since the Schools these Days (When Their NOT Recoverin' from Bloody Massacres) Try ta Make ALL a Their Students "EQUALLY" Mediocre (by Takin' the BEST Students OUT and Puttin' 'em with OTHER "BEST" Students, and Takin' the "Troubled" Students OUT and Puttin' 'em with OTHER "Troubled" Students......Now THERE's a Really "Brilliant" Idea from Y'all HIGHER Learnin' Types... AND Takin' "Slowwwer" Students OUT ta Be Put with Even "SLLOOOWWWWWER" Students), So that NO ONE Will Feel "Unique" and "Different" and EVERY Student Can Feel the PRESSURE of Bein' "EQUALLY" Mediocre......Can Ya Imagine YET Why They Tat and Pierce ThemSelves???.... WELLLL......Let's JEST Dig a Little DEEPER "Under the Skin" at This "Infected" Sore Point Then.....

When I Went ta School "Back in the Days" as a "Little" NIPer, We Sang Patriotic and "Folksy" Songs, We Square Danced and Played "Educational Games Like "HORSE", and HopScotch, and Jump Rope, We Participated in the Activities Sponsored by the President's Council on Physical Fitness, We Listened ta Classical and Popular Music During Luch Breaks, We Acted in Plays and Skits, And We Even Had a Little Band Where I First Learned ta Play a Tune on the Trumpet, AND We Even Managed ta Do a Little Readin' Writin', and 'Rithmatic as Well, BUUTT (And That's a REALLY BIG BUUTT)... I Don't Know WHAT Their Teachin' or Doin' ta the Kids in School THESE Days....Do YOU???...

We ALSO Had Things Like "Achievement Awards", and "Valedictorians", and "Salutatorians", and "HONOR Societies", Sports Teams, and Drama Societies, And All KINDS of Ways ta Express Our "Individuallity" and "Uniqueness" that I Believe are Missing in Today's Schools, Not ta Mention the Fact That We Didn't Have QUITE the Restrictive "Dress Code" (Except That The Atheletes Were Required ta Wear Neckties on "Game Day" If'n They Wanted the Opportunity t' "Suit UP" Fer the Game), Because We Were "TAUGHT" a Little "BETTER" By Our Parents as ta WHAT was "Appropriate" School Atire and What was NOT......Am I Gittin' THROUGH t' Ya YET Why Kids Tat and Pierce ThemSelves???

WHEN We NEW Independece Party Thinkers/Members (NIPers) Take Over This Here GREAT GOD-Fearin' NATION of OURS in the "NEW" AMERICAN Revolution (One Voter at a TIME),

UNLIKE the "CURRENT" Administration of the Federal Governement, We WILL Be Makin' a Few "CHANGES" ta Git "Individuality" and "Uniquesness" (AND the "Appreciation" Thereof) BACK inta the School System (Amoung "OTHER" Places)...... And You Can "BANK" on That.......

Did THAT Crap Make ANY Sense to Y'all on Pages 87-88, or Am I JEST Funnin' Ya.....YOU Decide!!!

Chapter 31

Do Ya Really OWN Yer Home And Have "Money" in the "BANK" ???

And Speakin' of "BANKs", I'd Be Willin' ta Bet that a LOT a You Folks Out There THINK That Ya OWN Yer Home (House) IF'n It's Mortgage (And Second Mortgage, AND "Equity Line of Credit) is Fully PAID OFF, AND I'd ALSO Be Willin' ta Bet that Y'all THINK that Ya Have a Little CASH in the BANK (If'n Good Ole "UNCLE SAM" Ain't Stole Every Penny Ya HAVE Yet), BUTT (As USUAL Y'all'd Be "DEAD WRONG").......

Let's Start with the MYTH of "Money in the BANK" Before We Git ta the MYTH About Home (House, Property, and Possessions) Ownership.....Y'all Do NOT Have ANY Money in the "BANK".... In Today's Fast-Paced, "Buy it NOW", Highly Techological Society, You Have a Few Little Electronic "Bits" in a Computer (SomeWHERE !?!) That "Indicate" the "Possibility" That "SOME" of the Money in a BANK Jest "MIGHT" Be Available Fer You ta "USE" for a While (As LONG as Ya Pay it Right Back, with "Compound Interest")........AND It ONLY Takes the "Flippin'" of ONE "Bit" ta Turn Ya from a Millionare ta Someone Who is a Million Dollars in DEBT.....Now How's THAT Fer Them Thar Greedy "BANKS" a "Flippin' Ya OFF"???......Sounds ta ME Like Ya Otta Start "Flippin'" THEM the "THIRD" Use of the "Sign of the NIPers" (Reference Chapter 2).

Let's Let the "BANKS" Stew in Their Own "Greens" Fer a While, And BUST (BURST??) the MYTH That Y'all OWN Yer HOME (which HOPEFULLY Includes a House or Apartment, Some Small Portion "However Tiny" of Land/Acrage, And Various Personal Possessions): Y'all Do NOT Own Yer HOME (Even IF There Are NO Outstandin' Debts Against it).....You ONLY Have (at MOST) a Piece of Paper that MOST Folks "Recognise and Accept" that States that You OWN "Something", BUTT That Thar "Ownership" is ONLY as "Good as the Paper it is Written ON" (or RATHER.....Only as Good as the "Government" that "Protects and Serves" Who Can BACK it UP with the Full POWER of Justice and Righteousness of the LAW and Court System, AND a Few "Weapons" in the Hands of Them Thar LAW Enforcement Officers Trained in Their "Proper" USE). WITHOUT All a THAT CRAP (Like TODAY .....Where the "BIG Government" Feels it is Their "DUTY" ta SEIZE Yer HOME Fer the PUBLIC..... That Means Everyone BUTT "YOU".....GOOD, And the COURT System Operates on the Principle of "LEGALITY" Instead of "Righteousness and Justice", AND the LAW Enforcement Officers are FEW and "Far Between" And NOT Well Armed or Trained Due ta "Budget" Cutbacks), THEN You Are "On Yer OWN" and You ONLY "OWN" Whatever You Can HOLD By the Strength of Yer Resolve and a Few GOOD "Weapons" of Yer OWN.....AND HOPEFULLY You Have Gotten Training on Their "Proper" Use (Prefferably by Volunteering a Portion of Your Life, Time, and Effort to the "Protection of OUR FREEDOMS" by Serivng in the ARMED FORCES of the GREATEST NATION on EARTH), AND Have an "Abundant" Supply of Ammunition.

BECAUSE......as Almost ANY of Them Thar "DOOMSDAY Preppers" Will Tell Ya.....Our VERY "Fragile" Existence that is SOOOOO Dependent on Layer Upon Layer of Electronic Technology (the "DEVIL's TOOLS"......Ya KNOW......Like Flip Wilson's, "The DEVIL Made Me Do THAT!!!") Where it Takes a Computer ta Guide the Laser that Cuts the "NEW" High-Tech Material Thin Enough ta

Make an Even FASTER and MORE Efficient MicroChip Processor that Can Make Y'all Even MORE TOTALLY Dependent on Electronic Technology Fer Yer Very Existence AND ta Maintain Yer HIGH Standard of Livin',So Y'all Can KILL Each Other OFF with Even MORE POWERFUL and EFFICIENT "High-Tech" Weaponry......Y'all NEED ta Be "PREPARED" Fer the DAY When it ALL Comes a Tumbblin' DOWN Like a "House of Cards". Once AGAIN We NEW Independence Party Members (NIPers) Say that Ms Sarah Palin (with HER Survival Skills and "small GOVERNMENT Mind-Set" , ALONG With Mr Herman Cain's Business Savy And 9-9-9 Tax Plan, is the ANSWER t' the QUESTION that ALL of Y'all AMERICANS Out There SHOULD Be Askin', "WHO is the "BEST" Choice ta Steer OUR Ship of State Through the TROUBLED Waters Ahead???".......THINK About it VERY, VERRRY Carefully....We NIPers Have.....And to US.....the "CHOICE" is "Obvious".....Who's "Laughin'" NOW???.....

Did THAT Crap Make ANY Sense to Y'all on Pages 89-90, or Am I JEST Funnin' Ya.....YOU Decide!!!

Chapter 32

If'n Ya Can Laugh ALL the Way ta the Bank, Cain't the NIPers HOPE ta Laugh ALL the Way t' the White House ???

Humor is an Infectious Disease that CAN Break Down Yer "Natural Defenses" Against TRUTH and Logic. I Use Humor as a "Sugar Coatin'" Fer My "Informational/Inspirational" Time Bombs…..When Information (the More "Purely" TRUTHFUL the Better) is Combined "Correcctly" with Inspiration (the More "Purely" UPLIFTIN' the Better) it Forms a VERRY Volitile Substance that Has "Fueled" the Careers of Everyone from Adolph Hiltler to Mahatmas Ghandi. I Choose to "Sugar Coat" This "Bitter Pill" with HUMOR ta Git Ya ta "Swallow it" Before Ya KNOW it…..OR….I Wrap My Little Time Bomb of Information/Inspiration in a "Trojan Horse" of HUMOR, "Shoot" it Through Yer Defenses, And Capture Yer "Heart" Before Ya Even KNOW it.

Many Times People Who Use HUMOR Efficiently and Effectively to Further Their Careers (and Financial Status) are Said to "Laugh ALL of the Way to the BANK" AND in That SAME Vein, I and the NEW Independence Party (NIPers) are Goin' ta TRY ta Git ALL of AMERICA SOOOO Tied Up in "Hysterical Laughter" (or At the VERRY Least a Slight Titter or Giggle), So that WE Can "Laugh ALL of the Way ta the White House". At the Outset, This "Appears" to be a QUITE Daunting or Impossible Task, BUTT with Perseverance (and the AID of This Little "Baby" of Mine….And with the Aid of My Little www.YouTube.com Videos that NO One is "Currently" Lookin' at) WE NIPers Feel that it CAN Be DONE……And MUST BE DONE !!!

As I Said Above, HUMOR is an "Infectious Disease", BUTT The "Trick" in Gittin' the Disease ta "Infect" and "Spead Across" an Entire NATION is ta "Infect" the "Correct" CARRIERS. We NIPers are STILL Tryin' ta Git My Book and Videos inta the "Correct" Hands ta Git 'em ta Go "VIRAL", BUTT I'm SORRY ta Say that We're NOT Havin' Much "LUCK" at This Time (Reference Chapter 57). BUTT There IS Something that YOU (Gentle Reader) CAN Do to Assist US NIPers in Our Goal to "Infect" the ENTIRE "GREAT GOD-Fearin' UNITED STATES of AMERICA" Nation of OURS…..And THAT is to Pass This Book (Electronically OR via "HardCopy") to EVERYONE Ya KNOW (Friends, Family, Co-Workers, Yer Worst Enemy or Yer Mother-Out-Law……UnLess'n a Course Those LAST Two are ONE and the SAME……And THEN Ya Only Have ta Waist ONE Copy), AND ta Send "Links" ta My www.YouTube.com Videos as "Teasers" ta the Book……BECAUSE…….If'n Someone "LIKES" the Videos, Then They'll Probably "LOVE" the Book (My Little "Baby")…..BUTT…..If'n They DON'T "Like" the Videos, Then More than Likely They Will "HATE" My Little "Baby"…Boo..Hoo..HOOO!!!

Did THAT Crap Make ANY Sense to Y'all on Page 91, or Am I JEST Funnin' Ya…..YOU Decide!!!

Chapter 33

Do Y'all REALLY Know Who Yer Neighbor is, or Do Ya Even CARE ???

There's This Little Story I Heard "Once Upon a Time" from the UGMMHL (the "User's Guide and Maintenance Manual for a Human Life") That Talked About Who Yer Neighbor is, BUTT I Think There are a Whole BUNCH a Folks Who Missed the WHOLE Point o' That Little Story by What We NIPers See a Goin' On in the World Today…..With the WAY Folks Seem ta Treat Each Other…..SOOOO….. I Figgered I'd Jest Try ta Tell Ya That Little Story Agin……With a Little Bit of a "Different" EmPHAsis, and "SEE" If'n it Makes More SENSE t' Ya…….

In the UGMMHL (and MOST "Churches" Today), This Little Tail (Waggin' the Dog) is Called "The Story o' the GOOD Samaritan"…..Now If'n Ya Already "THINK" that Ya KNOW it (ALL)….Then Jest Skip ta Another Chapter and Don't Pay THIS Old Fool from Beauregard, AL No NeverMind…..BUTT… If'n I Jest MIGHT Have Earned Yer Respect Durin' the PREVIOUS Chapters….Or Ya Have a "Feelin'" That This Old Codger Has a "Brain Slap" Fer Ya UP His Sleeve (Even Though I'm a Wearin' One a Them Thar "Sleveless" Shirts)…..OR, Yer Jest Curious as ta What This "Sage o' the Age" from Sleepy Little Beauregard, AL Might Be UP to……Then Read On…..Gentle Reader…..Read ON……

MOST Folks Think that the Story o' the "GOOD Samaritan" is Supposed ta TEACH Us that Nearly EVERYONE is Our "Neighbor" (the World Over) and that We Should Jest "LOVE" Everybody, And as USUAL…..They'd Be DEAD WRONG!!! That Ain't the "Point" that MY GOD Was a Tryin' ta Make …..WEELLLLLLL….It IS (I Guess), BUTT It AIN'T TOO…..Let Me Explain it "HOPEFULLY" in a Way That Y'all Have NEVER Heard it BEFORE…….UnLessin' a Course Y'all FINALLY Checked Out Some a My www.YouTube.com Videos That Have Been OUT There Ferever and a Day, That Ain't NO One Lookin' at (Least Wise the "Dust Bunnies" in P.O. Box 2149, Tuskegee, AL 36083 Seem ta Indicate That Nobody's a Lookin'….BUTT….Maybe It's Jest that Their LOOKIN' BUTT Ain't Findin' Nuthin' a "VALUE" in 'em ta Make 'em Feel Obligated ta Send Me a Dollar or Three)…….

The KEY ta the Story of the "GOOD Samaritan" is the SAME as ANY a Them Thar Real Estate Folks Will Tell Ya……location…..Location……LOCATION!!!…….Because, Yer Neighbors Are the Folks "Physically" Near Ya (Like the Person Sittin' Next ta Ya in the Movie Theater Chattin' Away on Their Cell Phone Durin' the MOST Excitin' Part……or the Person Ahead of Ya in the Grocery Checkout Line Who Jest Had ta Have Their THIRD (a Trinity) Price Check……Or The $*^%*(^^& Fool $##^$#$&* Who Jest Cut in Front a Ya as You Was Tryin' ta Maintain the "Proper" Distance Between You and the Car Ahead a Ya……AND…..WEELLLLL…..I Think Ya Git the IDEA……Them Thar Folks is Yer Neighbors BECAUSE They ALWAYS Happen ta Be the Folks NEAR Ya…..and WHY Cain't Ya EVER Seem ta Find a COP (Excuse ME…….Police Officer…..We NIPers Think Them Thar LAW Enforcement Folks Have a TOUGH Job Tryin' ta Keep Y'all "Neighbors" from Killin' Each Other…..and Git VERRY Little Respect Fer it….SORRY Folks Fer Callin' Y'all COPS……PLEEEASE Fergive Me……AND As Long as Yer in a Fergivin' MOOD……I Gots These Here Parkin' Tickets……OOPS……I'm a Bit OFF Topic……I'll Git BACK ta Ya On Them Thar Parkin' Tickets a Little Later…..Thanks)…..Now ….. WHERE Was I…….Oh Yeah…..

Yer "Neighbors" are the Folks Physically "NEAR" Ya……That's Why the "OTHER" Two Fellas in the Story of the "GOOD Samaritan" Walked WAAYYYYY Over on the OTHER Side a the Road When They Passed the Beat UP Feller, BUTT the "GOOD Samaritan" Walked RIGHT (or LEFT) Up ta Him and HELPED Him Out. A LOT a Folks Think that Them Thar Folks in Foreign Countrys Like Africa and China are Our "Neighbors", BUTT They're NOT (Although it Does SEEM That Like That with That Thar DAMN Babble Box INVADIN' My Privacy by Bringin' ALL a Them Thar "GIMME…GIMME" Commercials Comin' inta My VERY Livin' Room……ACTUALLY the TV is in the Den…..And the Bedroom……AND the KITCHEN……BUTT "Livin' Room " Identifies Better with MOST Folks and We NIPers ALWAYS Try ta "Fit IN"……NOTT!!!......Anyhow Now…..), Because as I Said Before, Yer "Neighbor" is the Person "NEAR" You…….Let Me SEE If I Can Bring This "POINT" Home t' Ya By Tellin' Ya a More RECENT Story…..

Once Upon a Time (in the Not TOO Distant Past) There Was This Little Security Guard, Who Was a Doin' His Job as BEST He Could (Bein' that it Was CHRISTmas Time Again and Everyone Was in a Frantic Haste ta Git Their CHRISTmas Shoppin' Done So's They Could Git Home and Enjoy the Warmth and Love o'Their Families…..(UnLESS a Course Y'all Have a Family Like MINE…..'Nuff Said). Jest Before Openin' Time at the Store Where This Little Security Guard Worked (SOME of Ya Can SEE Where I'm a Goin' with This…….Some a Ya Don't……AND as USUAL…..MOST a Ya Hadn't Got a "CLUE"……BUTT, HUMOR Me This Time and Come Along Fer the "Thrill Ride"…..It Jest MIGHT Do Ya Some GOOD…)…..BUTT, When He Opened Up the Doors ta Let His "Neighbors" in ta Finish Their Last Minute Shoppin' (Or Git a "Jump Start" on Them Thar Great "Holiday Sales")…..In Their Headlong RUSH and "Feedin' Frenzy" ta Git the BEST Deal on Some a the "Cheap" Material Possetions of This Wolrd………They Tramppled That Poor Little Security Guard ta "DEATH"……

HE WAS THEIR "NEIGHBOR" Folks……They Were SOOOOO Near Him That Their "Foot Prints" Were All OVER Him…….He Was Their "NEIGHBOR" and They Trampled Their "Neighbor" ta Death …..What a WORLD We Live In…..MY GOD Gave Each of Us a "Smallish" Sphere/Aura of Love That Reaches Out a Few Feet ta Be Able ta TOUCH Our "Neighbors"…..the People "NEAR" Ya……and NOT the Folks Over in Africa and China……They Have "Neighbors" of Their OWN Over There ta Take Care o' Them (or at Least They SHOULD Have……Like We SHOULD Take Better CARE of the Folks Who are "NEAR" Us Here in the Good Old US of A, BUTT…….When Was the Last Time That Ya ACTUALLY "Talked" ta Yer Neighbor……Now I Don't Mean "On the Phone (Cell or Otherwise) or Via E-Mail or WORSE YET That ABOMMINATION of the DEVIL Known as TEXT MESSAGIN"… I Gots a Code 'er TWO Fer Y'all TEXT MESSENGERS……"FO"…er..."FU"…..See CHAPTER 55), AND If'n They DON'T (and Yer SOOOOO Damned "Concerned" About 'em, Then Go OVER ta Africa or Asia or CHINA and Stand Toe-t-Toe with 'em, And Then They WILL Be "Near" You AND Be Yer "Neighbors"……..Let's Take a Little Paragraph Break And I'll Try it from a "Different" Direction…..

If'n YOU Send a Wad a Money ta Them Folks "OVERSEAS" and Walk Right (or Left) Past a "So Called" "Homeless Bum" on the Streets of ANY GREAT United States City……Then YOU Haven't "Understood" ANYTHING I've Just Said……Ya DON'T "Understand" the LESSON of the "Good Samaritan"….AND Yer Part of the PROBLEM in This Good Ole US of A, Instead of Bein' Part of the SOLUTION of Gittin' This Country BACK inta the SHAPE, Like When it Was "Bright and GAY" (AND GAY Meant "Light and Airy" or "FUN Lovin'" And NOT What it Does TODAY). People USED Ta Keep Track o' Their "Neighbor's" Property and Respect it AND Their "Neighbors"……it WASN'T

Uncommon Ta Knock on Yer Neighbors Door and Ask ta Borrow a Cup a Sugar, And Be Invited IN Fer a Cup a "Joe" (or "Josephine") and a Little Chit Chat About That NEW So-and-So Neighbor Down the Street or Across the Way……We USED Ta NOT Be SOOOOOO Caught UP in Our OWN Affairs That We Didn't Have the TIME Ta Console a Grievin' Neighbor Who Had Lost a Loved One, INSTEAD of Havin' Ta Read About it in the NewsPaper (That is If'n ANY of Ya Read Them Thar "NEWSPAPERS" Anymore……Yer Always "Bloggin'" Or "Surfin' the "NET" OR WHATEVER the HELL Ya Do These Days OTHER Than Be Respectful, Kind, and Courteous ta Yer "Neighbors")…….I Think I'll Git Down OFF'n My "Soapbox" Now Cause I Don't THINK There's Any o' Ya Out There a Listenin' Anymore…

Y'all Don't REALLY Care About Yer "Neighbors" Any More…….And That's Just PART of the Reason This Here GREAT GOD-Fearin' Country of'n OURS is in SUCH Sad Shape…….And I'm Jest a WAISTin' (YEAH……I Gots a BIG "WAIST"…..What's it TO Ya…….a Little "Spare Tire" Never Hurt ANYBODY……I Remember This "Spare Tire" I Had Fer My 1991 Ford Explorer That We Flipped Over in the "Boonies"….Booneville, Missourri ta be EXACT…. While We Was a Travelin' "TOO LATE" at Night Between St Louis, MO and Kansas City, KS On Our Way Home ta See My DAD in Nebraska One CHRISTmas……BUTT…..That's Another Story….) My TIME Tryin' ta Git Y'all ta HELP Me Git Ms Sarah Palin and Mr Herman Cain Elected President and Vice-President (Respectively) on the NEW Independence Party (NIPer) Ticket as WRITE-IN Candidates Fer Them Thar Nov 2016 Elections…..BUTT….If'n I Gots ta Do it ALL By MYSELF…..I WILL !!!!!!!

Did THAT Crap Make ANY Sense to Y'all on Pages 92-94, or Am I JEST Funnin' Ya…..YOU Decide!!!

Chapter 34

If'n the "Definition" of INSANITY is ta Do the SAME Thing Over and OVER Again And Expect "DIFFERENT" Results, WHY Do Y'all KEEP Electing Those Lousy LEFT-Leaning Liberal Damn Democrats AND Rascally Radically Religious RIGHT-Wing Republicans Over and OVER Again….. When There is a BEST "Third Party" CHOICE Out There ???

How the HELL Should We NIPers KNOW….We Ain't Crazy or INSANE….Figger it OUT Yer OWN Damn Self !!! (A Note from the NIPers for Y'all that STILL Don't Have a "CLUE": Please Notice that the Shortest Chapter in This WHOLE Damn Book Has the Longest Damn Title…..This is Supposed ta Be HUMOROUS Folks…. Lighten UP a Bit and LIVE a Little….."Live WELL, Love MUCH, And Especially…Laugh OFTEN"…. Is a Sign My Wife Bought ta Hang Over the Door ta the Hallway that Leads t' the 3 (Y'all Should be Used ta Trinity's By NOW) Most IMPORTANT Rooms in Our House: 1) the Messy Cluttered Laundry Room; 2) the VERY Messy and Cluttered "Back Bedroom"; AND (Last BUTT Not LEAST, in the Position of HONOR…..) 3) My EXTREEMLY MESSY and CLUTTERED THRONE ROOM !!!.....Movin' ON…..

Did THAT Crap Make ANY Sense to Y'all on Page 95, or Am I JEST Funnin' Ya.....YOU Decide!!!

Chapter 35

If'n "COMMON Sense" = "Universal TRUTH" = "GOD's WORD", Then WHY Doesn't "GOD's Word" Make Any SENSE ???

Let's YOU and Me Play a Little Word Game Where I Use "Debater's Technique" ta Git Ya ta Agree with a Whole Buncha Things and THEN Give Ya a Good Old "Brain Slap" at the END......Whatcha Say??.......Are Ya UP Fer it????......OK.....Hold onta Yer Derriere's Cause Heerrrrre We GOOOO.....

First and Foremost, Y'all HAVE ta Believe That There's Such a Thing as "Common Sense" (Now I REALIZE That "Common Sense" AIN'T as "Common" as it USED ta Be And Really SHOULD Be Called "UNCommon Sense"…. Because So FEW of Y'all Out There Actually HAVE it Anymore, BUTT Fer the Sake of Yer Poor Bruised Egos, and This Debate, We'll AssUMe That Y'all HAVE Some and We'll Call it "Common Sense") OR There's NO Damn REASON ta Go ON and Y'all Can Jest SKIP ta Some Other Chapter…..

OK……Let's PLAY……Last CHRISTmas (…..Or Was it the CHRISTmas Before Last?.....Or the One Before THAT??.....Damn Fergitter is Workin' Overtime Agin….."Once Upon a CHRISTmas in the Last 3 Years"…..) My Lovely and THOUGHTFUL Wife Bought Me One a Them Thar "Spingy" Seats Fer My Little Garden Tractor (on Accounta My Tender Hind Quarters was a Bein' Banged ta DEATH on the HARD Old Seat that Came On it), and was Called a "Universal" Tractor Seat (I Can Only SUPPOSE Because it was SUPPOSED ta Fit Various Models o' Tractors……BUTT I Had One HELL of a Time Gittin' it ta Fit on MY Little Massey Furgesson 1225 Diesel "Baby"….BUTT I DID……Ain't Gonna Let No Damn "Springy" Tractor Seat Beat ME, I'm a Tellin' Ya……Not After MY Dear Wife Paid Good Money Fer it, No Sir'ee, by Jimminy……Now Where Was I…..Oh Yeah…), BUTT It Could a ALSO Been Called a "Common" Tractor Seat, Because it Fit Various Different Models (….Probably Fit Them Thar OTHER Models Jest FINE…..Only MINE that the Dad Burned Thing Didn't Wanna Fit on….), SO Fer the Purpose of This Little Debate the Words "Common" and "Universal" can Be Used Interchangably "CORRECT"?? OK…..Let's Continue…..

If'n You HAD t' Pick…..And Ya DO…..Which Would Make MORE Sense….the TRUTH….or a LIE (I Know….I KNOW…..That's NOT a "Yes" or "No" Question, BUTT I'm a Leadin' UP ta One….)??? HOPEFULLY Yer Like My Team Leader Mr Lewis and Ya HATE Lies and Liars, So Ya Said That "TRUTH" Makes More "Sense" than Lies….Therefore "TRUTH" and "Sense" are ALSO Interchangable (Fer the Sake of This Debate And Fer Sanities Sake), SOOOOO What We Have So Far is that "Common Sense" Equals "Universal Truth" (SOME of Ya Can SEE Where I'm a Goin' with This, So KEEP Yer "Damn Mouths" SHUT, And Don't SPOIL it Fer Them Folks Out There Who DON'T, AND Fer ALL a Them Thar Folks Without a "CLUE")……Now Here's Where it Gits a Bit "Sticky"…..

I Don't KNOW About YOUR God (Because Ya Ain't TOLD Me Yet), SOOOOO We're Just Gonna Talk About MY GOD……MY GOD Family (Y'all Should Remember by NOW That MY GOD is a "Family"……GOD the FATHER……GOD the SON, and……GOD the FATHER's Significant "OTHER") Said That (And I Believe THEM with ALL a My Heart and Mind….SOUL and SPIRIT)

"THEY" Created the Universe AND That "THEY" are OmniPresent (Meanin' That "THEY" Can Be EVERYWHERE in the Universe at the SAME Time), SOOOOOO Fer the Purpose of This Debate "GOD" and "Universal" are Interchangeable.......And FINALLY (Yer Jest About Ready Fer Yer "Brain Slap") MY GOD (Now Remember that We're Talkin' About MY GOD, and NOT Yers.......Unless'n They "Happen".....Ya KNOW, Like How "Stuff Happens"??..... ta Be the SAME GOD.....Because I Don't KNOW About YOUR God......Because Ya STILL Ain't TOLD Me Yet) Says in OUR NIPer Handbook (the "User's Guide and Maintenance Manual for a Human Life", the UGMMHL, "Holy Bible" Version) That HIS Word is "TRUTH"......Therefore, Fer the Sake a This Little Debate, MY GOD's "WORD" is "TRUTH", AND "MY GOD's WORD" Equals "Universal Truth"....

Here's Yer "Brain Slap" (Due ta the Postulate That 2 Things Equal ta the SAME Thing ARE Equal t' Each Other.....).....".Common Sense" = "Universal Truth" = "MY GOD's WORD" = "Common Sense". SOME a Ya Out There (Yeah.....I Can HEAR Ya......I MAY Be a Little Hard a Hearin' with My Little Case a Tinnitus, BUTT I Ain't THAT Deef) Are a Sayin', "BUTT God's Word Don't Seem ta Make Sense ta ME Sometimes.....), AND There's SEVERAL VERRY GOOD REASONS Fer That Statement. One is that a LOT o' LITERAL Meanin' is LOST in the Translation from the ORIGINAL Languages of Hebrew and Aramaic (in the OLD Testament) And Koine (or "Common".....the Language of the "Streets" and "Business" in "Olden Times", as "American Standard English" is "Today") Greek (the PERFECT Language......or at LEAST as "PERFECT" as a Language CAN Be When Created by "IMPERFECT" Human Beings.....Developed by "Alexander the GREAT").....

In Addition ta Errors from MisTranslation, There Are Errors Introduced by MisInterpretation....Like the "Camel Passin' thru the Eye of the Needle" that I Told Ya About in Chapter ??......Maybe I DIDN'T Tell Ya That One Yet (Damn Fergitter is in "Overdrive" Agin).....WEELLLLLL.....Take Yer Shoes OFF and Git Ya a Dr Pepper and a Piece o' RKC, and Git Comfortable While I Tell Ya the Tail (Waggin' the Camel) of the Camel and That Thar "Eye of the Needle".......Now I KNOW What yer a Thinkin'....Yer Thinkin' That I (and the "GOOD BOOK") Are a Talkin' About a Damn Sewin' "Needle" AND as USUAL Y'all'd Be "DEAD WRONG"......This Verse (for the MOST Part) is "Translated" Correctly, BUTT It is ENTIRELY "MISINTERPRETED" By MOST Folks, SOOOOO Let's Git it CORRECT.... By "CORRECTLY" Interpretin' That Verse in the "Idioms" of the Time in Which the UGMMHL Was Written.....

There Were Several Words that COULD Be Translated as "Camel", BUTT the One Used in THIS Little Verse is the One fer a "Heavily Laden Camel" (One With Bags and Sacks Tied All Over it), AND The "Eye of the Needle" was a Small Door in the Massive City Wall that was Left "Open" at Night (After the Street Vendors,Marketers, and Traders Had LEFT the City Through the Massive BIG DOORS That Were Locked and Guarded at Night)......Now the ONLY Way fer a "Heavily Laden Camel" ta Pass Thru the "Eye of the Needle" was ta "Humble" HimSelf and Crawl on His Knees ta Git from OUTSIDE of the Massive City Wall (Outside World) ta the Safety and Security of the CITY (Kingdom of Heaven).....This is What That Verse from OUR NIPer Handbook is Tryin' ta TEACH Us.......a "Rich Man" Has a Bit a TROUBLE "Humbblin' HisSelf" and Gittin' DOWN on His KNEES Before HIS GOD, SOOOOO He Has a HARDER Time Than the REST of Us LowLifes ta Git Inta HEAVEN.....Now Don't THAT Make "Sense" t' Ya??........THAT's The WAY I Heard it from MY "CORRECT" Pastor Teacher...."Junior"...

And FINALLY (in CASE Yer NOT Keepin' Track…..This is My Third, Trinity, "Point") Sometimes MY GOD's WORD Doesn't SEEM ta Make Sense Because of MisAPPLICATION…..Like When Y'all Think that Somethin' in the NIPer Handbook (e.g., The One About the "Mote" in One Persons Eye and the "LOG" in Another Person's Eye) APPLIES ta the "OTHER" Guy and NOT t' YerSelf……Remember WAAYYYYYYYY Back Up in Chapter One (Ages and AGES Ago) Where I Told Ya That the Person Lookin' BACK at Ya Outta That Mirror was the ONLY One that Ya Have the ABILITY ta CHANGE?? …..WEELLLLL….That's the "CORRECT" APPLICATION of This Verse from the UGMMHL NIPer Handbook. If'n Ya'd JEST Git OFF'n Yer HIGH HORSES Out There and Join the NEW Independence Party (NIPers), Then We Could REALLY Teach Y'all How ta Live Yer Lives Efficiently and Effectively (Accordin' ta the Values, Principles, and Standards of the NIPer Handbook) and ta Git This GREAT GOD-Fearin NATION of OURS Back ta Bein' the GREATEST NATION on EARTH (By Gittin' Ms Sarah Palin and Mr Herman Cain Elected President and Vice-President on the NIPer "Write-IN" Ballot Campaign in Them Thar Nov 2016 Elections) !!!

One ABSOLUTELY LAST Thing Before We Move ON ta the "Next" Chapter…….OUR NIPer Handbook Says that NOT a "Jot" or a "Tiddle" Should Be CHANGED (Because by "Addin'" or "Removin'" Somethin' As "small" As a "Jot" or a "Tiddle" COULD "Change" the ENTIRE Meanin' of a Verse…….Now WHAT the HECK is a "Jot" or a "Tiddle" Ya Say?!?......WELLLLL They are Two of THE 'smallest' PUNCTUATION Marks in the "Hebrew" Written Language…….Kindly a Like That Thar "Comma" and "Apostrophy" in the Standard American English "Written" Language…..AND THAT is Why I AIN'T Allowin' NO DAMNED "Editors" (Sorry About That Thar Comment…Y'all GOOD "Editors" Out There) ta "MESS" with MY "CaPiTaLiZaTiOn", "PUNC?UA?!ON", And "GRAMMAR" (GOD Rest Her "Ornery" SOUL)…….BECAUSE It Would "RUIN" All of the "Subliminal" CLUES, HINTS, And "ReEnFORCEments" That I Have "Subtly" Buried THROUGHOUT My Little "Baby".

Did THAT Crap Make ANY Sense to Y'all on Pages 96-98, or Am I JEST Funnin' Ya…..YOU Decide!!!

Chapter 36

IS the "GIFT o' Tongues" Alive and Well Today, AND Do I HAVE it ???

A LOT a Folks These Days are REALLY "Out in the Toolies" When it Comes taUnderstandin' the "Gift of Tongues"......MOST of 'em THINK That the "Gift a Tougues" Means ta Be Able t' Babble in Some "Foreign" Language, BUTT it Doesn't And NEVER Has.....the "PROPER" Definition of the "Gift of Tougues" is ta be Able ta Make the Values, Principles, and Standards of GOD (i.e., the "WORD" of GOD) Clear ta Yer "Neirghbors" in Words that They Can "Understand".

Back at the FIRST "Pentecost", When the 12 Apostle Disciple Followers of Jesus CHRIST Where "Filled with the SPIRIT", They Not ONLY Spoke in the "Foreign Languages" of the People "Near" Them (Their "Neighbors", Reference Chapter 33), BUTT More IMPORTANTLY, They Were Able ta Speak ta Them Using the "IDIOMS" of Those Languages. When "WE" Use the "Idiom" about "Burni' the Candle at Both Ends", It DOESN'T Always "Translate" Well inta Another Language, SOOOO ta Make the "Concept" of "OVER Workin'" or "OVER Stressin'" CLEAR ta Someone from a "Foreign" Country, a "Different" Idiom or Axiom MAY Need ta be Used.

I (and the NIPers) Have TRIED, in This Book, ta Make the Values, Principles, and Standards of OUR GOD "Clear" ta Y'all in Words that Y'all Could Understand and "Identify" with. WE Have TRIED ta "GENERICIZE" GOD's WORD, by Techniques as Simple as "Re-Branding" the "Torah", "Koran", and "Holy Bible" inta a "Generic" Category of the "User's Guide and Maintenenace Manual for a Human Life" (the "UGMMHL") in Order ta NOT "Offend" or "Exclude" ANYONE (Who HAS a God) from Bein' a NEW Independence Party Thinker or Member (NIPer). WE Have TRIED ta Show that OUR GOD Designed US ta Live in "Families" Through the "Model" of the "Holy Trinity" ("BIG 3") of GOD the FATHER, GOD the SON.....AND....the "Currently Politically CORRECT" Term of.....GOD the FATHER's SIGNIFICANT "OTHER".....Since There SEEMS ta Be "Confusion" About That "Third" Member of the TRINITY.....Holy "Ghost"....Holy "Spirit"....etc.

We Have ALSO TRIED ta Make a FEW of the "Stories" from the UGMMHL ("Holy Bible" Version) a "Little" More Understandable in a "Different" Sort of Way (e.g., the UGMMHL "Stories" of "The GOOD Samaritan", "David and Goliath", and "Adam and Eve", Reference Chapters 33, 63, and 18), AND We are "Constantly" Associating the Values, Principles, and Standards of the UGMMHL with the NIPers (e.g., "The FIRST Shall be LAST, and the LAST Shall be FIRST", "The Stone Which the Builders Have REJECTED, We Have Made the Head of the Corner", "Cast Your Bread Upon the Waters and it Will Return ta You 10 Fold", etc.), AND We Have EVEN TRIED ta Give Y'all a Little Religious "Brain SLAP" with "Theoretical and Heretical Concepts" Like Y'all Found (Will Find??) in Chapters 4, 24, 25, 35, 43, 45, 51, 55, 57, 58, And 59.

BUTT, Whether I HAVE the "Gift of Tongues" or NOT Will Be Fer You and YOU ALONE ta..... DECIDE!!!

Did THAT Crap Make ANY Sense to Y'all on Page 99, or Am I JEST Funnin' Ya.....YOU Decide!!!

Chapter 37

ARE We Here ta LEARN What We Need to Learn, DO What We Need ta Do, and TEACH What We Need ta Teach, or NOT ???

With ALL of the "NEWS" Which is Gittin' Kinda "OLD" About That Thar Tragedy of Them Thar Kids Gittin' Slaughtered at the Sandy Hook School in Newtown, Connecticut, We NIPers Figgered Ya Just MIGHT Wanna KNOW Why the GOOD Die Young (And Especially Our Military SUPER-Troops). SOOOOOO....I Think it's About Time That I TELL Ya.....

We Are ALL Here on THIS Planet "Earth" (Sent by "OUR" GOD....Whoever THAT May BE) ta DO What We Need ta DO (with Our BODYs), LEARN What We Are "SUPPOSED" ta LEARN (with Our Minds/SOULS), AND TEACH Whatever We CAN TEACH (with Our Hearts/SPIRITS), AND Then We Are "Ready" for the GREAT "HereAfter" ("Happily EVER After"..... HOPEFULLY). WE Are the "Test Case" that My GOD is Using ta "PROVE" ta Satan/Lucifer/Devil/Whatever that HE (GOD) is JUST in Throwin' Him (Satan) and His "Followers" (Fallen Angels/Demons, Devil Worshipers, Atheists, ETC.) into the "Bottomless Pit" and/or the "Lake of Fire". We Have Been Given the FREEDOM and the FREE WILL ta Make Our OWN Decisions in Life AND Our OWN Decision FOR or AGAINST Our GOD (AND, of Course, We Hafta SUFFER the "Consequences" of Them Thar "BAD" Decisions OR REAP the "Benefits" of Them Thar "GOOD" Decisions).

BUTT, WHAT Does THAT Have ta Do with "Why the GOOD Die Young".....WEELLLLL....That's Pretty "Simple".....the "GOOD" Who Die "Young" Have ALREADY DONE What They Needed ta DO with Their BODYs, LEARNED What They Were "SUPPOSED" ta LEARN with Their Minds/SOULS, AND TAUGHT Whatever They Could (or Were "ALLOWED" ta TEACH) with Their Hearts/SPIRITS. ALSO, in the Case of Military SUPER-Troops, GOD "Allowed" Their BODYs ta Be "Sacrifieced" in Order ta Give Them a "Promotion" from United Sates Military Service to Service in the Prestigeous..... "ARMY of the LIVING GOD". Remember THAT the Next Time that a Military Family Member "Dies" Serving This GREAT GOD-Fearin' NATION of OURS While Protecting Our FREEDOM and RIGHT ta Run This Country inta the Ground.....My GOD Has Given Them a "PROMOTION" Away from Y'all UNDesrvin', UNGrateful, UNAppreciative AMERICAN CITIZENS to a Place of "No MORE Sorrow, NO More PAIN, NO More DEATH, For ("Them") the OLD Things Have Passed Away....Movin' ON...

Did THAT Crap Make ANY Sense to Y'all on Pages100-101, or Am I JEST Funnin' Ya, YOU Decide!!!

Chapter 38

What's the DIFFERENCE Between "Bits", "Bytes", and "MBs" (And NO Puppies, I Don't Mean "Milky Bones") ???

This is the "Digital" Age Where We are "Bound" to the Technology of Personal Computers, Cell Phones, and ALL Sorts of Electronic Media......Before Long Yer House Will Tell Y'all that Yer TOO Cold, Yer Refridgerator Will Remind Y'all that Ya Need ta Buy Milk, or Jest Order it from the On-Line Grocery Store, and Yer Damn Cell Phone Will Scream that Ya Have 13 Missed Calls, 7 VoiceMails, 33 Unasnswered Text Messages, and 144 Unread E-Mails, AND Could Ya Please Call Yer Mother Ya Damned UNGrateful So and SO........Oh, That's "Correct"......That Kindly a Crap is ALREADY Happenin' ta SOME Folks...Who Have More MONEY than CENTS...Maybe....(Review Chapter 31).

It's ALWAYS Amazin' ta Me How Our Modern Technology is Layered Upon Layer, Upon Layer of ONE of the Smallest "Bits" of Matter There is......the "Electron"......It's SO Small and "Insubstantial" that It Can Hardly Be" Seen" and Yet is the Basis fer Almost EVERY Technological Advancement in the Last 100+ Years. Jest "Watt" and How MUCH Does it "Take" ta Divert an Electron from it's "Current" Path, And Send it OFF in a "Different" Direction?? Are ALL of the Problems of Modern Technology Directly Attributable ta "BUGS" in the "System", or COULD it Be that Little Tiny "Gremlin Demons" are ACTUALLY Divertin' a FEW o' Them Thar Electrons JEST ta Make Yer Life "Interestin'" (Like the CHINESE Curse that I Mentioned in Chapter 64......Oh, THAT's "Correct".....Y'all Probably Haven't Got There Yet....Unlessin' Yer One a Them Thar Ijiots That Read the LAST Chapters FIRST and SPOIL the "Surprise" Endin's That We GREAT Authors Try SOOOOO HARD ta Build UP to.....TELL Me Yer NOT One a "THEM"!!!.....Say it Ain't SO!!!.....Because I Wrote Chapter 64 Jest AFTER I Wrote That Thar Chapter 65....Which I Wrote Jest AFTER I Wrote Chapter 66.... Which I Wrote Along About the Time I Wrote Chapter 8), And Git Ya ta Loose Yer "Faith" in Yer God??

Sometimes Them Thar Little "Gremlin Demons" Do Stuff that REALLY Tightens My Jaw....Y'all Know What I'm a Talkin' About......Somethin that REALLY "Bytes".....Like the Time I Was a Surfin' My Porn Sites and ALL of a Sudden I Gets This Screen FULL a "FBI Warnin'" That My PC Was Locked, and It Began a Sireen Like Sound a Sayin' that I Had ta Pay a (300$) Fine....Do Ya "Notice" Anythin' "Peculiar" about that "300 Dollar" FINE??.....WEELLLLL, I DID. In the GOOD Ole US of A, We Tend ta Put Our "Dollar Sign" on the "LEFT" Side of the Dollar "Amount" (Kindly a Like Them Thar LEFT-Leanin' Liberal DANM Democrats) INSTEAD a on the "RIGHT" like the "Brits" Do (And Kindly a Like Them Thar Radically Religious RIGHT-Wing Republicans), So I KNOWED it Warn't REALLY the FBI .....JEST Like Them Damn KIDS a Knockin' at the Door "Claimin' ta Be the "FBI" BACK in Chapter 19 or Up Ahead in Chapter 56. It Was Them Thar Little "Gremlin Demons" Jest a Tryin' ta Make My Life "Miserable"......and Failin' "Miserably" as USUAL......Like inThis Little Movie "Les Miserables" that Me and My Lovely Wife Seen LAST Month with Hugh Jackman Playin' a GREAT "Jean Valjean" ta Russell Crowe's "Javert".....And My Wife Said that Hugh Jackman MUST a Been GOOD If'n That Thar "Arrogant ASS" Russell Crowe Even Complimented Him on His Brilliant Performance. ALL o' the Cast Did a Really GREAT Job. My Wife Didn't KNOW that Ms Anne Hathaway Could Sing THAT Good, BUTT I Had Remebered Her Singin' from "Ella Enchanted" So I

Wasn't Surprised……DAMN…..There Ya Go AGAIN!!!…….Lettin' Me Ramble OFF Topic Again……
And With Me Only THREE (a Trinity) Chapters Away from Bein' DONE with This Here Little "Baby" a
Mine (Except Fer the MANY Hours of Editin' ta ENSURE That EACH Word is "Rightly" MISSpelled
and "Leftly" MISSused JEST SO……And That I USE My OCDOF…. Remember That's "Obsessive-
Complusive, DISPleasure ta OTHER Folks"…..ta NitPick My Little "Baby" ta DEATH……And THEN
There's ALL a That "Finish" Work, Like Puttin' in a Few Graphical Illistratory "Enhancements" (Thems
"a Few Pictures" ta Y'all "Common" Yahoos Like ME…..If'n I Don't Put in a Few a Them Thar Hoity-
Toity "HighFalutin'" Soundin' Words, NONE a Them Thar "Better'n Thou" Stuck UP Snobby "Critics"
Will Give it a "Good" Review)……As a Matter of FACT, I'm a Gonna Have a TOUGH Time Findin'
JEST the "CORRECT" Editor and Publisher Who Will TREAT My "Baby" with the Respect, Kindness,
and Courtesy (RKC) that it DESERVES……MOST Editors Figger If'n They Don't PISS All OVER Yer
Work with "RED INK" Then They AIN'T Done Their "JOB" Correctly…. Once They PISS All OVER
it, They THINK it "Smells (And SELLS)" Better, BUTT I Think THAT Jest "Stinks"……I NEED an
Editor and Publisher (Like AuthorHouse) Who Can "SEE" That MY "Baby" is "Unique", "ONE of a
KIND", And CAIN'T Be "Pidgeon-Holed" inta ANY "ONE" Category or Genre……MY "Baby" is as
"Unique", "RUGGEDLY Individual", and "OUTLANDISHLY UNOrthodox" (in the "Biblical" Sense)
as I AM Since it "Came" from the "Loins" of My Intellect……There Ya Go AGAAIN!!!!.....CAIN'T Ya
EVEN Keep Me "ON TOPIC" Fer One MINUTE……JEEEZZZZZ…..I Ain't NEVER Gonna Git This
Thing DONE at THIS Rate…….Now WHERE Was I "SUPPOSED" ta Be……Let Me Seee…..

   Y'ALL Are as BAD as the Puppys About Takin' a "Bit" a Time ta "Byte" My ASS If'n I Ain't Quite
Quick Enough Gittin' 'em Their "MBs" ("Milky Bones")…..Jest Like NOW When My Lovely Wife Was
a Kissin' Me Goodbye as She is OFF ta Inspect a Medical Laboratory Over Near Atlanta, GA and Gently
"REMINDED" Me That If'n I DON'T Pick the Garbage Bag "RIGHT" UP OFF'n the Kitchen Floor
Where I "LEFT" it……(See FOX Network……I Know How ta Keep "Fair and Balanced" TOO), Then
My "Dear SWEET Puppys" Will "REMIND" Me (in a Rather "Dramactic" and VERRY Messy Way),
"Daddy…..Ya "LEFT" the Garbage Bag "RIGHT" Where We Could Git AT it….. AGAIN!!!"……HOW
MANY TIMES Am I Gonna Have ta "TELL" YA…….KEEP ME "ON POINT", Or I'll Be FORCED ta
"POINT" That Out ta YA "Where the Sun Don't Shine"…….Now What WAS We "SUPPOSED" ta Be a
Talkin' About…..Let Me Go BACK a Page and Check the Title a This Here Chapter Again and Start
ALL OVER Again……What a Wasted "Bit" a Time and Effort……It Really "Bytes" Ya Know……Sone
Times it Even "MegaBytes" My ASS……

   MY GOD "INTENDED" Fer US "Homo Sapiens" ta Live "Simply"…..Like They Did WAAYYYYY
Back When the NIPer Handbook, the "User's Guide and Maintenance Manual for a Human Life" or the
UGMMHL ("Holy Bible" Version) Was Written…….Kindly a Like Them Thar "Amish" Folks LIVE
Today. He "Designed" the Planet Earth ta Operate Efficiently and Effectively Accordin' ta THAT There
"LifeStyle", BUTT (There's That BIG BUTT Again, So Ya KNOW What's a Comin'…..DONTCHA!?!)
THE "DEVIL" Stepped in with His "Better" Way ta "LIVE" and Got Y'all DEPENDENT on ALL a This
"Electronic" Technology and Made Ya "SOFT" and "WEAK": in BODY…..Couch Taters…..in Mind…
"Internet" and "BoobTube" Junkies…..AND in SPIRIT…AFRAID ta "STAND UP" Fer Yer FREEDOM
And ta JOIN or at Least "STAND BESIDE" US NIPers as We Attempt ta Start the "NEW" AMERICAN
Revolution (ONE Voter at a TIME) of the NEW Independence Party (NIPers) and Git Ms Sarah Palin
And Mr Herman Cain Elected President and Vice-President (Respectively) on the NIPer "WRITE-IN"
Ticket in Them Thar Nov 2016 Elections.

AND DONTCHA Fer a MOMENT Believe That This "Softness" and "Weakness" of These Here GREAT GOD-Fearin' UNITED STATES of OURS Has Gone UNNoticed By the REST a the WORLD. WHY Do Ya THINK That There are SOOOOO Many Folks Out There a Stirrin' UP "Trouble" Fer US AMERICANS These Days......"THEY" Know that We're "Soft" and "Weak" of Body, Mind, and Spirit ....Except'n (THANK GOoDness) Fer OUR COURAGEOUS And DEDICATED "LADYs" And "GENTLEMEN" of the US ARMED FORCES (at Least Until That Thar Tit-TURD Obamma Ramma "GUTS" 'em with the "DEATH of a Thousand (Budget) CUTS".....And UNTIL We Git a "LEADER" with the CORRECT "Mind-Set" BACK in the White House ......in the SAME Vein as Teddy Roosevelt or Ronny Reagan), Then Them Thar "OTHER" Obnoxious "BRATS" Around the World Are a Gonna KEEP "Testin' Our Strength and Resolve (ta Do the "CORRECT" Job, in the "CORRECT" Way, at the "CORRECT" Time.......Which Means "Takin' the TIME ta DO the Job "CORRECTLY" the VERRY FIRST Time".....Do THOSE "Slogans" Sound "Familiar" to Ya??.....Do They MEAN ANYTHING to Ya???.......Am I Gittin' THROUGH to Ya?????.......Or Do Ya Even "CARE" Anymore???????

MY GOOD LORD Has Been a "Bit" Fiddlin'.....Y'all DO Know What "Bit Fiddlin'" is Dontcha?? .....WEELLLLL Kick Yer Shoes OFF, Sit BACK in Yer Seats, and Git Comfortable, Because This is Gonna Take a While and I Can "SEE" That Ya NEED a Little "Break" from This Here "HEAVY" Stuff That I Been Throwin' at Ya......Now THIS Ain't the SAME as Gittin' OFF "Point".....This is More the "Tip" of the "Point" I Was About ta Make.......WAAYYYYY Back When the DEVIL "First" Got Us ta Designin' and Buildin' Them Thar Fancy Computers That Y'all Are SO Dependent on Fer Yer Very Lives (or at Least "LifeStyles"), Them Thar Computers Would Fill a WHOLE ROOM (And Not Be NEARLY as POWERFUL as the "Smart Phone" That Ya Probably Have "Glued" ta Yer Ear (or Maybe Semi-Detached by a Wireless or BlueTooth Ear Bud) at THIS Very Moment......CAUGHT Ya Didn't I?????......Jest CAIN'T Put That Dad Blasted Thing Away Fer Even a "SECOND" ta Hear Somethin' IMPORTANT from SOMEONE Who ACTUALLY Has Sumthin' ta SAY That's WORTH Listenin' to ......And "Speakin' of Somethin' "WORTH" Listenin' to".......I STILL Ain't Findin' NUTHIN' of "VALUE" in P.O. Box 2149, Tuskegee, AL 36083......the "Bounty" on "Dust Bunny" Hides AIN'T What it USED ta Be.......SOOOO a Dollar or Three (Since We NIPers LOVE ta Deal in Trinitys) Would Go a LOONNNGGGGG WAY Toward Makin' Me Fergive Ya And Fergit That Ya KEEP Lettin' Me Wander OFF TOPIC Like This All a the Time.......a WORD (or Three Thousand) ta the "WISE" Should Be Sufficient.........So I Guess There Ain't Enough WORDS in the WORLD ta Git Through YOUR THICK Sculls and HARD Heads........"Bit Fiddlin' (Y'all Thought I Fergot What I Was a Larnin' Ya UP on Didn't Ya??.....) is What Them Thar "Early" Computer Programmin' "Wizzards" Used ta DO Before Them Thar "HIGH LEVEL" Computer Languages Like Assembly Language, Basic, COBOL, and FORTRAN Were Invented (WHAT !?!?! Even THEM THAR Languages Are "Before Yer Time"??..... DAMN.....I AM Gittin' ON in YEARS.......I'd Better Take Me a Little Paragraph Break......Not ta Mention a Little Potty Break, 'Cause I THINK That That "Water Pill" I Took a While Ago is a Kickin' IN "with a Vengence" that I Took Fer My Swollen Feet and Ankels......Oh SHIT........

That Was a "Close One" Folks......I Almost had a MESS ta Clean UP.....Now Where Was I Agin' Before That Thar Dad Gummed "Water Pill" Kicked My BUTT (Bladder)......Oh Yeah.......

Did THAT Crap Make ANY Sense t' Y'all on Pages 102-104, or Am I JEST Funnin' Ya, YOU Decide!!!

Chapter 39

If'n Dr Pepper Tastes Like Carbonated PRUNE JUICE, Then HOW Can "They" Git it PAST the Federal Inspectors (DAMN Revenoors) ???

This Chapter is Jest Fer Them Thar Folks that Make the OFFICIAL Drink of the NEW Independence Party (NIPers), So The REST of Ya Go ON to Another Chapter……There Ain't Nuthin' Here Fer Ya ta See…..Go ON……GIT !!!.......OK, Now That We Done Got Rid of the RIFF RAFF……I'd Like ta Take the Opportunity ta THANK Y'all Dr Pepper Folks a WHOLE HEEP Fer Lettin' Us Use Yer Catchy Jingle ta Git the NEW Independence Party (NIPers) Started……We're Gonna Git This Party Started……We'er GONNA Git This Party STARTED…..WE'RE GONNA GIT THIS PARTY STARTED…….YEAH !!!

Now, Y'all Dr Pepper Folks MAY Have Noticed that We NIPers Kindly a "Indicated" That Yer Little Drink Tasted a BIT Like Carbonated Prune Juice (So's We Could Try ta "PULL IN" the Agin' Baby Boomers inta the NIPer Flock), AND Ya MIGHT Be Worried that the "Feds" (Them SAME Dad Blasted "Revenoors" that Keep Tryin' ta Find My "Shine" Still) MIGHT Try ta Persecute (Prosecute ??) Ya Fer False Advertisin', SSOOOOOOOO……We NIPers Don't WANT Ta See THAT Happen ta the Makers of OUR OFFICIAL NIPer Drink (and YOU Won't Either If'n We Git Sarah Palin, Who Jest LOVES Them Thar Dr Peppers, Elected President, and When She Goes ta "Wet Her Whistle" Durin' Her Little Inaugeration Speech and She Hoists Up a Can or Bottle of Dr Pepper…..Are Ya Gittin' the Picture ??)

WELLLLL……We NIPers Have a Little "FIX" Fer That: We'd be Willin' ta BET That Y'all Dr Pepper Folks have a Whole Bunch a 5, 10, 15, or 20 Thousand Gallon Tanks (or BIGGER) of Dr Pepper Jest Sittin' Around Waitin' ta be Bottled, AND (I Already Done Checked Yer Lable) Ya Don't Have "Prune Juice" Listed as One a Yer Ingredients in Yer Dr Pepper Drink…..SOOOOO….Here's Whatcha DO: Ya Go Down ta Yer Local 7/11, or Yer Local Zippy Mart (or Some Such) and Buy Ya a Quart Bottle o' ANY Kind a "Prune Juice" and a Shot Glass. THEN, Ya Take that Back ta Them Thar BIG Holdin' Tanks, and Ya Git Ya a Film Crew in There ta "Document"This, AND Ya Pour Ya a Shot Glass "PLUM" FULL (Git it??……" PLUM" Full o' "PRUNE" Juice…….DAMN Y'all Are "Sour" Pusses… Y'all'd Think I was Talkin' About Usin' Lemon Juice Instead a "PRUNE" Juice) Inta Them Thar Tanks and THEN Ya CAN Add "Prune Juice" as the LAST Ingredient on the Lable And Them Thar Dad Gumm "Revenoors" Won't Be Able ta Do a THING About it and Ya CAN Join the NIPers in Tryin' ta Git Them Thar Agin' Baby Boomers (Who Are a "Significant" Percentage of the Population These Days) to Buy Yer Dr Peppers AND Join the NEW Independence Party……It's a WIN-WIN Proposition…..

Did THAT Crap Make ANY Sense ta Y'all on Page 105, or Am I JEST Funnin' Ya…..YOU Decide!!!

Chapter 40

How Long DOES it Take ta Git a "NEW" Political Party Started, And HOW Can I HELP ???

That's the 640 Million Dollar Question That I WISH We NIPers KNEW the Answer to…..It SEEMS That the Requirements fer Startin' a "NEW" (as in the "NEW" Independence Party) Political Party Vary GREATLY from State t' State. Jest STARTIN' the Party is NOT the MAIN Problem….the "MAIN" Problem is Gittin' a "Place" on the "OFFICIAL" Election Ballot……BUTT We NIPers Figger That SINCE We Have Decided ta Run an "Outrageous" and "Foolishly Futile" ("OFF") WRITE-IN (or "WRITE ON") Campaign, Then We Won't Be "LEFT OFF" of the Ballot, Since EACH Ballot SHOULD Have a "WRITE-IN" Field "RIGHT" ON Each "Official" Election Ballot…..Have I Got Ya TOTALLY And Irrevocably Confused YET…….GOOD……Now Let's "Simplify" Things Fer Ya…….

When We NEW Independence Party Thinkers/Members (NIPers) FINALLY Git Ms Sarah Palin and Mr Herman Cain ta Git "ON-BOARD" the NIPer Train (or 13 Bomb-Bustin' Bus 50 State Campaign Tour CONVOYYYYY Fer Them "Three" Trips Around the GOOD Ole US of A), THEN When We Come Around ta Yer HOME State (on the FIRST Trip), We'll Find OUT What the Requirements ARE ta Git a "NEW" Third Party "Option" (as "OPPOSED" ta the Severely "LIMITED" Choices a Them Thar Lousy LEFT-Leanin' Liberal DAMN Democrats AND Them Thar Really Radically Religious RIGHT-Wing Republicans) And We Will Ask SOME a Y'all ta HELP OUT (As NEW Little NIPers) ta Fulfill Them Thar "Requirements", THEN On OUR SECOND Trip ta Yer HOME State, We'll Find OUT What HELP from US That Y'all Might NEED ta Overcome Road-Blocks, Git Petitions "Signed", And ALL a That "OTHER" Crap Them Thar LEFT-Leanin' Liberal DAMN Democrats AND Them Thar Radically Religious RIGHT-Wing Republicans Are a Pullin' On Ya ta "DE-Rail" the NIPer "Train" (BUTT Jest Y'all Remember That We Ain't Gonna Be Takin' No "Train"…..We Don't NEED No Stinkin' TRAIN ….. We're Gonna Have a 13 Bomb-Bustin' Bus CONVOYYYYY…..And FINALLY, On Our "THIRD" (a TRINITY) Trip ta "Meet and GREET" Ya in Yer HOME State, We'll HOPFULLY Have Enough a Them Thar "eLOOSive" Campaign Funds "aMASSed" (From ALL a Them Thar Folks Who Have Done "LOOSened" Up Their "Purse Strings" ta Fund ANYONE Who Will Run AGAINST the "Hand-Picked" Successor ta the CURRENT "MASSa" President, BECAUSE We Don't NEED ANOTHER'n LIKE THAT… And I ASSURE Ya Mr Herman Cain is NOTHIN' Like the "CURRENT" Yahoo "Occupyin'" the ONCE Prestigeous "Office of the President" of the GREATEST GOD-Fearin' NATION in the WORLD…..Like the "OCCUPIED" Sign on a Port-a-Potty ……), AND We'll Be "READY" Fer the Radically Religious Right-Wing Republican "Candidate" as WELL (If'n "THEY" Can Ever Git Their Act Together and "….DECIDE!!!" on One……Which is DOUBTFUL…….

We NIPers Figger We Got's a PURTY GOOD "Chance" a WINNIN' the Nov 2016 Elections with JEST ONE Minor "Problem" (at THIS Time) Which We HOPE Will Be Resolved ta OUR NIPer Satisfaction SHORTLY……We CAIN'T Seem ta Git Ms Sarah Palin's and Mr Herman Cain's Attention ta Git 'em "Convinced" ta Be OUR NEW Independence Party (NIPer) Presidential and Vice-Presidential Candidates (Respectively)…..Do ANY a Y'ALL Out There KNOW Ms Palin and/or Mr Cain, So's Ya Could Put a Little "Bug" in Their Ear(s)…. (or Maybe a Little "NIP"….for the NEW Independence

Party… in Their Coffee…..or Dr Pepper…..JEST ta Git 'em "In the MOOD" Fer a "Bit" a Politickin').
My Brother –IN-Law OUT in Washinton State MAY Be "Correct" When He Said that Ms Palin and Mr Cain were "OUT a My LEAGUE", BUTT We in the NEW Independence Party (NIPers) Believe That NO One is "OUT a OUR League" Unless'n They WANT ta Be……AND Before I (and the NIPers) Believe that Ms Palin and Mr Cain are "OUT a OUR League"…..We'd JEST Like ta HEAR it From Their OWN Lips (and NOT Depend on a "THIRD-Hand"….Even Though it IS a Trinity….Account).

HOWEVER…..We NIPers Feel That This Here "Baby" a MINE is the KEY that Will Open the DOOR ta Ms Palin's and Mr Cain's Hearts and Minds…..And MAYBE Even ta the VERRY Fickle Hearts and Minds of the HIGHLY "Independent" (Although Their VOTIN' Record SURELY Doesn't Reflect it) Thinkin' AMERICAN PUBLIC…..And On THAT Note (a Two Octave Above the Flag "STAFF", HIGH "C")….I THINK We'll CUT OUR Losses and……Move ON……

Did THAT Crap Make ANY Sense ta Y'all on Pages 106-107, or Am I JEST Funnin' Ya, YOU Decide!!!

Chapter 41

WHY Would Arnold Be a GOOD FBI Man AND Jessie Be a GREAT Head of the (CIA)…… (SHHHHHH…... It's a "Top Secret SCI KYDEOI "……… Don't TELL Nobody!!!) ???

I'm Terribly SORRY……."NOT"…….BUTT This Here Chapter is STILL Under Construction in My Confused and Addled Brain, So Ther Ain't Nuthin' Here ta SEE Yet……So, Move Along…….I SAID, "MOVE ALONG"….No LOITTERIN' HERE…..Now GIT….Until I TELL Ya that Y'all Can Peek!!!

Due to "National Security" Restraints, This Chapter Has Been "Classified" as "TS SCI KYDEOI" and ONLY the Information Provided in "OTHER" Chapters a This Here Book is "Permitted" ta Be Released ta the "General Public" (And THAT Means YOU "Bubba Gump"). WHAT "OTHER" Chapters Y'all Say?? We Ain't Gonna Tell Ya…..We AIN'T GONNA "TELL" YA !!!!....ha….HA….HAAWWWW !!!

BUTT, We NIPers WILL Tell Ya That a "TS SCI KYDEOI" Clearance is For Information that Has Been "Classified" as "TOP SECRET, Special Compartmented Information, KEEP YER DAMN EYES OFF IT!!!".

Did THAT Crap Make ANY Sense ta Y'all on Page 108, or Am I JEST Funnin' Ya.....YOU Decide!!!

Chapter 42

WHY Haven't We WON a War Since WWII ???

Couldn't Y'all Come Up with Somethin' HARD??.......That's TOO Easy!!! In WWI and WWII We Had a Different "Mind Set".....We Set Out from the Start to KILL the Enemy Until They Were ALL Dead or Until the Ones that Were Left Put DOWN Their Weapons, Put UP Their Hands, and Said, "We UNConditionally Surrender.....Whatever YOU Say GOES!!!". We Haven't Won a War Since WWII, Because We Don't Fight Wars that Way Any More. We Came Pretty Close in "Desert Storm", BUTT We Stopped SHORT of the Goal and Left SOME of Them Alive WITHOUT Makin' Them Surrender UNConditionally, So "THEY" Felt That They Had WON a Victory (Even Though "WE" Declared a Victory Which We Didn't Earn).

We NIPers Want to Put the FEAR of US and Our GOD, BACK inta the Hearts and Minds (Souls and Spirits) of Our NON-Allies the World Over. Remember "Back in the Days" When There was a Family Gatherin' and One of the ADULTS (at the BIG Table) Yelled BACK ta the Disobedient Heathens (at the "KIDS" Table), "Behave YerSelves.......You Don't WANT Me ta Come OVER There!!!". And it Put the "FEAR of GOD" inta the Upstarts......WEELLLLLL......OUR Federal Government USED ta HAVE that Kind of Power, and We NIPers Want ta RETURN ta Them Thar "GOOD Ole Days". We Want ta Be Able ta Say, "Behave YerSelves.......You Don't WANT US ta Come OVER There!!!". And Have Who EVER We "Tell That to" ta BELIEVE That We MEAN it AND that We Are Willin' ta Back it Up with the POWER of the US Military Forces, BUTT We Have LOST Our "Credibility" Due to "Weak" and Totally INEFFECTIVE Leadership in the Executive Branch of the Government, and It is HIGH TIME that We NIPers Change That Fer Ya.

We NIPers Believe in Our Handbook (the UGMMHL) that Says, "Ye Though I Walk Through the Valley of the Shadow of Death, I Will Fear NO Evil.......For I am the LEANest, MEANest, SumBeech in the Valley, and MY GOD Can Kick YOUR God's ASS Any Day of the WEEK, Especially on MONDAY after HE's Had a GOOD Rest on SUNDAY".....or Somethin' Like That. We NEED ta Support Our Fine MILITARY Troops with the MOST Modern Weapons and the MOST Effective Armor and Armament that Can be Invented, Procured, and Provided. AND When They Return, Each and EVERY One a Them SHOULD Return to the BEST HEROES Welcome that We "GRATEFUL" AMERICANS Can Provide. The "Men" and "Women" (NO....I Meant "Ladies" and "Gentlemen"......There IS a BIG "Difference") of OUR Military Services WHO Put Their Lives "On the Line" fer US "Ordinary Citizens" Every Day to Protect the Freedoms, Rights, and Privieldges that We Take for Granted, BUTT MANY of Those Brave Souls Serve in Lands Where They SEE the LACK of Those Freedoms, Rights, and Priviledges Each Day.

One LAST Thing (in the Position of HONOR) Before We Close This Chapter is to Propose a Little "CHANGE" that Will Limit the Freedoms, Rights, and Priviledges that These Ladies and Gentlemen of the Military Services Fight to Protect.......Just as it is ILLEGAL to Shout "FIRE!!!" in a Auditorium, Theater, or Other Crowded Building, So TOO, Under a NEW Independence Party (NIPer) Administration Will it Be ILLEGAL to Hold ANY Kind of PROTEST or ASSEMBLY that the "Family" Deems to be INAPPROPRIATE within 10 Miles of the "Last Rites" (to Include "Visitation", "Funeral", "Wake",

"Internment", etc.) of ANY Deceased Military Member, and Eventually to Extend to ANY AMERICAN Citizen. Even Though We NIPers Do NOT Grieve Over the Decaying ("Dead Meat") "Husk" of the Body that the Departing SOUL/Mind has Left Behind, We DO Understand that Not ALL Cultures Believe as We Do. Instead of Grievin' Over a "Trussed UP" Corpse, We NIPers Prefer ta CELEBRATE the "Life" that was Lived Here on this Earth and the GREAT Reward that Will Be Received in Heaven.

Whenever Loved Ones of a Departed Military Member ask, "Why Did a Lovin' GOD Have ta Take Our Child at SUCH a Young Age??", We NIPers Give Comfort By Lettin' Them KNOW that Their Loved One MUST Have Been Pretty "Special" For OUR GOD to Take Them from the Trials and Tribulations of This Earth (at Such a Young Age) to Serve in The ARMY OF THE LIVING GOD !!! They Must Have DONE Everything They Were Supposed to DO (with Their Body), LEARNED Everything that They Were Supposed to LEARN (with Their Mind/SOUL), and TAUGHT Everything They Were Supposed TEACH (with Their Heart/Spirit), So that There Was No More Reason for Them to Continue on This Earth and They Continued ON to Their "Reward" Where There is "No More Sorrow, No More Pain, No More Death for the "OLD" Things (of This Earth) Are Passed Away (for Them), and They Are Absent from the Body and Face-to-Face with the LORD…….Isn't That Jest "Special" as the "Church Lady" Would Say………I LONNGGGGG ta BE There…..When My Time Comes…..

SOOOO That MUST Mean That I STILL Have Things to DO (with This Old Decrepit Body, Like Writin' Y'all This Book), Things to LEARN (With My Feable Mind with its Fergitter Workin Overtime), AND/OR Things to TEACH (ta Dad Gumm DUNDERHEADS Like Y'all Who DON'T Git My Jokes So's I Hafta Always Explain 'em and Ya DON'T Answer My E-Mails When I ASK Ya ta Comment on My Book, and Y'all Probably AIN'T Gonna Git a Passin' Grade on That Nov 2016 Multiple-Choice Test, Jest Like Ya Failed Miserably When Ya Took the Nov 2012 Test, AND We'll Git ANOTHER One o' Them Thar LEFT-Leanin' Liberal DAMN Democrats Or WORST YET One o' Them Thar Radically Religious RIGHT-Wing Republicans, AND The WHOLE DAMN Country's Gonna Go ta HELL in a Hand Basket, and I'm Gonna Have ta Move ta CHINA When the GOOD LORD Gives UP on Ya and SHIFTS HIS BLESSIN' Across rhe Sea, AND……AND……And I'd Better Be Movin' ON…..

Did THAT Crap Make ANY Sense ta Y'all on Pages 109-110, or Am I JEST Funnin' Ya,YOU Decide!!!

Chapter 43

HOW Can We Convince ALL o' Them Thar RIGHT-ta-LIFErs that "Capital Punishment" is a "Good Thing" (NO...."Verry GOOD Thing"...NO....."EXTREMELY GOOD Thing")???

On the Surface, That Seems Like a Fairly "Impossible" Task, BUTT We NIPers Jest See That as a Bit of a Challenge.....We NIPers Make the HARD Tasks Look EASY.....It's Jest the "Impossible" Tasks That Take Us JEST a Wee Bit Longer ta Accomplish than Usual. MOST of Them Thar Right-t-LIFErs "PROFESS" ta Be CHRISTians with a Belief in the Everlasting Life of the SOUL, BUTT No REAL Understanding of it, SOOOOOO......Y'all Heathen godLESS Atheists Can Sit This One Out While We NIPers Have a Little Chit Chat with Them Thar "CONFUSED" CHRISTians Out There.

The Reason We Have SOOOO Many Murderers, Rapists, and Child Molesters (Like Chester the Molester Fer Y'all "Girly" Magazine Fans) Out Walkin' Our Streets, And Continuin' ta Murder, Rape, and Molest Y'all AMERICAN Citizens, IS Because of Y'all DAMN Right-t-LIFErs Who Are SOOOO DAMN Concerned about the "Lives" of the Criminals that Ya Fergit About the INNOCENT "LIVES" of the VICTIMS. Y'all Have ta Remember that the BODY (Which has a Beginnin' at "Conception" and an Ending at "Physical Death") is Mearly a Tool/Mechanism Used to Carry Out the Actions Dictated by the Human Mind/SOUL (Which has a Beginnin' at "Birth" and NO Endin') Contained Within it.

Just Like a Hammer Can be Used to Build a Bird House or Bash Someones Head in, or a Screwdriver can Be Used to Fix a Doorknob or Rip Someones Guts Out, or a Knife Can be Used to "Cut the Cheese" or Slit Someones Throat, SOOOOO the Human BODY Can be Used as a Weapon to Murder, Rape, or Molest Another Human Being or it Can Be Used to Save One or More Lives (as Police Officers, Fire Fighters, Doctors, ParaMedics, Nurses, Coremen, etc. Do Almost Every Day). When a Police Officer Apprehends a Criminal, They Disarm Them By Taking Away Any Weapon They May Have to Keep Them From Harming ThemSelves, Other Police Officers, and Other Innocent People. We New Independence Party Members (NIPers) Want to Do the SAME Thing......

We Want to Take Away the Body (Weapon) of Criminals Convicted of a "Capital" Crime by Killing it in Whichever "Humane" Manner that the Criminal Chooses: by Hanging, Firing Squad, Gassing, Lethal Injection, Be-Heading, Electrocutiion,Torn Apart by Wild Beasts, Crushing Like a Wreched Car Body, etc. The ONLY Options that Are NOT on the Table are Dying of Old Age, "Natural" Causes, or Slow Death by Disease......We NIPers Want it Quick, Realtively Clean, and as Close to Painless as Possible (VERRY Unlike the Torture of Mind and Body that the Criminals Put Their Victims Through). We NIPers Want to Kill the Criminal's Body and Send Their Immortal Soul to Their GOD for Judgement.

MOST CHRISTians Misunderstand the Body and SOUL Connection; the Body is Transient and the Soul is Immortal. They ALSO Don't Understand GOD or Heaven.......They are SOOOOO Afraid of Killing an "Innocent" Criminal that They Force Us Tax Payers to Give Them "Convicted" Criminals a "Lifetime" of FREE Meals, a FREE Place to Stay with Clean Linens and Laundry Service, FREE Clothes to Wear, and ALL of the "Comforts" of Home (Bathroom Facilities and Showers, TV/Radio and Even

Sometimes Computers, Books, Records, Tapes, CDs, DVDs, Etc., Ad Inifinitum, Ad Nauseum) When We Have "Homeless" INNOCENT Folks on the Street Who Would Do ANYTHING (Except Commit a Crime) to Live That Well. We NIPers Want to Tell Those SO CALLED "CHRISTians" that IF'n We NIPers Happen ta KILL the Body of an "INNOCENT" Soul that OUR GOD (We Don't KNOW about YOUR GOD) Will Make it UP ta that Person Above and Beyond Whatever They Could EVER HOPE or DREAM, and If We KILL the Body of a "GUILTY" Soul, Then OUR GOD Will Make SURE that the CRIMINAL Gits Exactly What's Comin' to 'em. We CAIN'T KILL the SOUL of a Criminal, Since it IS IMMORTAL and Created by GOD, AND Would Therefore Make US More Powerful Than GOD (Since Even HE Won't "KILL" a SOUL….JUST Send it Inta Everlastin' Torment In the "Lake of FIRE" …… We NIPers Just Want ta KILL the BODY that the Criminal's Mind/SOUL was Usin' to Commit the Crimes Against INNOCENT People. Kindly a Like Takin' Away Their "Weapon" ta Keep 'em from Hurtin' the Bodys and Minds of Innocent Victims OR Forcin' Us "Law Abidin" and "TAX Payin'" Citizens ta Maintain That Body Until it Dies of "Natural" Causes (Like Bein' Killed by Another Convict in a "Turf" Brawl, or Killed by a Prison Guard While Attemptin' ta Escape or Tryin' ta Inflict Harm on Another Prisoner or Prison Guard).

The More Criminal Bodys that We KILL, the Less There'll Be Fer Us Tax Payers ta Maintain in the Jails and Prisons, and the Less There'll Be ta Parole Back onta the Streets ta Muder, Rape, and Molest Again. Because, We NIPers Believe that Murder, Rape, and Child Molestation SHOULD be "Capital" Crimes that Require the "Death Penalty"……We Are HOPIN' ta Git MOST AMERICANS to Agree.

JUST One MORE "Brain Slap" Fer YOU SO CALLED "CHRISTians" Out There Before We Git BACK ta Talkin' About Things That Them Thar godLESS Atheists NEED ta Hear……That There Fifth Commandment That Yer SOOOOO Fond a Bandyin' About is MISTRANSLATED From the Original HEBREW Language…….There Are SEVERAL Words that COULD Be Translated as "KILL", BUTT the ONE Used in the Fifth Commandment SHOULD Be "PROPERLY" Translated as "MURDER" (the "KILLIN'" of an INNOCENT Person), THEREFORE the "KILLIN'" of a Convicted Criminal OR the "KILLIN'" of the "ENEMY" in War is an HONORABLE Duty Because it PROTECTS the LIVES of INNOCENT People and "KILLS" Those Who Would INFLICT Harm OR Their WILL on Others….. SOOOOOO Say We NEW Independence Party Thinkers/Members (NIPers) !!!

Did THAT Crap Make ANY Sense t' Y'all on Pages 111-112, or Am I JEST Funnin' Ya, YOU Decide!!!

Chapter 44

Did Ya KNOW that a Sadomasochistic Dominatrix (with Very HIGH Moral Character) in Skin Tight Red Leather is Called a "Mord Sith" ???

My….My…..MY !!!….. What an Interesting Question to Ask…..That Can ONLY Mean that Mr Terry Goodkind (Who I Believe to be a Psuedonym for Terry "Badevil", But I Love His "Sword of Truth" Series Anyway) is One of Your Favorite Author's (as He is One of Mine). I'm a BIG Science Fiction Fan (as are MOST of the NIPers) and ALSO Enjoy the Work of Christopher Paolini ("Inheritance" Dragon Rider Series), Anne McCaffrey ("Dragonriders of Pern" Series), J K, Rowling ("Harry Potter" Series), J. R. R. Tolkien ("Hobbit/Lord of the Rings" Series), Rick Riordan ("Heroes of Olympus" Series), and the MANY Works of Robert A. Heinlein, Andre Norton, Terry Brooks, and MANY More. HOWEVER, in This Chapter on Favorite NEW Independence Party (NIPer) Authors, I'd Like to Concentrate on Just 3 (a TRINITY…..of Course)…….

First Let's Take Mr Terry Goodkind's "Sword of Truth" 11 Book Series (Not Counting the Later "The Law of Nines" and "Omen Machine"). I ONLY Have ONE Bad Thing to Say to Mr Goodkind: You SHOULD Have Put a WARNING Label on Your Series to Keep Parents from Buying it for Their Little Kiddies (Thinking with a Title Like "Wizard's First Rule" that it Might Belong Side-by-Side with J. K. Rowling's "Harry Potter" Series), SOOOOOO……Parents Out There……This is a WARNING from Us NIPers that IF'n Ya Don't Want Your Child to Know that a Sadomasochistic Dominatrix (with Very HIGH Moral Character) in Skin Tight Red Leather is Called a Mord Sith, Then PLEASE Don't Buy Mr Terry Goodkind's "Sword of Truth" Series for Them, BUTT All of You More Mature Baby Boomers Out There Who Just Woke Up from Your Naps (WHAT !?! Did He SAY !!!) Feeling a Little "Frisky" May be Very INTERESTED in Knowing that a Sadomasochistic Dominatrix (with Very HIGH Moral Character) in Skin Tight Red Leather is Called a Mord Sith. In Which Case, We NIPers HIGHLY Recommend Mr Terry Goodkind's Series. Each Book (Except for the Final 3, which Form a Trilogy) Stands on it's Own, BUTT is Also Well Integrated into the Whole. The Protagonists (Richard, Kahlen, and Zed, Another Trinity) Contiuously Exemplify the Values, Principles, and Standards of the NEW Independence Party (NIPers), So We are HAPPY to Recommend Them to YOU.

HOWEVER, If You Parents Want Something for the Kiddies, Then J.K Rowling's "Harry Potter" 7 Book Series is Just the Thing. The Protagonists (Harry, Hermione, and Ron…..WOW, Another Trinity) ALSO Exemplify the Values, Principles, and Standards of the NEW Independence Party (NIPers), BUTT Without NEARLY as Much Rape, Pillage, and Gore (RPG) as Mr Terry Goodkind's Books. If I Ever Get to Meet Ms Rowling, I'd be VERY Interested in the Answers to the Following 3 Questions:

1. Was Your Major Theme of the "Harry Potter" Series ("The last enemy that shall be destroyed is death", I Corr, Chap 15, Verse 26) Devine Inspiration, Random Chance, or Concious Decision???

2. Is the Fact that the 4 Houses of Hogwarts School of Witch Craft and Wizardry Align Perfectly with the 4 Quadrant Leadership/Management Model I have Been Taught Over the Years (Griffendor=Director, Ravenclaw=Intellectual/Technician, Huffelpuff=Socializer, and

Slimey Slitherin=Relationship) by Devine Inspiration, Random Chance, or Concious Decision??? (MORE in Chapter 44…..No This is 44…..I Meant 28)

3. Was the Initial Intellectual/Literary Concept to Write the 7 Book Series by Devine Inspiration, Random Chance, or Concious Decision???

I (and Inquiring NIPer Minds) Would be Very VERY Interested in the Answers to Those Questions. ALSO, Since We NIPers ALWAYS Like a Happy Ending, We're VERRY Glad Your Series HAD One.

AND Last, But Definitely NOT Least, the Youngest of Our Favorite NIPer Authors, Mr Christopher Paolini is ALSO a Writer Who's Work We Recommend for the Kiddies. I was a Bit Disappointed in the Ending, BUTT it Does Teach that HOPE Springs Eternal (and Sequels Too Maybe), and I Would be Interested in ANY of Your Future Work (Although I was Really Glad When You FINALLY Got OFF'n Yer DEAD ASS and Got That FINAL Book of Your "Four" Book "Triology" Finished……I Was Afraid I'd be DEAD Before You Got it Done, AND I'd Have to WAIT Until You"Finally" Joined Me in Heaven to Know How it Ended). BUTT, I REALLY Enjoyed that Interview with Your Editor on the Last CD. I Find that I Have Less and Less Time to "Read" Books these Days and Have to Resort to Multi-Tasking by Listening to "Books on CD" While I Do Some of My More Mudane Tasks (Like My Lovely WIFE's HoneyDO List).

HOPEFULLY, Each of You Authors in This Chapter Will Realize a Significant Increase in Sales of Your Work, and (in the Terry Goodkind Concept of "Value for Value" which We NIPers Adopted from Your "Sword of Truth" Series) Will at Least CONSIDER Donating a Portion of the Profits to the NEW Independence Party (NIPers) to Help Us Get Ms Sarah Palin and Mr Herman Cain Elected President and Vice-President (Respectively) On the NIPer Ticket for the Nov 2016 US Elections. Now Ms Rowling….. On the Surface, You Might NOT Think that the US Presidential Elections are of Any Concern to You….. Until You Realize that OUR US Leaders Have to Work in "Coordination and Cooperation" with YOUR British Leaders to Protect Freedom the World Over, So PLEASE, Dear Lady…… PLEEASE at Least "Consider" Donating a Portion of Any SIGNIFICANT Increase in Profits to Us Poor Little NIPers.

Did THAT Crap Make ANY Sense ta Y'all on Pages 113-114, or Am I JEST Funnin' Ya,YOU Decide!!!

Chapter 45

HOW Can We NIPers RESOLVEe the Conflict Between Creationists and Evolutionists ???

WOW....I Must be SICK or Needin' a GOOD Stiff NIP a "Shine". I Don't Know WHAT Happened in That Thar "Last" Chapter. My Nebraska "Twang" Perverted Southern "Drawl" Jest Up and "LEFT" Me High and Dry. Thank GOoDness I Had Me a Bit a HOOCH Stashed "RIGHT" Behind My "Throne" (ONLY Fer EMERGENCY Medical Conditions of Course).....Now Where Was I???.......Oh Yeah....I 'member Now.

How Can Us NIPers POSSIBLY Resolve the Age Old Conflict Between Them Thar GOD-Fearin' Creationists and Them Thar godLESS Atheist Evolutionists??? Do Ya Want the "Shrt" Version or the LONNGGG Version.......WHAT the HELL Ya Think This IS...a DEMOCRACY???.....Yer Gonna Git BOTH and Be DAMN Glad ta Have 'em......So THERE.....Put THAT in Yer Pipe and Smoke it.....I Gariantee Ya it's Gonna be Better'n ANY o' That Thar MaryJaWanna Stuff Y'all Been Smokin' Lately.

The 'shrt' Version is that GOD CREATEd the Universe, and it EVOLVEd from There......Now fer the LONNGGG Version: MOST Folks (CHRISTians Mainly) MISREAD the First Few Verses in the NIPer Handbook (the "User's Guide and Maintenance Manual for a Human Life" UGMMHL, "Holy Bible" Version) ta Read that GOD "CREATED" the Earth a Few Thousand Years Ago. Before I Go ANY Further, Let Me Make THIS Disclaimer: ANYTIME Our NIPer Handbook "SEEMS" ta "Conflict" with Scientific FACT, It Simply Means that the COPY of the NIPer Handbook that You are Using as a Reference Has Been MISTranslated (from the Original Languages of Hebrew and Aramaec in the OLD Teastament, and Koine Greek in the NEW Testament), and/or MISInterpreted (Due to Changes in Culture and Vocabulary Since the Original was Written), and/or MISRead (Due to the Ambiguous Nature of the Standard English Language).

Let Me Give Y'all a Little TEST ta SHOW Ya How Ambiguous the Standard English Language Can Be.......I'm Gonna Make 3 (Trinity) Statements, and Then Ask 1 Question, and Give Ya 2 Answers ta Pick from.......Let's Jest SEE If'n Ya Can Pick the "CORRECT" Answer....Are Ya Ready???....OK...

1. I Bought a Car
2. The Car was Wreched
3. I Fixed the Car

Now Here's Yer Question:

Tell Me (Jest Based on the 3 Staements Above): Did I Buy a Wrecked Car or Was the Car Wrecked AFTER I Bought it???

Because of the Ambiguousness of the Standard English Word "was" Ya Cain't be SURE Can Ya???

Let Me REPHRASE That (So's Y'all Don't MISRead it)

1. I Bought a Car
2. My Car Came to be Wrecked
3. I Fixed My Car

Now It's Pretty Clear (Ta the Most Casual Observer) That the Car Was Wrecked AFTER I Bought it, and NOT That I had Bought a Wrecked Car.

Now I Told Ya THAT One Ta Tell Ya THIS One: Let's Use that SAME Trick (Which Confoms ta the "Correct" Translation from the Hebrew Language) on the First Verse of the UGMMHL:

"In the Beginning (Billions and Billions of Years Before GOD Created HomoSapiens.....In a Single Moment of Time........in One Emerald Lugasi BIG" BANG") GOD Created the Heaven and Earth. And the Earth was (or Came to be, After the Dinosaurs, After the Cro-Magnon Beasts, After the Neanderthal Beasts, After ALL of the Various Animal Forms that the "Sons of GOD" or Fallen Angels, or Demons if You Will, had Tried ta Breed ta Make Up Fer the Fact that GOD and HIS Angles Clearly Outnumbered Him 2 t' 1) without form, and void (without "Defined" Shape, Due to Being Locked in the Ice Age, AND DeVOID of ANY Lifeform, Plant Nor Animal), and darkness was on the face of the deep (the Darkness bein' Due ta the Partculate in the Atmosphere Due t' the Volcanos, or Commet Strike, or Meteor Strike, and/or etc.....etc....etc......HELL...... This Here Aint No Bible Study Class..... It's a Political/Religious Satire........If'n Ya Want a GOOD Bible Study Class Where We NIPers Larned ALL a This Stuff YEARS Ago), Y'all Can "Google" (OR www.ask.com) the Father of Robert B. Thieme, III and Git it from the "DAD" Gummed SOURCE HisSELF...... Ain't That Correct....."Junior"...???

OK.....So Ya Don't Buy THAT One......Well DON't Spit it Out Just Yet.....CHEEWWWW on it a While and See If'n it Don't Begin ta Taste Better t' Ya. Sometimes When Folks Taste Somethin' a Bit "Different" with Their Mouths (or Their BRAINS), They Have the Tendency ta Spit it OUT Right Away, as an Autonomic Reflex Action That's a Built-in Protection Against Poison to the Body (or MIND), BUTT Many Times "Different" Foods (or "Different" Thoughts) are NOT Poisonous, Jest "Different" (Kindly a Like the Very First Time Y'all Tasted Calimari, or Escargot, or Sushimi, or Pate' Foie Gras, or Drambuie, or Any NUMBER of "Unique" and "Wonderful" Flavors of LIFE). In the Same Way that "Different" Foods (when Prepared by Lovin' Hands) are Tollerated on Yer Tounge, and the MORE Ya CHEW the Closer Ya Git t' "Acquirin' a Taste" Fer a Particular Food, There are Many MANY Ideas and Concepts that We NIPers Have "Lovinly" Prepared Fer Yer Mind/Soul Between the Covers (OR "Top" and "Bottom" If'n Yer Readin' the "Electronic" Version) of This Little "Baby" (Book) That May Need ta be CHEWED a While Before Ya Even BEGIN t' Acquire a Taste Fer 'em......ALL That We NIPers Kindly Ask is that Ya Keep an "Open Mind" as We "Talk" the "Walk"........And Keep Yer DAMN MOUTH SHUT...... Cause.....HEY!!!..... I'm a Talkin' Here........

Did THAT Crap Make ANY Sense ta Y'all on Pages 115-116, or Am I JEST Funnin' Ya, YOU Decide!!!

Chapter 46

How DO Ya "Effectively" and "Efficiently" Take the MEASURE of a Man/Person ???

We NIPers are REALLY Gald Ya Asked That, Because We Heard Tell that SOME of Y'all Out There are ACTUALLY Tryin' ta Evaluate the Performance and Character of Folks by the Scribblin's on a Few Pieces of Paper…..tsk…..Tsk…..TSK……SHAME ON YA !!!!!……Here's the NIPer Way…..

Ya Cain't Take the "Measure of a Man" (Sorry Ladies….."Measure of a Man" Jest "Sings" Better'n "Measure of a Person"……BUTT…..If'n YOU Prefer "Measure of a Person", Jest Go Ahead and Use it That Way…..We NIPers Don't Mind……The IMPORTANT Thing is the "Concept" and NOT the Words Y'all Use ta "Express" that Concept) by Lookin' at Some Scribblin' on a Few Pieces of Paper…..Here's the "Correct" Way ta Take the MEASURE of a Man Usin' ALL 6 (That's "Correct" I Said SIX) of Y'alls Senses:

1. First, Ya Stand Toe-t-Toe with 'em and "LOOK" 'em in the Eye and Guage the Content of Their SOUL. We NIPers Heard Tell that "The EYES are the Windows to the SOUL", and We Believe That, So Be SURE ta Take a Peek Through Them Thar Windows (And HOPEFULLY They've Used a Little Windex on 'em Lately So's Ya Git a Good CLEAR View…..AND While Yer at it, Make SURE Y'all Have Used a Little Windex on Yer OWN "Windows" So that YOUR Soul is Clear ta "Them" Too……And Not "Clouded" by "Deception"…..)

2. Second, "LISTEN" fer the SINCERITY or INSencerity in Their VOICE. Listen to the Volume, Pitch, Emphasization, Intonation, Rhythm, Rhyme, AND Don't Fergit the Non-Verbals (Back ta the LOOK, from Step 1) Like Facial Expression, Body Posture, Coordinated Hand and Arm Movements, Personal Space…..etc….Ect…..ETC……ta Ensure that They Appear to "Match" the "Words" Yer a Hearin'.

3. Third, "SMELL" the SWEETness or the SOURness o' Their BREATH (and HOPEFULLY They'll Have Taken a Breath Mint or Two So's Ya Cain't Tell that They Had Liver and Onions, Garlic, or Limburger Cheese fer Lunch).

4. Fourth, "TASTE" Their PASSION fer LIFE on Yer Tongue. This May SOUND a Little Silly to Ya, BUTT Some Folk Have Such a STRONG Passion fer LIFE that You Can Actually TASTE it on Yer Tongue……Some of Ya Out There KNOW What I'm Talkin' About……Some of Ya Don't…..And….as USUAL……MOST of Ya Hadn't Got a "CLUE"…..Movin' ON…..

5. Fifth, Reach Yer Hand Out in Friendship and "TOUCH" Their FLESH……Now I Jest HAVTA Pause Here and Tell Y'all This Little Story about the Lieutenant I Knew in the Air Force When I was Stationed in Germany: We Would Periodically Have "Functions" that We Would Have ta Attend t' "Meet and Greet" Different Folks……Now I Can Handle "Meet and Greet", BUTT…. The First Time that Lieutenant Called it "PRESS the FLESH"….it Gave Me the "WILLIES"…. I Don't Even Wanna "TELL" Ya The THOUGHTs That POPed inta My Head When That Thar Lieutenant Feller Said, "PRESS the FLESH"…OOooWWWooOOOOWWeeEEEEE…..So If'n Ya Want ta EVER Take MY HAND in Friendship, please….Please….PLEEEASE…"Meet and Greet" Me, BUTT PLEASE DON'T "PRESS MY FLESH"…..Thank You….Movin' ON…

6. And FINALLY Sixth (YES, We DO Have 6 Senses, And NO, I'm NOT Talkin' about Mental Telepathy.......I'm Talkin' about That There "GUT Reaction".....the "EMOTIONAL" Contact We Human Beings FEEL When OUR Spacial "Aura" Comes Close Enough to Another Person ta Make Contact (Connection) with THEIR Spacial "Aura". Haven't Y'all Ever Been Pretty Close ta Someone (Without Ever Sayin' a Word to 'em or Hearin' a Word from Them) and Ya Either Felt a Stong "Attraction" (NO I'm NOT Talkin' about "Sexual" Attraction......Git Yer Minds Outta the Gutter) OR a Strong "Repulsion" (the Feelin' That Ya Should Vacate the Area of This Person IMMEDIATELY Fer Fear o' Yer LIFE). WELLLLL.....This is Yer "GUT Feelin' or Yer "Sixth Sense" in Action, Tryin' ta "TELL" Ya Somethin'. Be SURE Ta Listen ta Yer "SIXTH Sense", BECAUSE It Can Do TWO VERRY IMPORTANT Things Fer Ya: 1) It Can SAVE Yer LIFE........When Ya Accidentally (or On Purpose) Put YerSelf inta a Seriously LIFE Threatinin' Situation, AND (Even MORE IMPORTANTLY) 2) It Can SIGNIFICANTLY IMPROVE Yer LIFE......by Allowin' Ya ta RECOGNIZE Yer "SOUL MATE" When Ya Meet 'em......Yer "Sixth Sense" is an INFALLIBLE Method of Recognizin' Yer "Soul Mate" When ALL Other Methods Fail (If'n Y'all Will Just LISTEN to it and NOT Try ta INFLUENCE it by the Application of "Logic" and "Reason"....'Cause it Jest Don't WORK That Way).....

SOOOOOOO.......Now That Ya Know the PROPER Way ta Take the Measure of a Man/Person, Ya Can Do it "Correctly" and THEN Just "Document" That Evaluation on One o' Them Thar Pieces a Paper...

Did THAT Crap Make ANY Sense ta Y'all on Pages 117-118, or Am I JEST Funnin' Ya, YOU Decide!!!

Chapter 47

WHAT's the "DIFFERENCE" Between a "Value Added Tax" (VAT) and a FREEDOM Tax ???

Whenever We NIPers Hear About a Value Added Tax (VAT), it Puts Us in Mind of a BIG "VAT" o' "PORK FAT" That Them Thar Congress Folks Can Dip Inta ANYTIME They WANT to. We NIPers Prefer a 9% SALES (See Chapter 17) or "FREEDOM" (Federal Reserve Expense Elimination and Debt Overcomin' Measure) Tax that Will be Solely and Exclusively Used ta Pay Down the National Debt. We NIPers Feel that This Would be The BEST Method Because the MORE AMERICANs SPEND ta Boost the Economy, the FASTER We Pay Down the National Debt (and Git Out from Under CHINA's BIG "Thumb" Before it Squishes Us). We NIPers See THIS as a WIN-WIN Proposition......How About Y'all???

Have Y'all EVER Heard Them Thar LEFT-Leanin' Liberal Damn Democrats or Even Them Thar Radically Religious RIGHT-Wing Republicans Come UP with Anything Even CLOSE ta as Logical, Reasonable, and Rational as That???......WEEELLLLLLL......Why the HELL NOT.....Could it BE That They're Just TOO Wrapped UP in Their Own Self-Importance That They Cain't Pull Their Head's Outta Their Anal Orifices Long Enough t' See What's Goin' ON in This Country and What We Can be Doin' ta FIX the Economy. SOME a Them Thar Legislative Branch Folks Have Their Head's SOOOOO Far UP Where "the SUN Don't Shine" That They are Blinded t' a Simple Soultion Like the "FREEDOM" Tax as a Part of Mr "Future Vice-President" Herman Cain's 9-9-9 "Flat" Tax Strategy (Reference Chapter 17).

Did THAT Crap Make ANY Sense to Y'all on Page 119, or Am I JEST Funnin' Ya.....YOU Decide!!!

Chapter 48

WHY Do We NIPers FEEL that When Ms Barbara Walter's Put Together Her Little "MOST Fascinating People" Specials, She MIGHT've Missed Jest ONE or TWO of Us Out Here ???

WEELLLLL……If'n Ya Haven't Figgered THAT One Out Yet, Then Yer Purty DENSE (like a "Box a Rocks", a "Clean Slate" , a "Dull Wazzu", a "Rusty Mouse Trap", etc... Etc…ETC….Ad Infinitum... Ad Nauseum), And NOT the Little NIPers (Like a "Bag a Donuts", a "Slate Covered with Einstein's Theory and Equations",a "Sharp Wit", a "Stainless Steel Bear Trap", a…..Weelllll… I HOPE Y'all Git the General Idea) that I THOUGHT Ya Were. Now, PLEASE Don't Git Me WRONG…. I Definitely AIN'T Accusin' that GREAT LADY (And FUTURE NIPer…..Once She Answers Her "Call to Service") Ms Barbara Walter's o' Bein' DENSE……She's Jest IGNORRANT…….(WHOOPS !!!.....I'd Better CLARIFY THAT Statement NOW……."Cause I'd Be Willin' ta BET That Y'all Don't KNOW the TREMENDOUS "Difference" Between "Ignorance" and "Stupidity"…..AND it Makes ALL of the "DIFFERENCE" in the World).

IGNORANCE Means that Ya Jest Don't KNOW any Better (AS with that GREAT LADY Ms Barbara Walter's Havin' NEVER Met Me NOR My Little Executive Assistant Couldn't POSSIBLY KNOW That There Was Anything "Fascinatin' about Either One of Us)…..BUTT….. STUPIDITY Means That Ya KNOW Better, BUTT Ya DO (with Yer Body), or THINK (with Yer Mind/Soul), or BELIEVE (with Yer Heart/Spirit) Somethin' Against Logic, Reasonableness, or Rationalousness…..Rationaliousness….. OH HELL…..Y'all KNOW What I'm a Tryin' ta Say…….Rationality……. That GREAT and GRAND LADY Ms Barbara Walters is IGNORANT of the Fascination of Me and My Little Executive Assistant, BUTT She AIN'T STUPID……Now That She KNOWS We're Out Here, Im SURE that She's Gonna WANT ta Talk ta US on an Hour er Two of FOX Netwrok "Prime Time"…….

Which Reminds Me……YO!!!....FOX Network!!!....Did Ya Git My"MEMO" (My Little E-Mail I Sent Ya a While Back about Them Thar 3 (Trinity) Proposals I Had ta BOOST Yer Ratin's…… WEELLLLL… If'n Ya Fergot, Here They Are Again:

1. First, an Hour or Two of Yer "Prime Time" (Where Ya Cain't Seem ta Git a Very GOOD Market Share) ta Have a Bit of a Chit Chat with Ms Barbara Walters ta Try ta Convince Her That She MIGHT a MISSED Jest One or Two of Us Out Here When She was a Puttin' Together Her Little "10 MOST Fascinatin' People" Specials (AND Jest MAYBE Convince Her ta Answer Her "Call ta Service" in the NEW Independence Party).

2. Second, a "War of Wits" Between Me and Robin Williams (or Any OTHER Two or MORE "Witty" Fellers or Gals o' Yer Choice) Durin' an Hour or Two of "Prime Time" Where Yer NOT Gittin a Very GOOD "Bang Fer Yer BUCK" (And I Heard Tell the Other Day That Y'all Were Purty BIG on Gittin' Them Thar "Bangin' BUCKS"….AND Market Share).

3. Third, (and MOST IMPORTANT, Since it is LAST, in the "Position of "HONOR") a Little Chit Chat Between ME and Sarah Palin (And Herman Cain, If'n Ya Can "Manage" it, AND the "ENTIRE" NIPer CORE Constituency that Were "Called to Service" in Chapter 3) ta TRY and

Convince Her (Them??) ta Be OUR NIPer Candidate Fer President (Or OUR NIPer Candidates Fer President and Vice-President, And Other Major Cabinet and Federal Government Positions??) on the NEW Independence Party(NIPer) Ticket in Them Thar Nov 2016 Elections (Ya KNOW…..That Little Multiple-Choice Test Y'all Take Every 4 Years that Ya Keep SCREWIN' UP And Gittin' the WRONG Answer on…..Like THIS YEAR….. or LAST YEAR……or WHENEVER……Dependin' How LOOONNNGGGGG It Takes Ya ta Git Around ta Readin' THIS and LISTEN ta THIS Old Fart from Beauregard, AL…. DAMN… I Got OFF Topic Again……And I Was a Doin' SOOO Good…..Oh Well…..).

Now, BEFORE Y'all Git TOO Excited About Them 3, FOX Network Folks, Let Me TELL Ya HOW it's GONNA GO….. I Got a Roof that's Needin' Fixin' Fer a WHILE Now (MY Wife's About Ready ta Divorce Me Over it), and I'm Gittin' Purdy Fed UP with the Way That BIG Government Organization I Work Fer Has Been a Treatin' Me Lately, And I Got Some Repair And Re-Modlin' Ideas Fer the BARN, HOUSE, AND SHOP Buildin's That I've Had in Mind FerEVER…..WEELLLLL… I THINK Ya Git the IDEA….. I Have a Few "Material" NEEDS That Could be Adequately Satisfied by a WAD o' CASH Money, SOOOOOOOO Hears the "DEAL"…..Take it 'er Leave it:

I'M the "IDEA" Man Here…….Y'all Would NEVER Have Come UP with ANY of This Without ME, SOOOOOO……Whatever Ya Pay Ms Barbara Walters Fer the "MOST Fascinatin' People" Update, Y'all Will Pay ME "TRIPLE" (Trinity)……Whatever Ya Pay Robin Williams (OR WHOEVERE Y'all THINK Can Replace Him), Ya Pay ME "TRIPLE" (Trinity)…… Whatever Ya Pay Sarah Palin (And ?? Herman Cain, AND "OTHERS"…...the MORE the "Merrier/Wealthier"), Y'all Pay ME "TRIPLE" (Trinity)…….Now If'n Yer SMART (And I Have My "Doubts"), Y'all Will TRY ta Convince Ms Barbara Walters, Mr Robin Williams (OR Others), AND Ms Sarah Palin (And Mr Herman Cain, AND "OTHERS" ??) ta Do it Fer FREE ('Cause 3x0=0, THREE Times ZERO Equals ZERO, Fer Those of Y'all Who Cain't SPELL…..in Mathematics…OR 3xKnot is Knot….is it NOT??).

As a SIDE Note ta Ms Barbara Walters, Mr Robin Williams (OR Others), AND Ms Sarah Palin and Mr Herman Cain, AND "OTHERS"……..I Don't KNOW If'n YOUR Monetary "NEEDS" Exceed Mine or NOT…. BUTT…. (There's My BIG BUTT Again)…… If'n I Were YOU….. I'd SOAK Them FOX Network Foks Fer EVERYTHING They Are Worth Fer DARIN' ta SUGGEST That This STUPID Old "Hick from the Sicks" from Beauregard, AL Deserves Anything NEAR "TRIPLE" What YOU "Fine" Folks' Time and Effort is Worth ta Do These "Suggested" FOX Network "Specials"…..Ignore MY E-Mails Will Ya FOX Network…….Make ME Go ta National Public Broadcstin' (NPB) ta Try ta Git SOMEONE's Attention Will Ya…… I'll Show YOU Who Has Their Brains in They're BUTT…And it "SURELY" AIN'T ME !!! (And NO……...I Ain't Tryin' ta Call Y'all "Shirley"……..I Wouldn't DO THAT……Or ….. WOULD I ???..... "…..YOU DECIDE !!!").

And THAT Reminds Me……or Was it Sumthin' on the LAST Page…..Let Me See……OH Yeah…. I Remember Now….Speakin' of "Missin' One or Two of Us Out Here"……I'd Be a Willin' ta BET That Long About Now Yer a Wonderin' Jest "Where IS Beauregard, AL", Because I'd ALSO Be Willin' ta BET That Y'all AIN'T Been Able ta FIND the "Magically" Sleepy Little Community of Beauregard on Any MAP; Jest Like the Magically "SLEEPY" Little Community of "BRIGADOON" That I Heard of Once in a Little "Play" Done by the Thespian Club When I was Attendin' Grand Island Northwest High School Jest Outside a Grand Island, Nebraska:

HAIL !!! Northwest Vikings, We Will MARCH Onto VICTORY !!!

We Will Fight…FIGHT…FIGHT to WIN for OUR Dear BLACK and GOLD !!!

HAIL !!! to Our STRENGTH and COURAGE !!!

We'll NEVER Be DISCOURAGED !!!

Fight…..FIGHT…..FIGHT…..AND WIN For OUR DEAR BLACK and GOLD !!!

GOOOOOO VIKINGS !!!   GO Grand Island NORTHWEST "VIKINGS" !!!!!   CLASS of '73 !!!!!

OOOPS……Fergit That LAST Line (a Little TOO Much Information There)…..Before I Had That Little "Blast" from My PAST, I Was a Gonna Tell Ya HOW Ya Jest MIGHT Be Able ta FIND That Thar "Magically" Sleepy Little Community Called "Beauregard"…..BUTT…..Before I DO…..Have Ya EVER Heard the Description: "It's a NICE Place ta Visit, BUTT I Wouldn't Want ta LIVE There" ???………. WELLLLLL……Beauregard is a VERRY NICE Place ta "Visit", BUTT….We Don't WANT Ya ta Live HERE…..Y'all Can Come Fer a "Visit"……And THEN GIT Yer ASS HOME AGIN, 'Cause We Don't NEED or WANT Ya HERE !!! Auburn and Opelika Been Tryin' ta "Take US Over" ("ANNEX" US) Fer YEARS And They AIN'T Managed ta Do it YET…….They Git a Little "Piece" a US from SOME Danged FOOL Every ONCE in a While, BUTT……….We "Hornets" (the Beauregard High School "HORNETS") Will "STING" Ya If'n Ya Try ta "MESS" with OUR FREEDOM. GOOO "HORNETS"!

We LIKE OUR Sleepy Little "Community" (NOT a Town Nor Even a "TownShip"….Jest a Sleepy Little "Community" with a High School, Water Authority, and Volunteer Fire Department……ALL a the "Bare" ("Bear"??) "Necessities of LIFE"…..That the LAW Abidin' Citizens of Beauregard WANT or NEED) JEST the Way it IS…….And We Don't Need ANY a Y'all Comin' in HERE and a MUCKIN' it UP (Like the "MUCK" I Clean Outta the Horse Stalls Every Weekend). BUUTTTTT (There's That Thar REALLY BIG BUUTTTTT a Mine Agin, So's Ya Can IMAGINE What's a Comin' Dontcha……SOME a Ya DO…….Some a Ya Don't…….AND as USUAL……MOST a Ya Hadn't Got a "CLUE"……So Let Me "CLUE" Ya IN) Ms Sarah Palin……Dear LADY……And Mr Herman Cain…….Kind Sir…… AND ALLL a Y'all NEW Independence Party (NIPer) CORE Constituency Members Who Were "Called to Service" WAYYYYY Back in Chapter 3……If'n Ya WANT ta MEET Me (Face-t-Face and Toe-t-Toe ta "Take the Measure" of the "Content a My Character"……and I Been Told MANY Times That I Am QUITE a "CharACTOR") Then HERE's a "Suggestion" Fer Ya….The "Tea Party" Had a Little "Rally" Here on the Plaza in Front of the Opelika (Lee County Seat) Court House a Couple a Years Ago…..And We Have the "Beauregard High School" Available Fer "Inclement Weather"…..And a FEW Other Places That Can Handle a "Fair ta Middlin' Crowd"…….SOOOOOO ta "Prevert" the Words of the "VOICE" from Kevin Costner's Little Movie "Field of Dreams"…….If Y'all "Schedule" it…..I WILL Come !!!

OH…..THAT's "Correct"……I AIN'T Told Ya HOW ta Find "Beauregard" Yet HAVE I??? I'd Be Willin' ta BET That Ya Jest MIGHT Have a Little MORE "Motivation" ta FIND it NOW (Than Ya Did When Ya STARTED Readin' This Here Chapter)…..MAYBE???......WELLLLL Let's Git ON with the "Revelation" of the "Location":

Ya CAIN'T "Find" Beauregard on NO "Physical" Map That I Know of (Because it is a "Magical" Place That ONLY Exists in "CyberSpace"……So Ya Need a iPAD, SmartPhone, PC, or Tablet with a

MAP App to "FIND" it). Go Git Yer iPAD, SmartPhone, PC, or Tablet and Open UP the MAP App…..
We'll WAIT on Ya……………………………………………..DAMN Yer Place MUST Be as Messy
and Cluttered as MINE If'n it Took Ya THAT LONNGGG…….OR Have Ya NOT Been Keepin' UP Yer
VIRUS/MALWARE/ADDWARE Protection So's Yer Apps Open UP Quickly…..OR Do Ya Have TOO
Many a Them "FREE" CRAP Apps a Tyin' Up Yer Processor Time and Memory Space…….OH Well….
NO Matter HOW Many Times This Old Computer Network Manager Tries ta Give Ya GOOD Advice ta
Make Yer "Computin' Life" Easier…….SOME a Ya Will NEVER Learn……ANYHOW Now…….

ZOOOOMMM in on the GREAT State of ALABAMA So's it "Fills" the Screen. Notice The "Point"
on the Eastern Boarder that We "Share" with Geogia…….ZOOOMMM in On THAT Area Until the Two
"Sister" Cities of Opelika (Lee County Seat) and Auburn (They Play a Little Football There from Time ta
Time…..And EVEN Git ta Be "National Champs" Now and Then……."ROOLLLLL TIIIDDE"…..JEST
Kiddin'…….I Meant "WARRRR EAGLE" and "GOOOOOO TIGERS" !!!). Notice That US Highway
51 (Marvyn Parkway) Travels (WELLL It DON'T Really "Travel", BUTT If'n You Was ON it in a Car
or SUV, or Truck, or Motor Cycle……without a Helmet Ya DANGED FOOL…..Ya DESERVE ta Ba a
"Future Organ Donor"…..OOPS…..Where Was I??.....Oh, Yeah….) Then Ya COULD "Travel" About 4-
5 Miles South ta the Little "Trinity" Intersection Where Lee County Road 46, Lee County Road 400, and
Marvyn Parkway Join Together….AND….There Ya ARE in the "Magical" Community of "Beauregard".

SOMETIMES (BUTT Not TODAY……Because the Little Computer "Gremlin Demons" is a "Playin'
GAMES" with My iPAD II) If'n Ya ZOOOMMMM Out or In VERRRY SLOOWWWLY the Name of
"Beauregard" Will "Magically" Appear and Disappear "Near" That "Trinity" Intersection I Jest Told Ya
About in the LAST Paragraph, …………………BUUTTTT I Jest Checked My MAP App on My Little
Verizon Motorola Droid Bionic SmartPhone and it Looks Like the Dad Blamed "Gremlin Demons" Was
Either Sleepin' on the Job OR They Fergot About it ALL Together, Because I GOT "Beauregard" ta
"Magically" Appear in IT…….Try it YerSelf with YOUR iPAD, SmartPhone, PC, or Tablet MAP App
and Jest "SEE" Fer YerSelf if'n I'm a Funnin' Ya or NOT………

Did THAT Crap Make ANY Sense ta Y'all on Pages 120-123, or Am I JEST Funnin' Ya, YOU Decide!!!

Chapter 49

How WOULD the NEW Independence Party Handle Foreign Relations ???

WELLLLL…..We NIPers Don't Have the Time ta Tell Ya How We'd Handle EVERY Itsy Bitsy Problem with EVERY Little Pissant Country Out There, SOOOOO…..for This Chapter We're Jest Gonna Pick On One…..Let's Take CHINA (That Seems a GOOD Choice Since Their Holdin' MOST of Our Debts, and I Heard on the News the Other Day that a Bunch a AMERICAN Businesses are Beginin' ta See the ERROR o' Their Ways and Findin' that CHINA Ain't the "Holy Land" that They Thought is Was….. Their Beginin' ta SPOT All of Them Thar "HOLES" Now (Like "Piracy" of Their Innovations, Hidden FEEs and COSTs, Labor Problems, Language/Culture Barriers, ect., Etc., ETC…..) Since We Have a Recent "CURRENT Administration" Debaucle to Use as an Example.

Herman Cain….Kind Sir….This Here Chapter is "Correctly" Up Your Alley (I Already Told Ya Why We NIPers Avoid the Word "RIGHT" Like the Plague…..Didn't I??.....I Thought I Did….Let Me Check Again……You're "Correct"……That's Not Comin' Up Until Chapter 55…..GOOD Catch….). Us NEW Independence Party Members (NIPers) Figger You Already Know This, BUTT We Jest Wanna Have Ya "Confirm" fer Our Loyal Readers Out There That You Would "Agree" with the NIPer Way of Handlin' This "RECOMMENDATION" ta the "CURRENT Administration" on the "PROPER" Way ta Handle "Foreign" Relations…….YOU Listen UP TOO (PLEEASE) Ms Oprah Winfrey (as Our NIPer Choice ta LEAD the Department of State) And Be SURE ta Make YOUR Voice Heard If'n Ya "Agree" with the NIPers Plan……

We (the GREAT GOD-Fearin' US of A……REPRESENTED by the "CURRENT Administration") Hosted the LEADER of CHINA (Who Holds MOST of OUR Debts, Is a MAJOR Wolrd POWER, AND to Where MANY AMERICAN Businesses Have "Fled") and Treated Him Like a Second Class US Citizen (and THAT's Pretty BAD These Days ta Be a Second Class US Citizen). We Treated Him ALMOST as Shabbliy as We Treated the LEADER of GREAT BRITAN (Another MAJOR "World POWER" and One of Our MOST VALUABLE ALLIES) When We Gave 'em a Bunch a Cheap CDs Fer a GIFT. I COULD Go Point-by-Point as ta HOW the "CURRENT Administration" Screwed the Pooch in Their Treatment of the LEADER of CHINA, BUTT (There I am Showin' My BIG BUTT Again) We Would Rather Follow Our MOTTO (that We Stole from Mr Terry Goodkind's "Sword of Truth" Series): "Concentrate on the SOLUTION and NOT the PROBLEM" (We ALL KNOW that the "CURRENT Administration IS the "PROBLEM"), So Here is the NEW Independence Party (NIPer) SOLUTION:

Whenever We NIPers Discover/Realize that We Have Made a Mistake We Do Three (a Trinity) Steps in Rapid Succession:

1. Admit/Confess the Mistake/Error IMMEDIATELY (If'n Not SOONER)
2. Apologize fer it Dearly and Sincerely (a Little Grovelin' at This Point is NOT Out of Order)
3. Make Ammends/Compensation (as BEST We Can) and Move ON……

If (NO….WHEN) We NIPers Take Over the Federal Government, We Plan to IMMEDIATELY FIX Our Relationship with the LEADER of CHINA in This Way:

We Are Gonna Take the "Initiative" and Contact the LEADER of CHINA and Admit that "WE THE PEOPLE of the UNITED STATES of AMERICA.....Under the INCOMPETENT "leader" That SOME MISGuided, DUPED, And "BOUGHT with WELFAIR BUCKS" Folks MISTAKENLY Elected to the US Presidency) Treated Him Shabbily the Last Time He was Over Here (Due to the INCOMPETENCE of the "PREVIOUS Administration"). We Will Then Apologize Dearly and Sincerely (and a Little Grovelin' MAY Be Required Since He Was "HONORABLE" and WE (the US Federal Government) Were the Ones Who Acted Like Little TIT-TURDS. And THEN We Will Invite Him (and Anyone ELSE He Wants ta Bring Along) to a Jam Bang Up GOOD "Old Fashioned" NEW Independence Party (NIPer) Inaugeral..... "HOE DOWN" ("Country Western Style" BALL Fer Y'all "City Folks").

We NIPers are Gonna Teach the LEADER of CHINA Our "Country Western" Ways" of Kickin' Our Heels UP and Lettin' Our Hair DOWN. If'n He Wants ta Wear His "Traditional" Button Down Collar CHINESE Uniform That's Jest FINE with Us NIPers, BUTT (Y'all Should KNOW by Now What's Comin' When I Show Ya My BIG BUTT) If'n He Wants ta Git "a Little Bit COUNTRY" with Us, Then We're Gonna Pull Out ALL of the STOPS and Deck Him Out in a BIG Old 10 Gallon or Stetson Cowboy Hat, a Leather Vest and Chaps (with ALL of the Fringes, Bangles, and Spangles that He Wants), LEE and or Wrangler Blue Jeans, a Western Style Shirt with the Pearl Inlaid Snaps instead o' Buttons, a Leather Bolo Tie with an Expensive BUTT "Appropriate" Cinch Clasp, And Shirt Garters If'n He Wants 'em, AND of COURSE the BEST COWBOY BOOTS that MONEY CAN BUY (Cause If'n Ya Don't Figger We, "the AMERICAN People" OWE Him ALL of That After LETTIN' the "CURRENT Administration" Snub Him Like We DID......Then Yer NOT the HONORABLE and COURAGEOUS Folks that We Want or NEED in the NEW Independence Party (NIPers)......IF'n I'm a "LYIN'"...I'm a "DYIN'".....

Did THAT Crap Make ANY Sense ta Y'all on Pages 124-125, or Am I JEST Funnin' Ya, YOU Decide!!!

Chapter 50

HOW Can Y'all "Beat" ANY Lie Detector Test EVER Created ???

Since MOST a Them Thar LEFT-Leanin' Liberal Damn Democrats AND Radically Religious RIGHT-Wing Republicans Already KNOW This, We NEW Independence Party Members (NIPers) Figgered We'd BUST (BURST??) Their Bubble and Let Y'all in on the Little Secret. There are Probably a Trinity o' Ways ta Beat ANY Lie Detector Test, BUTT I'm at Home with a Head Cold (Stay Back a Bit So's Ya Don't Cetch it), and the Meds is a Foggin' My Brain, So Only a Couple a Ways Come ta Mind (Go And Figger Out the 3rd Way Yer OWN Damn Self). Ther's a HARD Way and a EASY Way, So Here's the "HARD" Way First.

The HARD Way ta Beat a Lie Detector Test is t' Make a "Lie" SEEM Like the "Truth". Some Folks CAN Do it, Because They Got No Concience (The Sum Total of Yer Mother's Scoldin's and Yer Father's Beatin's), and it Don't Bother 'em a Bit ta Tell a "Baldfaced" Lie and They Can Do it with a "Straight" Poker Face (or Sometimes a "FLUSHed" Poker Face, or a "Full House" Poker Face, or a "Jacks 'er Better, Trips ta Win".....WELLLLL....I Think Ya Git the Idea......I Really ENJOY Playin' Poker.....) without Battin' an Eye (Because If'n Ya "Bat Yer Eyes" Around SOME Folks Too Much They MIGHT Git the Wrong Idea about Yer Sexual Persuasion and........Oh HELL......Ya Let Me Wander OFF Topic Agin). If'n Ya Wanna KNOW This Stuff, Ya Need to Do a Bit "Better" ("BEST") about Keepin' Me ON Topic. Now Where Was I........OK, I Got it......... There's ALSO Some a Them Thar Swarmy (or Swamii, or Swany River) Folks......Y'all Know......Them Thar "Yogi" Bear Types Who Can Contort Their Bodies Inta Trees, and Camels, and Frogs, and Dogs, and Cats, and Sun Salutations (and a ALL That Thar Other Crap), and Can Even Control Their Heart Rate, and Breathin', and Sweat Glands, and WHATEVER, BUTT If'n That's a Bit More'n You Can Handle, There IS a MUCH Easier Way.....

The EASY Way ta Beat ANY Lie Detector Test EVER Devised is ta Simply Make the "Truth" SEEM Like a "LIE". IF'n Y'all JUST Keep FIRMLY in Mind that EVERY SINGLE QUESTION is Designed to Trap Ya, And Destroy the Lives, Careers, and Reputations of Yer Family, Friends, and Loved Ones (Which Y'all Would THINK ta Be the SAME Thing, BUTT We Don't ALL of Us Sometimes "LOVE" Our Friends and Family Like We Otta), AND That YOUR "ANSWERS" ta Them Thar DAMNable "QUESTIONS" Will Ensure Your Loved Ones Lives are in "Immanent Danger", THEN ALL of Yer Answers (True of NOT) Will "Appear" ta Be a LIE, Which Will INVALIDATE the Lie Detector Test. When They Ask Ya Whether the SKY is BLUE, Remember the Last Day When the SKY was GRAY, and Say "YES" (And ALSO Remember That You JUST Condemned Yer Loved Ones to DEATH). If'n They Ask Ya How OLD Ya Are, Say "58", While at the Same Time, Knowin' in Yer Mind that You are 58 Years, 2 Months, 19 Days, 5 Hours, 34 Minutes, 17 Seconds (Giver 'er Take a Few) OLD, AND That Ya Have JUST Sentenced Yer Loved Ones ta Neverending Torture.

Now ALL of Y'all "Criminal Types" Out There (Like Y'all Lousy LEFT-Leanin' Liberal DAMN Democrats AND Y'all Rascally Radically Religious RIGHT-Wing Republicans) KNOW How ta Beat ANY Lie Detector Test EVER Devised, SOOOOOO Y'all Feel Pretty "Confident" Now HUH!?! Before Y'all Git TOO Cocky, Ya'd Better "Flip" (Like US NIPers "Flipin'" Ya the 3rd USE of the "Sign of the

NIPers, Reference Back ta Chapter 2) Over ta Chapter 46, Because We NIPers (and MOST Law Enforcement Agencies) Don't Depend on JUNK Like Lie Detector Tests ta Take the "Measure of a Man/Person".

Did THAT Crap Make ANY Sense ta Y'all on Pages 126-127, or Am I JEST Funnin' Ya, YOU Decide!!!

Chapter 51

Why Do "THEY" Say "Y'all Can't Take it WITH Ya", When There's at LEAST 3 (a Trinity) Things that Y'all CAN Take with Ya ???

Y'all Should Know Better'n ta Ask Questions Like THIS by Now, 'Cause Ya KNOW I'm Gonna Pull an Answer Out a My Anal Orafice (Without Wipin' it OFF) that Will Knot Yer Panties inta a Wad…. Here GOES…….RRRriiipppPPP……POP!!! The Infamous "They" Like ta Try and Convince Ya that Ya Cain't Take ANYTHING ta Heaven with Ya, So's Ya Might as Well Live it UP While Yer Here and Make "Right" SURE Ya Ain't Got NUTHIN' "Left" (or Better YET….."THEY" Will Try ta Convince Ya t' GIVE it or LEAVE it ta "THEM"), BUTT Me and the NEW Independence Party (NIPers) are Here ta Tell Ya that "THEY" are ABSOLUTELY WRONG (as "THEY" Usually Are). There are Actually Three (You Should ALSO Know by Now that We NIPers Jest LOVE ta Deal in Trinity's) Things that Y'all CAN Take with You.

The First Thing that Y'all CAN Take with Ya are ALL of the Memories of ALL of the "Wild and Crazy" Things Ya Did with Yer BODY While Ya was Here on the Late GREAT Planet Earth. All of the STUPID Things Ya DID with Yer BODY…..ALL of the WONDERFUL Times Ya Had Doin' ALL of Those STUPID Things…..All of the Memories of ALL of the BEAUTIFUL Folks Ya MET and Came ta LOVE Durin' Those WONDERFUL Times Ya Had Doin' ALL of Those STUPID Things…..AND of Course, ALL of the FANTASTIC Places ABOVE, ON, and BENEATH the Surface of This Planet that Y'all Went ta MEET Them Thar BEAUTIFUL Folks Durin' Those WONDERFUL Times Doin' ALL of Those STUPID Things (That Yer So Dad Gummed Fond a Tellin' Me About over, and Over, And OVER Again that I've Heard SSOOOOOO Many Times That I Think I'm Gonna PUKE If'n I Have ta LISTEN to it ONE MORE TIME!!!........I Know……I Got "Off Topic" Again……..Movin' ON…….

The Second Thing that Y'all CAN Take With Ya is ALL of the "Knowledge and Wisdom" of Yer Mind/SOUL that Y'all Have Gained About YerSelf and Yer Environment. Y'all Will Take with Ya the FACTS: that Ya "Like" the Color Blue, That Yer Favorite Hymn is "Amazing Grace", That the Sight of Purple Wild Flowers on the Meadow Combined with the Smell of Fresh Cut Wild Onions Remind Ya of Springtime in Alabama, That There Ain't NO Purttier Sight than a Rainbow after a Gentle Summer Rain. AND Y'all Will Not ONLY Know Beyond a Shadow of a Doubt that GOD DOES Exist, BUTT Y'all Will Understand That GOD Exemplifies: "Takin' the TIME ta Do the Universe "Correctly" the Very First Big Bang", "Do SALVATION the Correct Way at the Correct Time for the Correct Reasons.", AND of Course, the MOST FAMOUS, "How May Your GOD Help YOU Today??".

The Third and MOST Imortant (Since it is LAST, in the Postion of HONOR) is That Y'all Will be Able ta Take the Knowledge Y'all Have Gained About Your God in Your Humn Spirit/Heart. ALL of the Wonderous Values, Principles, and Standards You Have Learned and APPLIED Over the YEARS of Your Earthly LIFE from the "User's Guide and Maintenance Manual for a Human Life" Will Be EVEN "MORE" APPLICABLE in Heaven Than They Are Here on Earth. AND Speakin' of Heaven…..A LOT of Folks (Mainly CHRISTians) Are VERRY Impressed that the Streets of Heaven are Paved with Gold, Silver, and Diamonds……I Don't Know about YOU, BUTT That Sounds Pretty UNCOMFORTABLE ta

Me. I SURE Hope I Run inta Dr Scholl Up There So I Can Git Some Gell Inserts. HOWEVER, What Interests Me the "Most" About Heaven Will Be ta Check in With Johann Sebastian Bach, Ludwig van Beethoven, Franz Liszt, Fre'd'eric Chopin, Johannes Brahms, Rembrandt Bugatti, Salvador Dali, Pablo Picasso, Vincent van Gogh, Michelangelo Buonarroti, Leonardo da Vinci, François-Auguste-René Rodin, William Shakespeare, Jules Verne, Robert Heinlein, Mary Shelley, Henry Wadsworth Longfellow, Robert Frost, John Keats, Julia Child and Thousands Upon Thousands of Other Artists, Authors, Painters, Poets, Playrights, Sculptors, Chefs, Kings and Cabbages. MANY of them Havin' Been in Heaven fer Centuries. Can You Just Imagine How MUCH Their Talents Must Have EVOLVED Since Their LIVES Were First CREATED Here on the Earth?? I Can Hardly WAIT ta Get t' Heaven ta Bathe in the Artistic Sights, Sounds, Tastes, Smells, and All Sorts of Tactile Sensations......How About YOU???

   It is My and the NEW Independence Party's (NIPer's) HOPE that Each of Y'all Find Something in This Book That You Will be Happy to "Take with You".

Did THAT Crap Make ANY Sense ta Y'all on Pages 128-129, or Am I JEST Funnin' Ya,YOU Decide!!!

Chapter 52

Is Jehovah, Allah, and GOD Almighty Jest the SAME "Supreme Being" Doin' a Little "RE-BRANDING" Fer a "Bit" a FUN in a Pretty BORIN' Universe ???

I Don't KNOW About YOUR God……BUTT….(There's My BIG BUTT Jest Hangin' Out There by ItSelf Again…..)…..MY GOD Has a Sense o' HUMOR (AND If'n Y'all Don't Believe THAT, Then Y'all Haven't Seen a Duck-Billed Platypus Lately)…..And This is Somethin' That MY GOD Would DO:

GOD the FATHER Told the "OTHER" TWO……"Watch THIS……I Told THOSE Folks Over There that MY Name was "ALAH"…..And I Told THOSE Folks Over There that MY Name was "BUDDAH" …. And I Told THOSE Folks Over There thar MY Name was JEHOVAH……AND I Told THOSE Folks Over There that MY Name was "LORD GOD ALMIGHTY"……Let's See What THEY DO with it…..hee…..Hee…..HEEEEEE…….".

And GOD the SON Said….."Yeah, I Did Somethin' Similar…..I Told THOSE Folks that MY Name was JESUS……And…..I Told THOSE Folks MY Name was MOHAMMED……And……", AND at This Point GOD the FATHER Interrupted HIS SON (and Like an OBEDIENT SON….HE Shut HIS Damn MOUTH and Listened to What HIS ELDER Had ta Say)…..And Said, "HOW the HELL Did Ya Do THAT???"…..And GOD the SON Said, "WEELLLLLLL….I'm a Chip OFF'n the Old BLOCK Ain't I??......I'M a GOD TOO Ain't I??......MY DIETY Can Be EVERYWHERE in the UNIVERSE at ONCE Jest Like YOURS.... Remember???"

AND GOD the FATHER's Significant "OTHER"……Jest Looked On and Smiled…..Now Isn't That JEST Like the "Significant Other" in Your Family???

Chapter 53

What IS the "DIFFERENCE" Between Righteousness /Justice and "LEGALITY" ???

WEELLLLL.......That Kindly a Depends on What Yer Definition of "IS" Is (ta Steal a Quote from One a Them Thar EX....Thank GOoDness….. Presidents o' Ours……NAHHHH….Jest Kiddin'…..He WAS a Pretty Goodin' (Even IF He Couldn't Manage t' KEEP His "Little Wild Willy" in His Britches).

Let Me Give Ya a Little Example from Chapter 3 of This Book: I Made a "Call to Service" to the Father of Robert B. Thieme, III…..Who I Jest Call "Junior"….. Now If'n YOU are the QUALITY of Little NIPers I THINK Ya Are, Then Y'all Have Probably Figgered Out the Name of My (And the NIPers) "Correct" Pastor Teacher……BUTT……(There's My BIG BUTT Jest Hangin' Out There By ItSelf Again….So Ya KNOW What's Comin' Don'cha??......That's "Correct"…..a BIG Old "Brain Slap" …..)….. I Was VERRY "Legal" and "Literal" in NOT Mentionin' the NAME of Robert B. Thieme, III's Dad…….BUTT….. I Wasn't Very Righteous or Just….. BECAUSE, I KNEW That the "Intention" of Robert B. Thieme, III Was that I NOT Connect the "Personnage"… The "Essence" of His Father with My Books (Past, Present, or Future) or My NIPers (the NEW Independence Party)….. BUTT….. That's NOT What He "Said" ("Wrote")……He SAID (WROTE), Fer Me "Not ta Mention" the NAME of His Father in Connection with My Book Projects or the NEW Independence Party….. BUTT He (Robert B. Thieme, III) Did NOT Say that I Couldn't Use HIS (Robert B. Thieme, III's) Name in Connection with My Little "Baby" (Book Project) NOR The NEW Independence Party (NIPers).

The "Difference" is Subtile and YET Makes ALL of the "Difference" in the World (I've TOLD Ya Before Folks……Don't Leave This Old Coot from Beauregard, AL a "Loophole" 'Cause I'll Drive a Truck….Train….. or 13 Bomb-Bustin' Bus CONVOY Through it, Reference a LOT a Chapters in This Here Little "Baby" o' Mine). What I've Done in This Book (Regardin' the WISHES of Rev Robert B. Thieme, III) Was NOT "Righteous" or "Just"…..BUTT…..It WAS "Legal"……That is the REASON That We (the AMERICAN Public) Have SOOOOO Many Murderers, Rapists, AND Child Molesters (Like "Chester the Molester") Walkin' UNMolested on Our Streets Today……. WE (That's YOU and ME) Have ALLOWED the Courts (and the "JUSTICE" System ItSelf) ta Operate on the Principle of "LEGALITY" (Satans Way), AND ABONDONED the Principles of "RIGHTEOUSNESS" and "JUSTICE" (My GOD's Way)…..

Did THAT Crap Make ANY Sense to Y'all on Page 131, or Am I JEST Funnin' Ya…..YOU Decide!!!

Chapter 54

WHY is the WORST Thing Y'all Can Do TO Someone AND the BEST Thing Y'all Can Do FOR Someone the SAME Damn THING ???

By This Point, Y'all Should a Figgered Out that There's a Method ta My MADNESS, and That Y'all Got a BIG Ole "Brain Slap" a Headin' Yer Way, BUTT Y'all STILL Ain't Gonna See it Comin' Until It's WAYYYY TOO Late. SOOOOO….."BIG AL"…..How Are Ya Plannin' on Sneakin' Up On Us THIS Time (Yer Sayin' ta YerSelf)??? This Chapter Coordinates Well with Several Others, BUTT it is MOST Closely Associated with Chapters 37 and 51.

Let's Give Ya the BAD News First, and Git it Outta the Way: The WORST Thing Y'all Can Do TO Someone is ta Let Them SUFFER the Consequences of the Erroneous "Beliefs" of Their Hearts/Spirits, the Poor or Faulty "Decisions" of Their Minds/Souls, and the Inefficient/Ineffective "Actions" of Their Body. That is a Triple (Trinity) Whammy That Can Really Put the "Fear of GOD" in Ya. It ALL Starts with Them Thar "Erroneous Beliefs", Because "Beliefs" of the Heart/Spirit, Drive "Decisions" of the Mind/Soul, Which in Turn Drive the "Actions" of the Body, SOOOOOOO If'n Ya REALLY Want ta Have a Chance of Gettin' Someone ta Change Their Behavior (Actions of the Body), Then Ya Have ta Give Them TRUE and ACCURATE Information Upon Which ta Make a Voluntary and Conscious "Decision" ta CHANGE Their "Beliefs". This is VERRY Difficult, Because it's Jest Like Swimmin' Upstream Against a Strong Current. The "Flow" is SUPPOSED ta Go FROM "Beliefs" (the Basis of WHO We Are) to "Decisions" (That Shape Our Actions), BUTT When Information is Discovered That "Challenges Our Basic Beliefs, Then the "Flow" Must be "Reversed" and We Have to Decide With Our Mind/Soul Whether to Continue to Make "Decisions" Based on "Doubtful" and Possibly "Erroneous" BELIEFS, OR to Abandon or MODIFY Those "Beliefs" to Conform to the Newly Accepted Information. Once the NEW Beliefs are Cemented into the Foundation of the Heart/Spirit, then Better Decisions of the Mind/Soul, Improve the Actions of the Body (Which Can be Viewed by Others as Improved "Behavior").

OK, Now That the BAD News is Outta the Way, Let's Hurry On ta the GOOD News: The BEST Thing Y'all Can Do FOR Someone is to Allow Them to Reap (That Means to Harvest, NOT to Violate Sexually) the REWARDS of the True and Validated Beliefs of Their Hearts/Minds, the Meaningful and Organized Decisions of Their Mind/Soul, and the Coordinated, Efficient, and Effective Actions of Their Body. This is the Reason I and the NEW Independence Party (NIPers) are Providing This Book (My Little "Baby") to Y'all in the HOPE that Each of You Will Find Something that Will Cause You to "Decide" Whether the "Beliefs" You Now Hold are REALLY the BEST fer YOU, Your Family and Friends, Your NEIGHBORS, and Your COUNTRY…….the GREAT GOD-Fearin' US of A.

Did THAT Crap Make ANY Sense to Y'all on Page 132, or Am I JEST Funnin' Ya…..YOU Decide!!!

Chapter 55

HOW Can I Find My SOUL Mate and WHAT Does it MEAN ta be "Mates" ???

I Was Jest Thinkin' About This the Other Day While My Wife Was a Fussin' at Me. You'd a Thunk by Now that She Would a Realized after 27+ Years a Marriage, that I Don't Pay Much Attention t' Her Fussin' (Especially after She Done Gave Me that T-Shirt that Read, "I.m Just Gonna Nod My Head and Act Like I'm Listenin'"), BUTT I was a Thinkin' that My GOD with HIS "Peculiar" Sense a HUMOR... (And If'n Y'all Don't Think that MY GOD Has a Sense a HUMOR, Then Ya Ain't Seen No Duck-Billed Platypus Lately......Cause Once Ya See a Duck-Billed Platypus......and I Seen One at a Zoo in Germany Once......Then Ya KNOW Fer Sure that MY GOD has a Sense a HUMOR.....I Don't KNOW About YOUR God, BUTT My GOD Has DEFINITELY Got a Sense o' Humor) ...Done Put Me and My Wife Together as "SOUL Mates" So's that We'd Drive Each Other Crazy And We'd BOTH Have Nobody ta Turn to BUTT "HIM".

Don't That Always Seem ta Be the Case that the Folks We LOVE the Most are the SAME Folks Who Can IRRITATE Us the Most?? I Figger that's My GOD's Way of Ensurin' that I Stay on HIS Good Side, So's I Gots Someone t' Turn to When I Git on My Wife's BAD Side (and it Sure Can be PRETTY "Bad" Sometimes). Maybe That's the Way Y'all Can Tell Ya've Found Yer SOUL Mate...... If'n Yer Always Fussin' and Feudin', Then Ya Should KNOW Ya Got the One Yer God Picked Out Fer Ya and That Y'all Probably "Deserve" (... I Meant "Were Made Fer"...) Each Other. If'n Yer Like Me and My Wife, Y'all "SOUL Mates" Stay Together Out There SOOOO Long Because Ya KNOW that Nobody ELSE Would Have Ya or Be Able ta Put UP with Ya Fer Very Long. Maybe That's Why There's So MANY of Them There Divorced Folks Out There......Ya Keep Tryin' ta Find Mr or Ms "Right" When Ya SHOULD be Lookin' Fer MR or MS "HELL NO.....NOT ON YER LIFE !!!"......Think about it......

Maybe it's the Term "Mates" that Yer Havin' a Problem with, So Let's Go "Down Under" (Where Them Thar Duck-Billed Platypuses (Platypusie......Platypussies.......Oh HELL, You KNOW I'm a Talkin' About..... More that One Platypus......Git Yer Head On Straight......) to Some a Them Thar Australian Folks Like Hugh Jackman, Mel Gibson, Russell Crowe, and Nichole Kidman (Now Ya Hafta Unnerstand that Hugh Jackman was the ONLY One Actually BORN in Australia, BUTT Them Others Spent a Whole HEEP a Their Personal, Public, and Acting Lives "Down Under", So They ALL Know What it MEANS ta Be "Mates" (And it AIN'T What Yer Thinkin'). I'd Be Willin' ta Bet that MOST a Y'all Out There Think that When an Australian Says "We Be Mates" That They Mean "We're Friends" AND Ya'd Be DEAD WRONG !!!

Them Thar Australian Folks Don't Pass Out "We Be Mates" Like Sugar Candy (or Like SOME Folks Pass Out "BFF".......And Speakin' of Text Messagin'......I Need ta Fill Ya in On MY View of Text Messagin' Before Y'all Make the BIG Mistake a Tryin' t' Text Message ME......I Have 2 and ONLY 2 Codes that Handle ALL of My Text Messagin' Needs.......For Text Messagin' Itself I Use "FO" and Fer ANY of Y'all STUPID Enough ta Try t'Text Message ME, I Use "FU"......Those 2 Cutesy Little Codes Fulfill ALL of My Text Messagin' Needs, Because THOSE Are the Kind of Words that Lend Themselves ta "Cutesy" Little Codes.......The Words I Tend ta Use, Like HONOR, COURAGE, DEDICATION, VALOR, SACRIFICE. INTEGRITY, PERSPICASITY, VERACITY, ETC. Don't Lend Themselves ta Bein' Depicted by "Cutesy" Little Codes, They are TOO Powerful and TOO Meaningful.....They Must Be Spelled Out in FULL.....Now Where was I Before Y'all Got Me Rantin' and Ravin' About That Thar OBNOXIOUS Text Messagin' Crap.......Oh Yeah......We Was a Talkin' About "We be Mates".....). When One o' Them Thar Australian Folks Says "We be Mates", They DON'T Mean "Friends". They Mean That They Would Be Willin' ta Lay Down Their Life Fer the Person They Call "Mate" AND They're Pretty Dog Goned Sure that Their "Mate" Would be Willin' ta Lay Down Their Life in Return. Isn't That "Correct" Y'all Australian Folks?? (Remember That We NIPers Avoid the Use of "Right" Like the Plague ta Avoid Gittin' the SAME Obnoxious Disease as Them Thar Radically Religious RIGHT-Wing Republicans....NOT ta Mention Them Thar LEFT-Leanin' Liberal Damn Democrats.... SOOOOOO....Let's PLEASE Not Mention THEM Here EITHER).

Now I Told Ya THAT One ta Tell Ya THIS One: Me and My GOD......"We Be MATES". HE Done Already Laid Down HIS Life fer ME a Couple Thousand Years Ago on a CROSS.....And I'll ALWAYS Remember that I Can NEVER EVER Repay that......And HE Dosen't Really WANT Me ta TRY.....HE Wants Me ta "Pay it FORWARD". Now There was a Little Movie a Few Years Back Called "Pay it Forward" and it Was a Cryin' Shame that it Ended with a Little Kid Being Killed (Like in That Thar "Sandy Hook" School in Newtown, Connecticut), Because it Made People Want ta Fergit About "Payin' it Forward" Rather than Makin' Them Want ta "Pay it Forward" MORE than EVER ta HONOR the VALOR of that Little Boy, and the Makers of the Movie. I'm Seein' on the TV that Because of the Tragedy at the "Sandy Hook" School There's a Few Legislators Who Have Pulled Their Heads Outta "Where the Sun Don't Shine" and Begun ta Look Around at Findin' a Way ta Keep Somethin' Like That from Happenin' Again ANY Time Soon......So I Got Some Advice Fer 'em.......REACT.....Don't OVER React.

AND Lastly......Speakin' of "Payin' it Forward", I DON'T THINK THIS IS GONNA WORK.....Ya Hear that LORD?!?!?!?..... I DON"T THINK IT'S GONNA WORK..... BUTT My GOOD LORD has Put a Burden on My Heart ta Put This Here Book ("Baby") of Mine Out in CyberSpace "Free of Charge .... FREE of Charge......GREAT GOD ALMIGHTY It's FREE OF CHARGE !!!" HE Said ta Offer it UP on the Internet "Free of Charge" and ta Put My Mailin' Address (P.O. Box Number 2149 Tuskegee, AL 36083.....NO, I Ain't STUPID Enough ta Give Ya My PHYSICAL Address or Ya'd ALL Be Over Here Tryin' ta BUM a Buck Off'n Me) On the Last Page a My Book (If'n ANY of Ya Git That Far) and Ask Fer Ya ta Donate Whatever Ya Think it's Worth t' Ya (Besides HE Tells Me the Really BIG Money Don't Come from the "Book".......He Says Ya Can ONLY Expect ta Make a Few Million from a Book Sale.....It's the "Movie" Rights Along with the T-Shirt, Ball Cap, Beach Towel, Coffee/Iea Mug, Bumper Sticker, and Yard Sign Sales Where Ya Make the Really "BIG" Bucks)......HOWEVER.....Them Thar AuthorHouse Folks Convinced Me That Wouldn't Be "FAIR" ta ALL of the Book Stores and eBook Stores that Would HELP Me ta Git My "Baby" inta the "Hands of the AMAERICAN PUBLIC".

If'n Yer One of the Few Who Decide ta Send a Dollar or Three ta P.O. Box 2149 in Tuskegee, AL 36083......Please Be Kind ta Ms Sarah, the Poor Little Ole AMERICAN-Africam (Reference Chapter 12) Lady (and Remember there is a Pretty BIG Difference in Quality of Character Between a "Woman" and a "LADY") and Don't Y'all ALL Send it at Once or Y'all Will Break Her Back. ALSO Remember that Whatever Donations (If'n ANY....'Cause I've Had My www.YouTube.com Videos Out in CyberSpace

Fer Over a Year Now Askin' fer "Value for Value" Donations and There Ain't Been Nuthin' But Dust Bunnies in P.O. Box 2149......So I Guess Nobody has Found ANY Value in 'em.....And Ya Probably Won't Find NO Value in My Little "Baby" Either) That Y'all Might Decide ta Send Will be Split Three (We NIPers Jest LOVE ta Deal in Trinity's) Ways:

One Third Will Go ta My Little Executive Assistant and His Wife Fer Their "Retirement Fund", So's He Can Quit that BIG Government Job a His and Help Me with the NIPers and Some of My "Future Book Projects".....AND Git His WIFE That House in the Middle of 600 Acres....fer the "Family"...

One Third Goes ta ME Fer My Retirement "Nest Egg" and ta Fund the Rest of My "Future Book Projects" (See the End of This Book Plus a Little Further).

AND Last, BUTT Definitely Not LEAST, the Rest o' the Donations are Gonna Go ta the NEW Independence Party (NIPers) ta Fund Their Efforts ta Git This Here GREAT GOD-Fearin' NATION a OURS Back ON TRACK (And On TOP a the HEEP) by Gittin' Ms Sarah Palin and Mr Herman Cain Elected President and Vice-President (Respectively) on the NIPer Ticket Through a Rediculous WRITE-IN Campaign in Them Thar Nov 2016 Elections (Reference Chapter 18).

Did THAT Crap Make ANY Sense ta Y'all on Pages 133-135, or Am I JEST Funnin' Ya, YOU Decide!!!

Chapter 56

If'n Y'all Cain't "BEAT 'em", WHY the in the HELL Would Ya Want ta "JOIN 'em" ???

I'm Kindly a Glad Ya Asked that Because I Actually DO Have a Pretty Good Answer ta That Thar Question. It's Kindly a Like When "THEY" Say, "When it's a WIN, It's a TEAM Win, AND When It's a LOSS, It's a TEAM Loss.", And THAT Kindly a Works, Exceptin' When Two or MORE Members of the SAME Team Have a Bit of a Tussle. Let Me Elaborate on that a Bit……If'n ALL Members of a Team Work Together in a Coordinated Effort, with Each Team Member Contributin' Their Fair Share as Their God Has Graced them with Certain Abilities and Strengths, and Takin' Notice and Praisin' the Abliities and Strengths of the OTHER Team Members to Successfully Accomplish a Goal, THEN it is a Team "WIN" ALL the WAY!!!

Now Let Me Throw Your Team a Little "Curve Ball", "Knuckle Ball", or "Change Up Pitch": If'n One or MORE Members of the SAME Team Git into a Little Scuffle and Decide Instead o' SUPPORT'n Each Other (in a WIN-WIN Scenario), They Decide ta Turn it inta a "Heads I WIN, Tails You LOSE" Scenario, Then (No Matter WHO Wins) it is a TEAM "LOSS". We NEW Independence Party (NIPer) Folks Believe THAT is What is "WRONG" with AMERICAN Government These Days. Them LEFT-Leanin' Liberal Damn Democrats AND Them Radically Religious RIGHT-Wing Republicans are SOOOO Busy Tryin' ta "Beat the Other Guy" that They Fergit That We Are ALL on the AMERICA TEAM (Until it Comes Time fer the Olymipcs and Then It's Just the SAME WIN-LOSE Senario on an "OLYMPIAN" Level……They Fergit That at the "Olympics" China, USA, Britain, France, Germany, Japan, etc. Are ALL Supposed ta Be on the "WHOLE Wide World in HIS Hands" Team…. And a LOSS fer ANYONE is a LOSS fer the TEAM). Remember That the Next Time Ya Go to a "Sportin' Event" and BOOOOOOO fer the Players on the "Other" Side of the Field.

Let Me Set Up a Little Scenario Fer Ya and SEE What Ya THINK of it: On the Playground of the District 38 School in Hall County Nebraska (When I was Jest a "Little" NIPer), Occasionally We Had a "Dispute" Between a Couple o' "Players". Let's Call them Little "Left Out" (Like Them Thar LEFT-Leanin' Liberal Damn Democrats), and Little "Right On" (Like Them Thar Radically Religious RIGHT-Wing Republicans), AND of Course We Have ta Have "Somebody" ta "Egg them ON" and Someone ta "Break them UP" (Do ANY of Ya SEE Where I'm Goin' with This??……Some a Ya DO…..Some a Ya Don't…….And as USUAL…..MOST of Ya Hadn't Got a "CLUE"……BUTT I'm about ta "CLUE" Ya IN…..). Once the Tussle Between Little "Left Out" and Little "Right On" Gits Encouraged by ALL of the "Egger's ON", Along Comes "Teacher….TEACHER!!!" ta "Break them UP". Now, I Don't Know WHAT Kindly aTeachers They Have in School THESE Days, BUTT Them Thar District 38 School Teachers Were Pretty Dog Goned Smart. (I Can See that Yer Gittin' a Bit Tired and Bored, So Let's Take a Little Paragraph Break.)

Now That an ADULT ("Teacher…..TEACHER!!!"….or the NEW Independence Party, NIPer) Steps in Between Those 2 Squabblin' Brats ("LEFT Out" and "RIGHT On") and Asks the One on the LEFT, "What's Your Tale", Then Turns to the One on the RIGHT and Asks, "What's Your Story", AND THEN

(Since We Had VERRY Smart Teachers at My School) the ADULT Teacher (NIPer) Would Ask ALL of Those "Egger's ON" (the AMERICAN Public)….. "How Do YOU See it??? Once the ADULT Teacher Had ALL of the Facts from "LEFT Out", "RIGHT On", AND Them Thar Little "Egger's ON", Then and ONLY Then Did the NIPer Make an Informed, Reasonable, Rational, and Logical Decision (Which was USUALLY to 'Tan the Hides" of One or BOTH of Them Thar Squallin' Little BRATS!!!).

Now Jest in Case Y'all Lost Track o' Things in All of the Confusion Let's Make it VERRY Clear fer Those of Y'all Who Hadn't Got a "CLUE"……We NEED a "Middle of the Road" "ADULT" Third Party Choice Like the NEW Independence Party (NIPers) ta "Referee" Between Them LEFT-Leanin' Liberal Damn Democrat AND Them Thar Radically Religious RIGHT-Wing Republican Squabblin' "BRATS", So's We Can Be Gittin' ON with Servin' the AMERICAN Public in the Manner They "DESERVE" And SHOULD Be Able ta "EXPECT" from Their Dully (or is it Dually) ELECTED (or Maybe Soon to be UNElected) Public Service Representatives to the Executive and Legilative Branches of the BIG (OVER-Sized….SUPER-Sized) Federal Government………Jest a Sec……Somebody's a Knockin'…..Somethin' About FBI……

Did THAT Crap Make ANY Sense ta Y'all on Pages 136-137, or Am I JEST Funnin' Ya,YOU Decide!!!

Chapter 57

What's the "DIFFERENCE" Between "Good" LUCK and "Bad" LUCK ???

Someone Once Told Me that There Was NO SUCH THING as "Luck", and We NIPers Believe That. There's a Very GOOD Reason that the Word "LUCK" Should Always be Spelled with ALL "Capital" Letters…..it is an Acronym instead of Jest a "Normal" Word. "Good" LUCK is the Lord's Unlimited Caring Kindness, and "Bad" LUCK is Lucifer's UNCarin' Counterfiet Knockoff. Isn't That the Way "LUCK" Plays a Factor in YOUR Life…..When Yer Relationship with Yer God is in "Good" Shape, Doesn't EVERYTHING Seem ta Go Yer Way and Everything Seem t' Fall inta Place Rather Nicely…… and Conversely……When Yer Relationship with Yer God Ain't So Good (and Ya Start Doin' Things that the Devil Would be Proud of Ya Fer Doin')…..Don't it Seem Like Everything Falls Apart???

Sometimes Our (Me and the NIPers) GOD Throws Us a Little "Curve Ball" or a Little "Change Up Pitch" ta See If'n We Can Handle it and ta See If'n We ENJOY a Little "Excitement" in Our Lives, And Every Once it a While HE Plays "HARD BALL" with Us (Instead of Givin' Us Them Thar "Easy" Sliders)….. Because HE Knows that What Don't KILL Us Makes Us STRONGER…..BUTT If'n Yer "Faith" Ain't TESTED Oncet in a While, It Can Git Pretty "Weak and Fragile", So's that When Y'all REALLY Need it in a CRISIS Situation, It "Fails" Ya, So the GOOD Lord Likes ta Keep Ya on Yer Toes So's That Yer ALWAYS Prepared Fer that NEXT Crisis……..Movin' ON…….

Did THAT Crap Make ANY Sense to Y'all on Page 138, or Am I JEST Funnin' Ya…..YOU Decide!!!

Chapter 58

Why WAS Jesus CHRIST SOOOO Dog Goned DEPRESSED All of the Time ???

WEELLLLL….ta Understand WHY Jesus CHRIST was Always So Dog Goned Depressed, Y'all Jest Have ta Remember That, in Addition t' Being a Human Being (And the Savior of ALL Mankind) He Was ALSO an Important Member of the "BIG 3" Trinity (GOD the FATHER….GOD the SON – Jesus CHRIST…. And…..GOD the FATHER's Significant "OTHER") and As Such is ALSO Omniscient (ALL KNOWIN'). How "GOOD" Do Y'all Think YOU Would Feel If'n Ya Knew EVERY SINGLE SECOND of Yer Life a Billion Years Before it Happened, in ADDITION t' Knowin' it Just a Second or Two Before it Happened, AND Ya KNEW that it Wasn't Gonna Turn Out Very Well??? Wouldn't That Be Enough t' Depress Y'all??? It SURELY Would Us NIPers (…and I'm NOT Callin' Y'all "Shirley").

Y'all Remember WAAYYYYYY BACK in Chapter 4 When I Said (Wrote), "As a Lamb before the Shearers, He Uttered NOT a Word" (or SOME Such)…… And I Told Y'all that "I'll Git ta This a Little Later On"….. WEELLLLL…..It's "Later On"….. I Just Wanted t' Repeat a Little Somethin' from My Little YouTube Videos that Ya Ain't Watchin' About "WHO Killed CHRIST". Ya Already KNOW that I Don't Like t' Chew My Cabbage Twicet, BUTT There are Jest SOME Things that Are IMPORTANT Enough ta Bear (Bare ???, Bere……Oh HELL….Y'all KNOW What I Mean) Repeatin', And This Seemed as Good as Anyplace ta DO it……..

A Whole LOT o' Folks Think that the "Jews" Killed CHRIST, BUTT We NIPers KNOW Better, So If'n Yer ONE o' Them Thar Folks ………LISTEN UP !!! Them Thar Jewish Folks, "Way Back When" (Along with Some a Them Thar ROMAN Fellers) Really Tried HARD t' Kill Jesus CHRIST, BUTT They Just Couldn't DO it. They Tortured Him UNMercifully (and If'n Ya Don't Believe ME, Just Check Out Mel Gibson's Little Film and You'll See) by "Chastisin' (ta Skin Alive with a Cat-o-Nine-Tails Whip Studded with Bits of Metal and Stone) HIM and Beatin' HIM with Their Fists, and Rammin' a "Crown of Thorns" Upon HIS Head, BUTT "As a Lamb before the Shearers, He Uttered NOT a Word" (or SOME Such)…… Cause THAT Warn't NEAR Enough t' Kill CHRIST, BUTT Just Before We (THAT'S What I SAID…..WE….And That Means Y'all and ME !!!) Killed CHRIST, HE Screamed BLOODY MURDER, Just Like a NEWLY BORN BABY's First PRIMAL SCREAM…..as MY Sins….Y'ALLS Sins….AND the Sins (Past, Present, And Future) of the ENTIRE WORLD Descended on HIS Body (in a Single Point in Time…..Like the Birth of a Child….or the Birth of the Universe in a "BIG BANG") On the Cross….. And OUR Sins KILLED CHRIST's BODY (BUTT Thank GOoDness HIS Immortal SOUL and HIS ETERNAL DIETY Wheren't Affected in the Least). SOOOOO….Keep the Faith Folks…..Because Now That HIS Sacrifice is COMPLETED…..HE Ain't Depressed NO MORE (Exceptin' When HE Thinks About ALL o' Y'all Out There That DON'T Believe in HIS Sacrifice and DON'T Believe on HIS Name).

WEELLLL……If'n We NIPers Cain't Git Y'all ta Believe In OUR Plan t' Git Ms Sarah Palin and Mr Herman Cain Elected President and Vice-President (Respectively) on the NEW Independence Party (NIPer) Ticket for Them Thar Nov 2016 Elections…Then I Guess We're in GREAT Company (Since the Lord Jesus CHRIST HISSELF Cain't Git Ya t' Believe in HIM Either…..Oh Well……Movin' ON…..

This Page Has Been "INTENTIONALLY" ("RIGHTly") "LEFT" BLANK.

(Exceptin' Fer the Chapter Trailer, And the Text Above, AND The Text Below This Line)

(There Ain't No More "Zork" Makers ta HONOR is There???....Then WHY the HELL Did Ya Leave This Here Page BLANK???.....I Don't KNOW…..I Thought YOU Put it in…..I Did n't Put it in……I Thought YOU Put it in……Let's Ask "Mickey"……Hey!....MIKEY!!!!!)

Did THAT Crap Make ANY Sense ta Y'all on Pages 139-140, or Am I JEST Funnin' Ya,YOU Decide!!!

Chapter 59

Why Do SOME Folks Treat Their GOD Like Their Mother-OUT-Law ???

I Don't Know if Any of Y'all Have Noticed it Lately, BUTT We NIPers Believe that We KNOW Why Them Thar godLESS Atheists are a Stealin' the Power of Y'alls GOD Away from Ya. Now I'm NOT Talkin About MY GOD, the "BIG 3" (GOD the FATHER, GOD the SON, and ......GOD the FATHER's Significant "OTHER") Who are Backin' the NEW Independence Party (NIPers), Because OUR GOD is with US 24/7 (Twenty-Four Hours a Day, Seven Days a Week), HOWEVER Most of Y'all Seem t' Treat Yer God Like Yer Mother-Out-Law (or Some Other Relative that Yer Not TOO Fond of).

WAYYYY TOO Many of Y'all Out There Put Yer Gods in a Little House All Their Own (Temple, Mosque, Synagogue, Church, Cathedral, etc.) and Go and Visit Them a Few Times a Week (Maybe Even ONLY a Few Times a YEAR), and Then Think Y'all Have "Done Yer Duty" and Go About Livin' the Rest of Yer Lives in "Peace and Quiet" (Raisin' a Little HELL and/or Goin' t' HELL in Yer Own Way), BUTT MY GOD (as is the Case with MOST NIPers) is with Me 24/7......They (the "BIG 3", Trinity) are There in My Messy, Cluttered House (Yes, I am a "Pack Rat", "Hoarder", Obsessive-Compulsive (OC) "Recycler", or Whatever Obnoxious Term Y'all Want t' Call Me These Days) When I Wake Up t' the Lord's Brand NEW Day (After Havin' Watched Over Me and Kept Me and My Extended Family SAFE Throughout the Night), "THEY" Tommy-Peep at Me While I Take My Shower, Shave, and Brush and Floss My Teeth (Yes, the GOOD Lord Has Seen Me Naked, BUTT I'm NOT Ashamed of it and Neither is HE).

The "Big 3" (SOMEHOW) Manage ta Find a Place t' Sit in My Messy Cluttered 1999 GMC Yukon as They Accompany Me t' Work (and Surround Me with a "Circle of Fire" t' Keep All of Them Thar Obnoxious Road Hogs, Lane-Hoppers, Tail-Gators, Slow-Polk's, Speed-Demons, and Future Organ Donors from Takin' My Life or Causin' Me t' "Flip" them the Third Use of the "Sign of the NIPers", Reference Chapter 2), and They Watch Patiently as I Provide My Customers TOP Quality Customer Service (Remotely, via Several Different Information Technology Tools) from My Messy, Cluttered Office, Until (Usually Well After the End of My "Normal" Duty Hours) I Drag My Tired Buttocks Back to My Messy, Cluttered SUV for the 30 Mile, 40 Minute Drive BACK t' My Messy, Cluttered House (Unless, of Course, I hafta Stop Fer Fuel, or t' Provide Roadside Assistance t' Someone, or I have t' Stop by the Grocery Store, or Pick Up a Pizza on the Way Home, or Any One of a NUMBER of Other Little Surprises "THEY" (OR My Lovely Wife) Have Concocted ta Test My Patience and Commitment ta Uphold the Values, Principles, and Standards (VPS) Found in the NIPer Handbook, the "User's Guide and Maintenance Manual for a Human Life", Reference Chapter 10).

I KNOW That MANY of Y'all Probably Think That Me and My Lovely Wife are "Heathens" of the WORST Sort, Because We Don't Go t' "Church" Very Often (Only to Appease the Pleadin' of Some of Our Relatives), BUTT When Ya LIVE with Yer GOD 24/7 Like We DO, it Just Seems Kindly a Silly t' Go t' Some "Strange" Place t' Worship "THEM" (the "BIG 3"). I Don't Know About Y'alls God, BUTT If'n Ya Want t' Know What MY GOD Thinks About "Churches" (Organized Religion), Then Just Check Out the First Few Chapters of the "REVELATION of John" at the End of the NIPer Handbook, BUTT I

WARN Ya in Advance that It's Not Very Flatterin' and Ya Probably Won't Like it. MOST Folks Jest Skip Over That Part t' Git Onta the GOOD Stuff in the Later Chapters of That Thar Book. HOWEVER, We NIPers Don't Like t' Miss a Single Word (Even Them Thar Never-Endin' "Begats") in the Cannon of Scripture. AND Speakin' of "Cannons", I Have Been Told by More than a Few Folks that I was a "Loose Cannon", BUTT (as MOST of Ya Already Know) the ONLY Safe Place t' Be When Yer Around One o' Them Thar "Loose Cannons" is ta Be Firmly Behind Them, Because If'n Yer NOT Standin' Firmly Behind a "Loose Cannon", Then YOU Are "IN THEIR LINE OF FIRE", and Believe You Me, Y'all REALLY Don't Want to be in MY (or the NIPer's) "Line of Fire"…a Word t' the "Wise" SHOULD be Sufficient……We'll See……Movin' ON….

Did THAT Crap Make ANY Sense ta Y'all on Pages 141-142, or Am I JEST Funnin' Ya, YOU Decide!!!

Chapter 60

Y'all MIGHT Have Heard of the "12 Days of CHRISTmas", BUTT …..Have Ya Ever HEARD of the "12 Answering Machine Messages of the Year" ???

I Figgered that Since Y'all Have Stayed with Me THIS Long, Ya Deserved a Little "Gift" from the NIPers and Me "Personally". These are the Answerin' Machine Messages that I Have Developed Over the Years, and I HOPE Y'all Enjoy Them. There is NO Copyright on Them (Exceptin' the One on This "Baby" a Mine…..And I Hereby RELEASE This Chapter FROM That Copyright), So Feel FREE to Use Them in Any Way You See Fit:

January (to Be Sung Inebriatedly and Slightly Snuffly to the Tune of "Old Lang Syne"):

> So YOUR Phone Call Won't BE Forgotten and NEVER Brought to MIND, (Hicup)
>
> We HAVE This ANSwering Machine InSTALLED upon Our LINE,
>
> Pleeaseeee LEAVE Your MESSage AT the TONE…Your NAME and NUMber TOOOOOOO,
>
> And WHEN We Get Back HOME Again, We'll Get BACK with YOU.
>
> HAPPY NEW YEAR !!!

February (to Be Sung Lovin'ly to the Tune of "SweetHeart" ???...Not Sure…Tough to Describe):

> I'M Out with My SWEETheart So We're NOT..AT..HOME,
>
> But YOU Can Leave a MESSage Since You're ON..THE..PHONE.
>
> LEAVE Your Name and NUMber and a MESS..AGE..TOOO,
>
> And WHEN We Get Back HOME Again, We'll GET Right BACK with YOU.

March (to be Said with a Sort of HIGH Pitch Irish Accent)

> This is PATRICK O'Brian the LEPrechan,
>
> I'm SORRY the Master (or Substitute Mistress) He's (or She's) NOT at HOME.
>
> He (or She) CAPTURED Me Pot o' GOLD from Me,
>
> And I have to Answer His (or Her) CALLS Ya See.
>
> So GIVE Me Yer MESSAGE and MAKE it QUICK,
>
> Or ON Ya I'll Play Me NASTIEST Trick.
>
> Leave Yer NAME and NUMBER at The TONE You DO…..

And Here's WISHIN' You a HAPPY Saint PATTY's Day TOO.

April (to be Sung Lightly and Tenderly to the Tune of "Peter Cotton Tail"):

THERE Goes Peter COTTON Tail a HOPPIN' Down the BUNNY Trail,

SORRY He's Not HERE to Talk to YOUUU…

If You'll LEAVE a Message THOUGH

I'll Be SURE to LET Him KNOW

Please Leave ME Your NAME and Number TOOOOO…

And May the GOOD Lord's Easter BLESSIN' Be With YOUUUU

May (to be Sung Spritely to the Tune of "Strolling in the Park"):

We're Out STROLLIN' in the PARK ToDAYYYYY

In This VERY MERRY MONTH of MAYYYYY

Leave a MESSAGE Just the SAAMMMMEEE

Leave Your NUMBER and Your NAAMMMEEEEE

And We'll GET Back with You WHEN We're Home AGAIN, THANK YOU!!!

June (to be Sung HOWEVER to the Tune of "Take Me Out to the Ball Game"):

WE"VE (or I'VE) Gone OUT to the BALL GAME….We've GONE OUT with the CROWD.

I'm SORRY We're (or I'm) NOT Here to ANSWER Your CALL,

But PLEASE Leave Your NAME and Your NUMBER and ALL.

We (or I) Will CALL You BACK when We GET HOME…..If WE Don't Then it's a SHAME

For it's ONE….TWO….THREE Strikes You're OUT in the PHONE TAG GAME!!!

July (to be Sung Patriotically to the Tune of "Yankee Doodle"):

I'M a YANKee Doodle DANdy….I'm a YANKee DOODle Do or DIIIIIEE

I'M SURE SORRY We're (or I'm) Not HERE RIGHT NOW,

But WHY Don't Ya GIVE This a TRYYYYY

Please LEAVE Your MESSage, Name and NUMber

Right HERE Upon Our LITTLE TOYYYYYY (or PAALLLLLL)

And WE (or I) Will Try to GET Back with You WHEN We Get Back HOME

For I AM a YANKee DOODle BOOYYYYYY (or GAALLLLLLL)

August (to be Sung "Hee Haw" Style to the Tune of "In the Summertime" ??):

In the Summer TIME, When ALL the TREES and LEAVES are GREEN

And the TELEphone RINNNGGGGGGSSSS, but WE'RE Not HEERRRE

So WE Cain't TAKE Yer CALLLL.

IF'n You'll LEAVE Your NAME and NumBERRR…And a Message Too

Then We Will CALL Ya Back When WE Git Home AGAIN

And If'n We DON'T…Jest Call AGAIINNNN

Cause in the Summer TIME, When ALL the TREES and LEAVES are GREEN

And the TELEphone RINNNGGGGGGSSSS, but WE'RE Not HEERRRE

So We Cain't TAKE Yer CALLLL.

September (to be Sung Wearily to the Tune of "School Days"):

SCHOOL Days, SCHOOL Days, Those AWful BACK to SCHOOL Days,

SORry We're NOT Here to ANSwer Your CALL.

PLEASE Leave Your NAME and Your NUMber and ALL.

We'll Get Back WITH You WHEN We CAN.

I'm SORry I HOPE You'll UNderSTAND,

We're BUSY PrePARING for SCHOOL to BeGIN

And There's SO Much to DO Until THEN.

October (to be Sung Creepily to the Tune of the "Adams Family"):

We're CREEPY and We're GHOULish, And THIS Month Sometimes FOOLish,

But LEST You Think We're BORish, We're SORRY We're Not HOME.

If YOU'RE a ConverSATor, Jest LIKE Our AliGATor,

We'll GET Back with You LATer, If YOU Will Leave Your NAME.

Leave Us Your NAME (Click, Click) (Snappin' Fingers Don't Work as Well as "Cluks")

Your Number TOO (Click, Click)   (Like Ya Was "Clukin'" Fer a Horse ta Gitty UP)

Leave Us Your NAME….Your Number TOO….That's What You DO (Click, Click)

November (to be Sung to the Tune of "We've Gathered Together to Ask the Lord's Blessing"):

We've GATHered ToGETHer to ASK the Lord's BLESSing.

I'm SORry We're NOT Here to ANSwer Your CALL.

If YOU'LL Leave a MESSage……Your NAME and Number TOO,

When WE Return AGAIN, We Will GET Back with YOU.

December (the First Strange Answering Machine Message, Record Sloowwwly and Play at 2X Speed):

This is SANta's LITTle HELPer, I'm SORry HE's Not IN,

But IF You'll LEAVE a MESSage, I'll PASS it ON to HIM.

Please LEAVE Your NAME and NUMber , and TRY Hard NOT to GRIN.

Have a VERy Merry CHRISTmas. When You HEAR the TONE BeGIN.

Well, If'n Ya Liked This Chapter, Then There's a Pretty GOOD Chance that Y'all will Like the Next One Too…..

Chapter 61

WHY Do Bears DEFECATE in the "National Park Service" FORESTS ???

We NIPers Don't REALLY Know Why Bears Defecate in the National Park Service Forests (Just Like We're Not REALLY Sure that the Pope is Catholic), But We're Pretty Sure that You and Your Youngin's Will Enjoy This Little Ditty (Even Though Their Ain't No Sound, I Guess Y'all Will Have t' Buy the CD of This Book t' Hear How it's Supposed t' Sound):

Smoky the Bear Song

With a Ranger's Hat and Shovel and a Pair of Dungarees,

You can Find Him in the Forest Always Sniffin' at the Breeze.

People Stop and Pay Attention When He Tells Them to Beware,

'Cause Everybody Knows that He's the Fire Prevention Bear.

Smoky the Bear, Smoky the Bear, Prowlin' and a Growlin' and a Sniffin' in the Air.

He Can Find a Fire Before it Starts to Flame.

That's Why They Call Him Smoky; That was How He Got His Name.

You Can Camp Upon His Doorstep and He'll Make You Feel at Home.

You Can Run and Hunt, and Ramble Anywhere You Care to Rome.

He Will Let You Take His Honey and Pretend He's Not So Smart,

But Don't You Harm the Trees 'Cause He's a Ranger in His Heart.

Smoky the Bear, Smoky the Bear, Prowlin' and a Growlin' and a Sniffin' in the Air.

He Can Find a Fire Before it Starts to Flame.

That's Why They Call Him Smoky; That was How He Got His Name.

You Can Take a Tip from Smoky that There's Nothin' Like a Tree,

Cause Their Good for Kids to Climb in and Their Beautiful to See,

So Just Take a Look Around You and You'll Find it's Not a Joke

To See What You'd be Missin' If They ALL Went Up in Smoke.

Smoky the Bear, Smoky the Bear, Prowlin' and a Growlin' and a Sniffin' in the Air.

He Can Find a Fire Before it Starts to Flame.

That's Why They Call Him Smoky; That was How He Got His Name.

If You've Ever Seen a Forest When a Fire's Runnin' Wild,

And You Loved the Things Within it Like a Mother Loves Her Child,

Then You Know Why Smoky Tells You When He Sees You Passin' Through,

"Remember, PLEASE be Careful. It's the Least That You Can Do."

Smoky the Bear, Smoky the Bear, Prowlin' and a Growlin' and a Sniffin' in the Air.

He Can Find a Fire Before it Starts to Flame.

That's Why They Call Him Smoky; That was How He Got His Name.

We HOPE Y'all Enjoyed These Last Two Sing-a-Long Chapter's, Because Now it's Back to the "HEAVY" Stuff.

Did THAT Crap Make ANY Sense ta Y'all on Pages 147-148, or Am I JEST Funnin' Ya, YOU Decide!!!

Chapter 62

If'n We TRUELY Live Our Lives the SAME Way Jesus CHRIST Did, Does THAT Mean We Will ALL End Up Being CRUCIFIED Fer OUR Beliefs TOO ???

We NIPers Don't Believe that JUST Livin' Our Lives the Way Jesus CHRIST Did, is ENOUGH ta Git Us "Crucified" fer Our Beliefs.....HOWEVER, If'n We Try ta MESS With Satan's Plan t' PROVE ta GOD that His Methods of Greed, Avarace, and Graft (GAG), OR Lies, Avarace, and WELFAIR (LAW) Can Rule the Earth "Better" Than GOD's Methods of Truth, Love, and Charity (TLC) by Tryin' REAL HARD ta Convince OTHERS t' Trust in GOD's Methods ....Like Me and the NIPers Have Been Tryin' ta Do Between the Sheets of This Book (My "Baby?")..... THEN and ONLY Then Will Ya "MARK" (Like the "MARK" a the "Beast") YerSelf fer "Crucifiction" fer Yer Beliefs.

SOOOOO.....If'n YOU (Gentle Reader) Don't WANT ta Put Yer LIFE, CAREER, and/or Your REPUTATION "On the LINE" fer Your God, Then PLEASE Don't Let ANY of This Make Sense t' Ya, PLEASE Treat it as "Strickly" a Book of HUMOROUS Outlandish Opinions from a Poor CRAZY Old Fart from Beauregard, Alabama......and TRULY Believe That I am Jest Funnin' Ya......Because If'n Ya Don't Take That Advice......and "HELP" Us NIPers Git Ms Sarah Palin and Mr Herman Cain Elected President and Vice-President (Respectively) on the NEW Independence Party (NIPer) Ticket in the Nov 2016 Elections, Then YOU TOO May Have Yer LIFE, CAREER, and/or REPUTATION Negatively Affected, ALONG with Being "Crucified" (or Killed in ANY Number of OTHER Horrid Ways) fer YOUR Beliefs TOO.....

Did THAT Crap Make ANY Sense to Y'all on Page 149, or Am I JEST Funnin' Ya.....YOU Decide!!!

Chapter 63

WHY Did David CHOOSE 5 Smooth Stones, And HOW Does That Apply ta ME ???

OK.....Yeah....This is the Story of David and Goliath, BUTT Unless Y'all Have Heard This from the Lips of the NIPers "Correct" Pastor Teacher (the Father of Robert B. Thieme, III....Who I Call "Junior" and My Wife Calls "Old LOUD Mouth"), Then Y'all Have NEVER Heard it Told Like THIS Before:

This is Just ONE o' the 10 Questions (5 from the OLD Testament and 5 from the NEW Testament) that I ask ANY Clergyman Who Says They Want Me ta Attend Their Particular "House of God". I Hadn't Found One YET Who Could Pass it, Exceptin' My "Correct" Pastor Teacher, "Junior". MOST Folks THINK They Know What GOD Was Tryin' t' Teach 'em with the Story of David and Goliath, BUTT After They Hear it the Way We NIPers Tell it, They Have a Whole Different Perspective on LIFE.

Y'all See, David Was a PREPARED Man o' GOD (Like Us NIPers) and By Chosin' 5 Smooth Stones for His Slingshot, He Was Displayin' This Preparedness. EVERYONE Knows About the Giant Named "Goliath" from the Philistine Army (Who Was Killed by David), BUTT What MOST Folks Don't Know (or Remember) is that the Philistine Army Had a Whole Basketball Team of 5 Giants.....And If'n Y'all Don't Believe That, Jest Look it Up in Our NIPer Handbook, the "User's Guide and Maintenance Manual for a Human Life" (Reference Chapter 10) in I Samuel, Chap 17, and Again in II Samuel, Chap 21. There Was Goliath's Brother Who is ONLY Called That in I Samuel, BUTT is Named as "Lah mi" in II Samuel (Killed by "El ha nan"); And There Was "Ish bi be nob" (Killed by "A bosh a l"); Then Thar Was Six-Fingers and Six-Toes (Killed by "Jon a than"); and Finally There Was the Giant Called "Saph" in I Samuel, and "Sip pai" in II Samuel (Killed by "Sib be chai"). Now If'n Y'all are Wonderin' Why This Last Giant was Called "Saph" in One Place and "Sip pai" in Another, It's Kindly a Like One o' Them Past Presidents Bein' Called "Bill" Clinton by SOME Folks, and "William" Clinton by Other Folks, and "That Horney Old....." by Still Others........

SOOOO......Now That Y'all Know There was Actually FIVE Giants in the Philistine Army, Y'all Know WHY David Picked Up FIVE Stones......He was PREPARED t' Kill ALL FIVE!!! BUTT..... THAT's NOT the Lesson We Should Learn. The Lesson that Our GOD was Tryin' t' Teach Y'all is: If'n Y'all Will Just Tackle the "Biggest and Baddest" of Yer Problems, the Others Will Just Flee Before Ya, Like the Other Four Giants Fled Before David (to Be Killed by Other Folks) Once They Saw He Had Taken ON "Goliath" and Prevailed. SOOOO Us NIPers Like t' Tackle the "Biggest and Baddest" of Our Problems, and Watch the Others Just Seem ta Melt Away. See If'n That Thar Advice from the NEW Independence Party (NIPers) Doesn't Give Y'all the Courage t' Tackle the NEXT "Big Bad" Problem o' Yours with a Little More Confidence, Courage, and Perseverance.

Did THAT Crap Make ANY Sense to Y'all on Page 150, or Am I JEST Funnin' Ya.....YOU Decide!!!

Chapter 64

WHY Do Us NIPers "HOPE for the BEST", "EXPECT the WORST", and "PREPARE Ourselves" fer WHATEVER Comes in Between ???

HOPE Springs Eternal for Us NEW Independence Party Thinkers/Members (NIPers), And We are ALWAYS Lookin' fer the "Silver Linin'" to Them Dark Storm Clouds, the Single Candle in the Darkest Places, the "Bright and Morning Star" in Our Heatrs and Minds......BUTT We AlSO Believe Whole-Heartedly in "Muphy's Law" ("Whatever CAN Go Wrong, WILL Go Wrong in the WORST Possible Way at the WORST Possible TIME."). BUTT (No Matter WHAT I DO, I Jest CAIN'T Loose that BIG BUTT......Everywhere I Go.......There it IS) Just Like Them Thar Doomsday Preppers.....We Know that REAL Life Usually Falls Somewhere Between Those 2 "Extremes" and We Prepare OurSelves Accordingly.

HOWEVER.....Let Me Give Y'all the Slightly "Different" Slant that We NIPers Put on "Muphy's Law" (and Remember that "Murphy" was an "OPITIMIST"): For This Little Example, We're Gonna Use that Little 13 Bomb-Bustin Bus 50 State Campaign Tour that We NIPers Want Ms Oprah Winfrey ta Plan and Execute fer Us. Ms Winfrey MIGHT be a Little Intimidated by This Logistical Nightmare and Figger that We'd Think LESS of Her If'n it Didn't Go OFF without a Hitch......and Nuthin' Could be Further from the TRUTH.......as a Matter of Fact, We NIPers "Secretly" HOPE that EVERYTHING Goes JEST Accordin' ta "Murphy's LAW".......Now WHY Would We Say a Darned FOOL Thing Like THAT???....

WELLLLL....I Told Ya THAT t' Tell Ya THIS: I Want ALL a Y'all ta Think BACK Over ALL of the Trips, Vacations, Cruises, Outings, Etc., that You Have EVER Been On.....And Ask YerSelf This ONE Question: Which of These "Departures from the Norm" Did Ya Find MOST Interestin', Excitin', and the ONE That Yer Friends, Family, and EVEN Strangers on the Street Want ta Hear ALL About.... 1) The ONE Where Everything Went Well with Absolutely NO PROBLEMS...... or 2) The ONE Ya Took with "Murphy" By Yer Side (OR "Sittin' on Yer Shoulders, as My WIFE Jest Said) the WHOLE Way, Where EVERYTHING Went as WRONG as it Could???...... There is an Ancient Chinese CURSE that Goes Somethin' Like....."May You Have a Most INTERESTING Life". If'n Y'all Don't Live an "INTERESTIN'" Life (Like Us NIPers) Then Your Life Must be BORIN' as HELL. We NIPers Would be BORED ta TEARS If'n We Didn't Have a Little Bit o' EXCITEMENT in Our Lives from Time ta Time.....Now Don't Git Me WRONG......a Little Bit o' Excitement Goes a LONNGGGG Way, So's We Don't TRY ta Overdo it, BUTT We DO Love LIFE, And We DO "LIVE" LIFE......If'n Ya Don't Believe Us, Then Come on OUT and MEET Us When We Come Around in Our 13 Bomb-Bustin' Bus 50 State Campaign Tour.....ALL 3 TIMES !!!

Did THAT Crap Make ANY Sense to Y'all on Page 151, or Am I JEST Funnin' Ya.....YOU Decide!!!

Chapter 65

Why IS a Raven Like a Writing Desk ???

We Don't Know Why a Raven is Like a Writing Desk......Go ask Lewis Carroll......Go Look it Up on the Internet......Find the Answer Yer OWN Dad Gummed Self. We NIPers Don't Have ALL of the Answers and We Don't CLAIM to.......BUTT I DO Hope that Y'all HAVE Had a Little "Revelation" and Discovered that We DO Have "Quite a Few" Answers ta SOME of the Problems Plaguing America Today, OR at LEAST a Little "Different" Way of Lookn' at 'em than Ya Have EVER Heard of Before (Especially from those Lousy Left-Leanin' Liberal Damn Democrats and those Really Rascally Radically Religious Right-Wing Republicans, Among "Others").

I Don't KNOW About Your God, BUTT Let Me Tell Ya a Little Bit About MY GOD Family (Ya Know....GOD the FATHER, GOD the SON, and……GOD the FATHER's Significant "OTHER").....Just Like Us NIPers, My GOD Family HOPES fer the BEST (that Everyone Would LEARN About Them, BELIEVE in Them, and Take Respectful, Kind, and Courteous "Actions" Based on Those "Beliefs"), BUTT EXPECTS the WORST (that NO One Will Believe, and We'll All Act Like a Bunch of Heathens godLES Aetheists or Republicans/Democrats), and My GOD Family is PREPARED fer WHATEVER Might Come in Between. Can Ya Say the SAME fer Your God and Yer "CURRENT" Political Party of Choice??

Throughout History, EVERY Great EVIL was Opposed by Great GOOD….. Satan was Opposed by GOD….. Hitler's AXIS of EVIL was Opposed by the ALLIES of GOOD….. Communism' Principles of EVIL Were Opposed by Capitalism's Principles of GOOD….. AND….. the "NEW World ORDER" of EVIL (When it Rears It's UGLY Head of EVIL)…… WILL Be OPPOSED by My Little "NIPers"….. the NEW Inedpendence Party (NIPer) Thinkers/Members of THIS GREAT GOD-Fearin' Nation of OURS!!!

If Ya've Made it This Far with Us, Then We Haven't YET Pissed Off EVERY Single AMERICAN Out There (BUTT I've Done My BEST to TRY). I HOPE that I Have CHALLENGED Yer Beliefs, and SHAKEN Yer Faith, and ROCKED Yer Boat, and UPSET Yer Apple Cart, AND Made Ya Question Yer LOYALTY to Yer CURRENT Political Party and to This GREAT UNITED STATES of AMERICA Country of OURS......etc......Etc......ETC..... If 'n "Right" Now Y'all Have Jest a Little "Bit" "Left" in Ya...There's Jest One MORE Chapter ta Go……

Did THAT Crap Make ANY Sense to Y'all on Page 152, or Am I JEST Funnin' Ya.....YOU Decide!!!

Chapter 66

And FINALLY (Thank GOoDness), "WHERE" Do We GO from "HERE" ???

As USUAL I am VERRY Impressed with Y'alls Grasp of the Esoteric......HOG WASH !!! Y'all Are The SAME Damned IDOITS Who've Been with Me Since Chapter ONE.....Y'all Cain't Fool THIS Old Fart with'n Yer HOT AIR Spoutin' from the Anal Orafice.... I MAY Have Been Born in the Afternoon, BUTT It Weren't YESTERDAY Afternoon. I Been on This Here Planet Fer Nigh onta 60 Years And I've Done a HEEP a LIVIN' in That Time. I Ain't Got a LOT ta Show Fer it in MONEY, FAME, or MATERIAL POSSESSIONS.....BUTT.....I DO Have a HEEP of "Wild" Actions of This Tired Old Decrepit BODY, "Outragious" and "Outlandish" Seemin' "Opinions" of My Mind/SOUL, AND Don't Ya DARE Fergit The "Wonderousness" of My Heart/SPIRIT......"WOOOW" !!! Fer Those of Ya Who STILL Don't KNOW Me and DON'T Have a "CLUE", That Was... "Wild", "Outragious" ,"Outlandish", "Opinions", and "Wonderousness" = "WOOOW"......DAMN......If'n I Got's ta Explain EVERY Dad Burned Thing to Ya, Yer NEVER Gonna Have a Happy LIFE......Figger it Out Yer OWN Dad Gummed SELF.......

Goin' BACK ta Chapter One.......Let's Review Whacha Larned......If'n Ya Wanna Know What's "Right" or "Wrong" with AMERICA.....Look in a MIRROR......Did the Person Ya See Lookin' BACK at Ya Find Any "VALUE" in This Little "Baby" of Mine?.....Did That Person "Pay That Value Forward" ta Their Family, Friends, And/Or Co-Workers??.....Did That Person Even Bother ta Send a Little "Bit" a Somethin' (Or Maybe Even 2 "Bits"= a Quarter) ta P.O. Box 2149, Tuskegee, AL 36083 in Return (ta Help Take Care of My Wife in the FEW Years She Will Have "LEFT" "RIGHT" Here on This Planet, After the Shot That Takes My LIFE....."Cause Ya KNOW That My GOD Made Me DO This and That's REALLY Gonna PISS OFF That Thar "OTHER Guy". He Cain't Afford ta Let Me LIVE......AND He Cain't Afford ta Martyr Me EITHER....What a Pickle.....

IF'n Y'all Ain't Figgered Out By NOW That We NIPers Like ta Deal in Threes (Trinity's) Then Yer HOPELESS, BUTT as "Partin' Shots, ! ! ! ", I'm a Gonna Give Y'all Three (Count 'em.....Three) Slightly "Different" Endin's ta My "Baby" (Book) ta Choose from:

1. If'n Ya Don't "LIKE" Any a This CRAP.....Then Take a "LOONNGGGG" Walk Off'n a "shrt" Peir, Pound Beach Sand UP Yer ASSanine Anal Orifice, and THEN GO Git YerSelf a "10 Cent Screw" (And Stick it UP There with the Beach Sand "Where the Sun Don't Shine") !!!

2. I Was On "DRUGS" (Fer a Cold and Flu and This Damned Swellin' in My Feet and Ankles) And Didn't KNOW What I Was a Doin' (MOST a the TIME), And I Believe That This WHOLE Book is JEST a "Pigment" of My "Rosy Colored" Immagination, AND That YOU (Dear Readers) ALSO Are JEST "FigNeutons" of My "Warped" (as in "Warp Speed") and "Twisted" (as in "Twisted Sister") HyperBolic (Where the HELL Did THAT Come from....Oh Yeah....the "DRUGS") Imagination.

3.   It is MY (and the NEW Independence Party's) HOPE that EACH of Y'all (Who Made it This Far) Found SOMETHING that Y'all Could "Take with Ya".

We HOPE that Y'all Will at Least CONSIDER Voting fer Ms Sarah Palin and Mr Herman Cain fer President and Vice-President (Respectively) on the NEW Independence Party (NIPer) "WRITE-IN" Campaign Ticket in the Nov 2016 Elections.

We ALSO HOPE that We Have Given Each of Ya JEST a "Bit" (or "Byte" in the ASS) of Worthless Information and a Little Inspiration that Y'all Can USE ta "Improve" (AssUMen' Ya GOT'S One) the Personal and Private Relationship Between YOU and Yer God (Exceptin' Fer Y'all GOD DAMNED godLESS Atheists).....BUTT If'n We Haven't, We Would Like ta Leave Ya with This FINAL Thought.....

Please, Please, PLEASE.......Before Ya Do ANYTHING Else.....Review YOUR God's (WhoEVER That God May BE) Version of the "User's Guide and Maintenance Manual for a Human Life" from Cover to Cover and Ask YerSelf the Following Question.........

Does ANY of This CRAP Make SENSE to Ya, OR Am I Jest FUNNIN' Ya......YOU DECIDE!!!

"Bye, Bye fer Now. Y'all Take Care of Each Other Out There. Don't Be Doin' TOO Much Fussin' and Feudin'. Be KIND to Each Other, AND "Above it All".......GOD BLESS AMERICA!!! as Quoted from the Collected Wit, Wisdom, and Outlandish Opinions of A. L. Nolram, the Bombastic and Beaudacious (YES, I DID MISSpell "Bodacious" on Purpose) Mouth-of-the-South (AND Curmudgeon at Large) from Beauregard, ALabama on www.YouTube.com

If You Have Found Any "VALUE" fer Yer LIFE (Miserable Though it May BE fer the NEXT FOUR YEARS) Between the Covers of This Book (OR The "Top" and the "Bottom" If'n Yer Readin' the "Electronic" Version), Y'all MAY Send Donations fer the NEW Independence Party (NIPer) Activities or Contributions fer the "BIG AL's Future Book Project Retirement Fund" to:

P. O. Box 2149, Tuskegee, AL 36083

Because If'n Ya DON'T, the SHAME, GUILT, and UNWORTHINESS (SGU) Will "GIT" t' Y'ALL.... AND If'n it DON'T...Then "SGU" YOU TOO....AND MY GOD's Gonna "GIT" Ya Fer THAT !!!!!!!

BBBUUUUUTTTTTTTT (And "THAT" is the "BIGGEST" BBBUUUUUTTTTTTTT of ALLLLL.... "BIG AL" KNOWS That SOME of Y'all Cain't Even AFFORD ta Send Me a "Single Penny" (Even Though Y'all Would "LIKE" to...) Because Ya NEED That Money ta Feed, Clothe, and House Yer KIDs, And I Don't WANT Yer Money........BUTT....Here's Something That ANY of Ya CAN Do Fer

"ME" That is Even MORE "Precious" ta ME Than "Gold-Pressed Latinum", BUTT Won't Cost Y'all NUTHIN' Exceptin' a Little Time and Effort……PRAY ta YOUR God (Whoever THAT May Be) ta "BLESS" Me, My "Family" (at Least Those a Them Who are NOT Tryin' t' Have Me Committed t' a "Mental Institution"), My "Friends" ("Fair Weather" and "Fowl"….Flyin' South Fer the Winter), My Co-Workers (Who Will ONLY Miss Me When I'm GONE……and They Figger Out JEST How MUCH I DID and HOW Much Work is Gonna Be ADDed ta Their Workload, 'Cause I'm NOT There t' DO it), AND Anyone ELSE Who Believed in Me (Few), Encouraged Me (Far Between), or "INSPIRED" Me (Only MY GOD)!!!

For MORE "FUN Stuff" from the NEW Independence Party (NIPers), The "Purple Pit-Bulls fer Palin AND ValleyGirl Violet Cantancerous Canines fer Cain" Please Visit Our WebSites:

www.GoNIPer.com

www.GoNIPer.org

Did THAT Crap Make ANY Sense ta Y'all on Pages 153-155, or Am I JEST Funnin' Ya, YOU Decide!!!

Marketing Plans

1. Fight Tooth and Nail with the Editors to Maintain my "Unique" Method of "CaPiTaLiZaTiOn", "PUNC?UA?!ON", And "GRAMMAR" (GOD Rest Her "Ornery" SOUL)

2. Print in 8.5 x 11 inch Oversize with Large Font ("Times New Roman 11 Pitch) to ensure that Sight Impaired can Read. Put CD Sleeves inside of Front and Back Covers (for Companion CDs, Read by Me in My "Unique" and "Unorthodox" Style).

3. Start with Paperback? If Good Response, Release in Leather or Simulated Leather with Embossed Lettering, so that "….YOU Decide" is of Similar Quality to "The User's Guide and Maintenance Manual for a Human Life" itself. Covers Should be Solid Black with White Letters that Either Shine, Shimmer, and/or Glow in the Dark.

4. Send Free Copies to All Talk Show Hosts, Fox News Major Players, and Other Celebrities to incite Chatter (BUT ESPECIALLY to ANYONE who Helps Me Improve My Little "Baby" with Their Comments and Criticism).

5. Release AudioBooks on Cassette Tape and CD Read by Author with "Easter Eggs" and Running Comentary So Those Who "Bought" the Book Would ALSO Want to "Buy" the CD/DVD. Retain Option to Release on DVD as Performed Before a Live Audience.

6. Refuse Exclusive Interviews. Allow ANYONE to Interview, Provided They Ask Respectfully, Kindly, and Courteously (RKC). Donate Proceeds of Interviews to a Charity to be Determined at Time of Interview??

7. Setup WebSite to Promote Book and Provide Supporting Contents, and ALSO to Promote NIPers and Future Projects. Be Prepared for Controversy and Bombardment. (See WebSite Thoughts)

8. If 1st Book "Sells" Fairly Well and Generates an Audience, Along with the Internet Junkies Pulled in by the WebSite, Use Proceeds to Fund "Future Projects".

9. Offer to Participate in Events like "American Idol" (Enough of These "Flash in the Pan" Youngsters…..It's Time for a "NEW" Yet More "Mature" American Idol) and "Dancing with the Stars" (and Try to Incorporate SquareDance, RoundDance, and Clogging Elements into the Routines to Promote These Healthful Folk Dances to the American Public) as Alternate Publicity Opportunities.

10. Consider eBooks and Ways of Linking from Them to WebSite and Supporting Documentation. Consider PayPal for Financing and Donations.

11. Distribute Book to Family, Friends, and Coworkers for "Review" and HOPE that They "Share" Book and www.YouTube.com Videos with Friends, Family, and Co-Workers, Worst Enemy or Mother-Out-Law (UNLess Last 2 = SAME Person)

12. Secure Copyrights to Individual "Slogans" as Well as Entire Book in Anticipation of "Anciliary" Sales (Caps, T-Shirts, Beach Towels, Coffee/Tea Mugs, Pens, Pencils, NIPer Campaign Buttons, Bumper Stickers, Banners, Lawn Signs, Neckties, Bowties, "Boater" Style Hats, Pennants, etc…Etc…ETC…

13. Distribute Book "Free of Charge…Free of CHARGE…..LORD GOD ALMIGHTY it's…….FREE OF CHARGE !!!" via FOX Network?? NPR/NPB, or Oprah Network ?? Ask for Donations Based on NIPer Policy Slogan of "Value for Value" and "GOD Will Provide" (Sometimes Through "Others") Recheck www.YouTube.com Videos for the Donation Request (MOVIE Rights?????)

Working Phrase / Brainstorming List (So I Don't Forget):

Everything is Changed from Stem ta Stern and from "HEAD" Wind ta "POOP" Deck

Mind Like a Steel Trap..... Don't Get Your Foot Caught in it

Mouth Like a Steel Trap....Have to Surgically Extract My Foot Sometimes

Slippery Slide Ride to Hell.....Long, Hard, Steep Climb to Heaven

BS on Top of RKC for SOUL (Don't Try This at HOME on RKC for BODY)

Any Time "Right" is Used Associate with Repubs to Knock 'em Down a Peg

Constantly Use "Right" in Connection with Left Dems to Balance Back to Center

Promotions for Investments:

       Dr Pepper, RKC, FOX Network, NPR/NPB,

       Books by: Christopher Paolini, J. K. Rowling, Terry Goodkind, Robert Heinlein, Rick Riordan, Terry Brooks,

Don't Count Out Foreign Contributions....Their Leaders have to Work with Ours...Vested Interest

Keep Up with Current Events via FOX Network to Keep Book Contents Current and Relevant

CONSTANT VIGILANCE.....CONSTANT IMPROVEMENT....CONSTANT STANDARD of EXCELLENCE !!!

Stay Humble......Wife Will Keep Me Grounded through Constant Disbelief....Believe Her...Not THEM

Be Patient.....All Things, Even Waiting Patiently... Work Together for GOOD to Those Called

Reflect in a Mirror Every Day......Do WHATEVER You have to DO to Get MY Message Through!!!

Constantly Associate EVERYTHING Good with the NIPers and ALL Else to Them "OTHERS"

Constantly Associate Values, Principles, and Standards (VPS) from UGMMHL to the NIPers

Keep it "Light".....Humor is the KEY....Hide the Info/Inspiration Bomb....Belly Laugh= Explosion

Leave them Laughing So that You are Gone Before They Know You've Stung Their Soul

They Shouldn't See the Brain Slap Coming, but SOME Will.....Be Sure to Give Them Something Special

Build Mole Hills of NIPers into Mountain....Landslide/Avalanch into the White House

It's Not the Destination....Its the Journey....Convince to Take 50 State Tour Whether Win or Loose

NIPers NOT North or South, East or West, Left or Right, Top or Bottom......Born in Heartland of USA

Beauregard Magic Place.....Show Now You See it...Now You Don't Trick with iPad

EnSure BassAkerds Magic Trick is Revealed in Dramatic Way at Dramatic Time.....Prep Family and Friends

Work on Logo (Sign of the Trinity).....Associate with NEW Trinity Psychological Model

Always be Prepared to Make Sense Out of Nonsence.....Lemonade out of Lemons

ALWAYS Make Sense.....They will Eventually Come Around.....Backup Plan...Learn Mandarin Chinese

Remember, Even If Loose Job, GOD Will Provide.......As Long as You Stay Focused on HIS Goal

Be Prepared for the 15 Minutes of Fame.......to Stretch the Opportunity into a Lifetime

Be Prepared for Setbacks and Road Blocks by those Damn Little Gremlin Demons

Substitute Every Occurrence of "Ancient Aliens" with "Angelic/Celestial Beings" and See if Still True

Remember this is the Devil's 2000 Years to Prove that He can Run the World Better with Greed, Avarice, and Graft (GAG) better than CHRIST can Rule the World in Millennium with Truth, Love, & Charity (TLC) or Instead of GAG Use Lies, Avarice, and Welfair (LAW ??)

Give NIPer Timeline for Rapture and Armageddon (Check Derrick's Info on Birth in 5 B.C.)...there's Time

Set Up ᶦSeparate Accounts When (IF ??) Money Comes in for NIPers and BIG AL to Preserve and Protect

Invest in Commodities.......Money in the Bank = Bits in a Bucket.....When Technology Falls...so Does it

Locate "Survivor/Doomsday Prepper" Sites, Barter Sights, DIY Sites, Back to Basics Sites, etc

Use NIPer Funds for Political Solution.....Use BIG AL Funds to Get That Land in Western Nebraska....Low Population...Good for Crops and Livestock...Fairly Flat and Easy to Defend.....Hone Skills to be able to Make Own Crossbow and Bolts

Hone and Enhance Basic Skills in Woodworking, Blacksmithing, Stone Masonry, Canning, Agriculture

Train "Big Baby" to Pull Cart, Plow, etc. Check with Amish during 50 State Campaign Tour

Get Current Maps of Each State to Plan Route to Avoid Devastated Cities in Future

Study Up on Blog Technology to Use Most Effectively and Efficiently until Technology Collapses

Keep Eyes and Ears WIDE Open During 50 State Campaign....Look for Innovations and Gets BluePrints

Remember You Need the BEST Processes and NOT Just the BEST Products.....They Work Together when Combined with the BEST Minds.......Leadership= People Do the Work.....NEED MANY MORE NIPers

Watch for the "Signs" (like the Meeting on 13 Dec 2011, at 1300) Told to Substitute Herman Cain for Me

Sarah Palin, Herman Cain and I Form the Basic NIPer Trinity……Work it into Everything

Refute Tim's View that SP, HC and Core Constituency are OUT of MY LEAGUE:

> All Started Out as Squallin' Brats who Peed their Britches and Crapped their Pants

> Made Different Life Choices by SAME Princ, Stand, Values, and Precep

> Wouldn't be at the NEXUS (Critical Turning Point) if Anything Happened Differently

> Only OUT of LEAGUE if One or Other DECIDES So…….Y'all DECIDE!!!   Convince Them

Prep for Publicity and PooperRatsy who Try to Catch Wife in Shower or Compromising Situation

Check and Perform Regular Maintenance on 9mm Automatic, 40 Cal Auto, 410 Shotgun and Practice More with Crossbow (Extra Ammo for ALL, Especially Crossbow…..SBD…..Least Technology)

Remember to Get Colin Powel on Board with Military Strategy and Tactics (+ SUPER-Secret List)

Acquire Funds for 13 Bomb-Bustin' Busses (go to Manufacturer with Security/Comfort Improve)

Today= "Ask NOT what You can Do for Your Country, but What Your Country can Give You"

Rocket Ships Didn't Get Us to the Moon, "Ask Not What….." Got Us to the Moon, If We Want to Get ANYWHERE in this Country, We Need to Get Back to JFK's Mindset

Did JFKs Princ, Stad, Values, and Princ Die WITH Him??   Will Mine?????????

Mates (RM +RW) Persecute Each Other (God Only Out)

Every Relig is Correct (for You) (Diet Plan, Gods Plan

Barney Miller Morn/Eve Shower

Solumn Duty, Sacred Honor, Praise to Lord

Only Deaf Understand Abs Silent

MLK Free at Last American African

Book of Eli Will have ability to complete task

Trinity Model Who's on Top?

PaperLess Environment= ALL Electronic=Easier to Destroy in an Instant

We NIPers Think Nancy Grace is a DEB (Demonic Evil Bitch)

If You Don't Believe in GOD, Then HE Doesn't Exist (for YOU).....The SAME for the NIPers

Belief of the Heart/Spirit Drives Decisions of the Mind/Soul Drives Actions of the Body

If You Want to Change Actions (Murder, Rape, Child Molest), Change Beliefs or DisArm

To Disarm Criminals , Kill Body and Send Soul to GOD for Disposition (Capital Punishment)

Lt Adkins: Press the Flesh and NCOs are Devious and Bare Watchng

Capt ??: Recommended to Buy MicroSoft (Kick Self in BUTT Several Times(

What IF Mental Illness (BiPolar, Manic/Depress, Paranoid/Scitz = GOD + SATAN Tug of War

To Win War, Kill All until All Dead or Until Ones Left Unconditionally Surrender (See WWII)

After Beaten UnMercifully, Give Hand UP, Dust Off, and Handshake (Japan, Germany)

Where is the President's Council on Physical Fitness Today?????   I Remember Fitness Tests in Dist 38

Senator Crapo arrested for DUI (Shudda Known)

Two Kinds of Folks: True/False (Right/Wrong) and Multiple Choice (Good, Better, Best)

How Do We Turn Welfare Back to Charity without Throwing Out the Baby with the Bathwater

Shame, Guilt, and UNWorthiness ("SGU" YOU TOO!!!)

Will Herman Cain's Tax Plan of 9-9-9 be Enough for the Changes the NIPers NEED to Make

Dentist Dr Lee 2 Jan 2013 1000 Cleanin' Appointment for Renee' (Set in Watch and Remind Her)

Blue "Water Pills" Make Ya "PEE Green Soup or Pea Green Soup" AZOs Make Ya Pee Bright Orange

The "BIG AL" Nolram Shipin' Co "We Pick 'em, Pack 'em, Ship 'em & Git 'em TO Ya" (Escape Claws)

Like Forrressttt....Forrressttt GUMP (Tom Hanks) I Think I'm DONE Runnin' (My Mouth) Now...

Call Dr Lee about Being a Corporate Sponsor for My Book/Videos

Try to Speak to Chamber of Commerce to Get MANY Corporate Sponsors for Book/Videos

Fix Tiff with Ms Rita by Wanglin' a Invite ta "Church" BUTT ONLY If'n "BIG AL" is Invited TOO

Need a Third (to be a Trinity) of Media Types: 1) FOX Network, 2) NPR/NPB, 3) Oprah ???

Need to Research How ta Git ta Oprah Winfrey and HER Media Capabilities

Tell that "ABSOLUTE SILENCE" is Also Needed for Opening Prayer at Each NIPer Meeting/Event

Heed to Develop Third (Trinity) Reason for the "ABSOLUTE SILENCE" Honoration (Sandy Hook Kids ???)

Sandy Hook Kids OK for NOW (because it's Current) BUTT Need to Broaden to "Others" (911, Columbine, Cancer Kids, Military Active/Retired/Deceased, Past "Leaders": JFK, MLK, FDR , (All are 3 Letter Folks ???)

Associate with JFK and MLK and BAN ("Big AL"), 2 Got Shot and VPS Died with Them (Don't Let it)

Our Living Room Closet is One of Those "Don't Open that Door McGee !!!" Types "Fibber McGee&Molly"

If CHRIST Had a "Perfect" Body, is it a "Downs Syndrome" Body ??? (Super STRONG + Super LOVE)

We NIPers Make the HARD Stuff Liik Easy....It's Jest the Impossible Stuff that Takes a Wee Bit Longer

I Mix My Metaphors, I Shuffle MY Similies, I Pervert My Punctuation ,and I Catastrophize My Capitalization, Along with Causin' My Grammar t' Spin Like a Pin Wheel in Her Grave

How Exactly Do You Change the Entire Thought Process of a HardHeaded Nation Like Ours, before it's Too Late??

These Actually May Make GOOD Questions for a Follow Up Book instead of "EXTRA Ordinary Life" Check with Editor Once You Select One (Remember to Stay LOYAL, Monogamous Relationship)

How Do I Convince VA Leadership that MY Plan for Training My Replacement is the BEST??

Give 'em 3 "Alt" Endings ta Chapt 66... 1) Good , 2) BETTER , and 3) "BEST" the "Current" One

Like This Show "Rick's Restorations" Where They Said "Lighten UP Bro and Git Some "Purple" in Yer Life, and Make Some "Changes"

Play with "a Stable in Beauregard" vs 'a Stable in Bethlehem" Fer a Bit

"NEW" Title "Does ANY a This CRAP Make SENSE ta Ya, OR Am I Jest FUNNIN' Ya.....YOU DECIDE!!!"

I Think That Will DO for Now.......

Sent ta FOX Network Shortly After the Sandy Hook School Massacre:

With the Nation in a State of Grief, You Would Think that Now Would NOT be the Time for Political Satire, BUTT If You Find Value in the Collected Wit, Wisdom, and Outlandish Opinions of A. L. "BIG AL" Nolram on YouTube, Then You MAY Want to Request a Current (as Yet Unfinished) Copy of "Does ANY of This Make Sense ta Ya, or am I Jest Funnin' Ya...YOU DECIDE !!!" from ALNolram@aol.com

_____

Changes as of: 21 Dec 2012:

      Additions: Chapters 50, 51, 54, 55, 56

      Significant Modifications: Chapters 5, 8,

Changes as of: 22 Dec 2012

      Additions: Chapters 46, 49, 52,

      Significant Modifications: Chapters 5, and Marketing Plans (And ALWAYS BrainStorming List)

            Such as: PaperLess Environment= ALL Electronic=Easier to Destroy in an Instant

Changes as of: 24 Dec 2012

      Additions: Chapters (No NEW Ones This Time, Been Busy Politicin' and CHRISTmasin' Just.....)

      Significant Modifications: Chapters 3, 53, and Marketing Plans (And ALWAYS BrainStorming List)

Changes as of: 25 Dec 2012

      Additions: Chapters 48, (I Took it a Little Easy Today Bein' CHRISTs Birthday....BUTT... I Didn't "Take It Easy on "FOX Network"...... Check it OUT.....and Be WARNED.....DON'T IGNORE My E-MAILs !!!)

      Significant Modifications: Chapters 51, 53, 65, 66 and Marketing Plans (And ALWAYS BrainStorming List)

Changes as of: 27 Dec 2012

Sorry about That Dear Readers, BUTT My Wife Caught Me a Workin' on My "Baby" on HER Time and I Had ta Make it UP ta Her (So's the Dog Can Git a Good Night's Sleep ALONE Fer a Change), BUTT We're "Back on Track" (WOW !!!.....I'm a Poet and Don't Even Know It)

Additions: Chapter(s) 3 (I Think I MIGHT be Done Twaekin' This One....Ir's a DOOZY as IS), Corporate and Individual Sponsors Pages Between Title Page and Table of Contents, (If'n Ya WANT Yer Names or Advertisin' Here Ya Have ta Send Me an E-Mail and SAY So......Otherwise I'll Jest Treat Ya Like the "Silent Majority" and Keep Hammerin' at Ya Until Ya Give IN)

Significant Modifications: Chapter(s) Title Page (Added "Curmudgeon at Large") and Marketing Plans (And ALWAYS BrainStorming List) (I'm SERIOUS Folks......the "BrainStormin' List" is Were I Jot Down My "Thought of the Moment"..... And USUALLY NOT at the "End of the List"......and Then Develop it inta a FULL Blown "Brain Slap" at My Convenience)

The Additions and Modifications Will be a Little Sparse Over the Holidays Here Since I Promised Renee' that I Would Put a Concerted Effort on Helpin' Her Clean the House and Make it at Least "Presentable" Enough that She Won't Cry Herself ta Sleep at Night for the "Shame" of NOT Bein' Able ta Invite Friends and Family Over. I'm Gonna Take a Few "BEFORE" Pictures with My iPad 2, So's Ya KNOW What I'm a Talkin' about When Ya Come Over Fer My Little "Baby"s Comin OUT Party, OTHERWISE Y'all Would Jest Think I Was a Pullin' Yer Leg.

Have FUN with Yer Friends and Families Over the Holidays, Because When the NEW Year (2013, My "LUCKy" Year) Starts.........I'm Gonna Be Goin' FULL "BORE" (Ya Know.....Kindly a Like "Boring"......BUTT BIGGER.......Like the "BORE" of a BIG "LOOSE CANNON".........."BANG ! !".......Tht's Three "Bangs" by the Way........"!" is Called a "Bang" TOO.....HELL.....If'n I Got's ta Explain EVERYTHING to Ya, It Jest RUINS the EFFECT !!!)

Changes as of: 28 Dec 2012

Additions: Chapter(s) 25. 42, 43,

Significant Modifications: Chapter(s) 1, 2, 3 and Marketing Plans (And ALWAYS BrainStorming List)

Renee' Is a Complainin' About "BIG AL" Bookin' it on "HER" Time Again, So I Gots ta Go Clean, BUTT I Jest Got's ta Say That These Changes are My BEST Yet.......YOU DECIDE !!!

Changes as of: 29 Dec 2012

Additions: Chapter(s) 18, 26,   (Be CAREFUL....There's Some Pretty Powerful Stuff Here)

Significant Modifications: Chapter(s) ?? and Marketing Plans (And ALWAYS BrainStorming List)

Changes as of: 30 Dec 2012

      Additions: Chapter(s) 19, 20,   (Be CAREFUL….There's Some Pretty Powerful Stuff Here Too)

      Significant Modifications: Chapter(s) ?? and Marketing Plans (And ALWAYS BrainStorming List)

ALSO, Dear Readers……I Double Checked and I Hadn't REALIZED Jest HOW Productive I Had Been Lately….. With Today's Additions, I Have 53 of 66 Chapters Rough Drafted Which Leaves…..You Guessed it….ONLY 13….My LUCKy NUMBER Chapters Left (or Right) ta GO…….Wish Me LUCK and I MAY Be Able ta FINISH Ny Little "Baby" By NEW YEARS EVE !!!!!

Changes as of: 1 Jan 2013   (Nope…..I Got Lazy and Didn't "Git 'er Done" in 2012, BUTT Watch OUT 2013 !!!)

      Additions: Chapter(s) 33, 35,   (Be CAREFUL….There's Some Pretty Powerful Stuff Here Too)

      Significant Modifications: Chapter(s) 24, 28-32, 36-38, 40-41 and "Corporate Sponsor" Page, Marketing Plans (And ALWAYS BrainStorming List)

Changes as of: 5 Jan 2013   (Nope…..I Got Lazy and Didn't "Git 'er Done" in 2012, BUTT Watch OUT 2013 !!!)

      Additions: Chapter(s) 29-31,

      Significant Modifications: Chapter(s) 1, .2, 3 (a Bit MORE "Pounce Fer the Once"….a Little Bit MORE "Punch with the Lunch" as I Munch and Chew Out "MASSA" President's ASSertions….This Should PISS Ya OFF Fer SURE….OR "FINALLY" Git Ya OFF'n Yer ASS and ON My Side…of the NIPers), 11, 12, 28, , 65, 66 and "Corporate Sponsor" Page, Marketing Plans (And ALWAYS BrainStorming List)

Changes as of: 8 Jan 2013

      Additions: Chapter(s) ALL a the REST a the Book (First Draft)

      Significant Modifications: Chapter(s) EVERY One INCLUDING the TITLE/COVER Page and Marketing Plans (And ALWAYS BrainStorming List)

Sent ta National Public Braodcasting (.org) Since FOX Network Ain't Been Answerin' My E-Mails:

A. L. "BIG AL"   Nolram   ALNolram@aol.com

Since FOX Network Don't Wanna Listen......Have I Gotta DEAL Fer YOU !!!!!

Ya Didn't Give Me Enough Room in that Little "Your NPR Station" Field ta Put, "WTSU-FM: 89.9 and WJSP-FM: 88.1, BUTT (There I am Showin' Ya My BIG BUTT Again) the GPR Staion is a WHOLE HEEP Better'n the APR Station" So's I Had ta Come BACK to This Field and Put it Here 'Cause It SHOULD Be Important ta Y'all ta KNOW That ONE a Yer Stations is a WHOLE HEEP Better'n One o' the Others....."Nuff Said....Movin' ON......

I'm Writin' a Little Book (Based on My www.YouTube.com Videos) Titled "Does ANY o' This Make SENSE ta Ya, or Am I Jest FUNNIN' Ya.....YOU DECIDE!!!" and I Jest Cain't Git Nobody ta Listen and Help Me Out......If'n Ya WANT ta "KNOW More" Then Send Yer Request ta Review My Book (as One o' My "Potential" Little NIPers...that's NEW Independence Party Thinkers or Members) to the E-Mail Address Above, OR If'n Ya WANT "No MORE" ta Do with This Little Old Fart from Beauregard, AL Jest Ignore Me Like EVERYBODY Else.......

Changes as of: 22 Dec 2012

          Additions: Chapters 46, 49, 52,

          Significant Modifications: Chapters 5, and Marketing Plans (And ALWAYS BrainStorming List)

                    Such as: PaperLess Environment= ALL Electronic=Easier to Destroy in an Instant

There's Some Pretty "Interestin' Stuff" in These Mods......I HOPE Y'all Enjoy Them......

from ALNolram@aol.com
M. P. Gosda, Executive Assistant for

A. L. "BIG AL" Nolram the Bombastic and Beaudacious Mouth-of-the-South from Beauregard, AL

"Bye Bye for Now. Take Care of Each Other Out There. Don't be Doin' Too Much Fussin' and Feudin'. Be KIND to Each Other, and Above IT All.....GOD BLESS AMERICA!!!" -- as Quoted from www.YouTube.com, the Collected Wit, Wisdom, and Outlandish Opinions of A. L. Nolram, the Bombastic and Beaudacious Mouth-of-the-South, from Beauregard, AL.

"The enlisted men, although stupid and oftentimes lazy, can be incredibly sly and cunning and bear considerable watching." This was supposedly from the US Army's Officer Handbook, ed. 1898 and Alleged to be a Quote from George Washington at Valley Forge. .

"BIG AL" .....It Ain't THAT Hard..... Danged !!!   (to Fill the Field "How to Pronounce Your Name")

I am TRYING to Get Someone (ANYONE) to View My www.YouTube.com Videos and Review My Book Titled "Does ANY of This Make SENSE ta Ya, or Am I Jest FUNNIN' Ya.....YOU DECIDE!!!" a Political and Religious Satire of Our Time, Under the Name of A. L. "BIG AL" Nolram, the Bombastic and Beaudacious Mouth-of-the-South (and Curmudgeon at Large) from Beauregard, AL. If You Would Like an Electronic Copy of the Book to Review or Can Offer ANY Advice or Assistance, Please Respond to ALNolram@aol.com.....Thanks and Have a Blessed Day.....Live WELL....Love MUCH.....And Especially.....Laugh OFTEN!!!
Since There's NOT Enough Room in the Field Below, My Stations are: WTSU-FM: 89.9 and WJSP-FM: 88.1,

Here's Some MORE "Usless" Things Yer NOT a Gonna "Appreciate" That I Have "Created", "Enhanced/Improved", And/or "Collected" Over the Last Several Years:

Attachment A = Anything and Everythimg

Attachment B = Biographical Pictorial Gallery

Attatchment C = "Crap" Shots (WHAT ELSE ?!?)

Grocery List

	Serving Size		Carb	Cal
	Unit	Qty		

Fruits (Fresh or Dried)

	Unit	Qty	Carb	Cal
Apple (Red / Green / Gala)	Each	1/4		
Apricots	Each	3		
Bananas	Each	1/2		
Blackberries	Each	5		
Blueberries	Each	5		
Boysenberries	Each	5		
Cantaloupe	Each	1/8		
Cherries	Each	5		
Chokecherries	Each	5		
Cranberries	Each	3		
Dates (Dried Only)	Each	3		
Grapes, Seedless (Red / Green)	Each	3		
Grapefruit (White)	Each	1/2		
Kiwi	Each	1/2		
Kumquat	Each	1		
Lemon	Each	1/4		
Lime	Each	1/4		
Mandarin Orange	Each	1/2		
Musk dines	Each	3		
Nectarine	Each	1/2		
Orange	Each	1/3		
Peach	Each	1/2		
Pear	Each	1/2		
Plum	Each	1		
Raisins	Each	10		
Raspberries	Each	5		
Scuppernongs	Each	3		
Star Fruit	Each	1/3		
Strawberries	Each	3		
Watermelon	Slice	1/4		

Vegetables

	Unit	Qty	Carb	Cal
Alfalfa Sprouts	Oz	1/2		
Artichoke	Oz	3		
Asparagus (Green / White)	Oz	6		
Beans (Green / Lima / Northern / Pinto / Various)	Oz	6		

	Unit	Qty	Carb	Cal
Bean Sprouts	Oz	1		
Broccoli	Oz	6		
Cabbage (Red / Green)	Oz	6		
Carrots	Oz	3		
Cauliflower	Oz	6		
Celery	Oz	6		

Vegetables (Cont)

	Unit	Qty	Carb	Cal
Corn (Ear / Kernel / Creamed)	Oz	4		
Cucumbers	Each	1/4		
Green Beans	Oz	4		
Lettuce (Iceberg / Romaine / Bibb)	Oz	4		
Leeks	Oz	1		
Okra	Oz	4		
Olives	Oz	1		
Onions (Green / Red / White)	Oz	1		
Peas (Blackeye / Early / Green / Snow)	Oz	4		
Peppers (Green / Red / Banana / Jalapeno)	Oz	1		
Potatoes (Red / Russet / Sweet / Instant)	Oz	6		
Spinach	Oz	4		
Squash	Oz	4		
Tomatoes (Large / Roma / Cherry)	Oz	6		
Radishes (Red / White)	Oz	2		
Water Chestnuts	Oz	2		
Zucchini	Oz	4		

Meats

Beef

	Unit	Qty	Carb	Cal
Brisket	Oz	6		
Franks	Oz	4		
Ground	Oz	8		
Patties	Oz	6		
Roast	Oz	8		
Steak	Oz	8		
Veal	Oz	8		

Bison

	Unit	Qty	Carb	Cal
Ground	Oz	6		

Chicken

	Unit	Qty	Carb	Cal
Breast	Each	1/2		
Legs/Thighs	Each	1		
Patties	Oz	6		
Tenders	Oz	8		

	Unit	Qty	Carb	Cal
Wings (Hot Sauce)	Oz	8		
Whole	Oz	6		
Fish				
Bass	Oz	6		
Catfish	Oz	8		
Cod	Oz	6		
Grouper	Oz	8		
Halibut	Oz	6		
Haddock	Oz	6		
Lobster	Oz	6		
Fish (Cont)				
Mackerel	Oz	6		
Salmon	Oz	8		
Sardines	Oz	6		
Shrimp	Each	7		
Tilapia	Oz	6		
Tuna	Oz	8		
Fowl				
Cornish Game Hens	Each	1/2		
Duck	Oz	6		
Goose	Oz	6		
Pheasant	Oz	6		
Quail	Each	1		
Turkey	Oz	6		
Pork				
Bacon (Thick Sliced)	Slice	4		
Chops	Each	1		
Cutlets	Oz	6		
Ground	Oz	6		
Ham	Oz	6		
Sausage	Oz	6		
Tenderloin	Oz	6		
Dairy				
Butter	Oz	1/2		
Cheese	Oz	2		
Cream	Oz	1		
Eggs (Brown / White)	Each	1		
DanActive	Each	1		
Ice Cream	Oz	4		

Grocery List

	Serving Size			
	Unit	Qty	Carb	Cal
Milk	Oz	8		
Sour Cream	Oz	1		
Yogurt	Oz	4		

Miscellaneous

Nuts

	Unit	Qty	Carb	Cal
Almond	Each	6		
Brazil Nuts	Each	2		
Cashew	Each	6		
Filbert	Each	4		
Hazel	Each	4		
Peanut (Cocktail / Redskin / Dry Roasted)	Each	8		
Pecan	Each	6		
Pine Nut	Each	8		
Pistachio	Each	6		
Walnut	Each	6		

Seeds

	Unit	Qty	Carb	Cal
Pumpkin	Each	10		
Sunflower	Each	10		

Processed

Breads

	Unit	Qty	Carb	Cal
Bagel	Each	1/2		
Black	Slice	1		
Cinnamon (Slice / Roll)	Each	1/2		
Corn Bread	Oz	4		
Croissants	Oz	4		
Dinner Rolls	Each	1		
English Muffins	Each	1/2		
Pancakes	Each	1		
Rye	Slice	1		
Waffles	Each	1		
Wheat	Slice	1		
White	Slice	1		

Cereals

	Unit	Qty	Carb	Cal
Cheerios (Regular / Honey Nut)	Oz	6		

	Unit	Qty	Carb	Cal
Corn Flakes	Oz	6		
Frosted Flakes	Oz	6		
Granola	Oz	4		
Grits	Oz	4		
Oatmeal	Oz	6		
Rice Krispies	Oz	6		

Crackers

	Unit	Qty	Carb	Cal
Cheezits (10 Each)	Oz	1		
Chicken Biscuit (6Each)	Oz	1		
Club (8 Each)	Oz	1		
Graham (1 Each)	Oz	1		
Oyster (8 Each)	Oz	1		
Ritz (6 Each)	Oz	1		
Soda/Saltine (6 Each)	Oz	1		
Townhouse (6 Each)	Oz	1		
Triscuit (6 Each)	Oz	1	20g	120
Wheat (6 Each)	Oz	1		

Dressings/Condiments

	Unit	Qty	Carb	Cal
Blue Cheese	Oz	1/2		
Catalina	Oz	1/2		
Catsup	Oz	1/2		
Cocktail Sauce	Oz	1/2		
French	Oz	1/2		
Herb	Oz	1/2		
Horseradish	Oz	1/2		
Horsey Sauce	Oz	1/2		
House	Oz	1/2		
Italian (Oil / Creamy)	Oz	1/2		
Ketchup	Oz	1/2		
Mayonnaise	Oz	1/2		
Mustard	Oz	1/2		
Ranch	Oz	1/2		
Tartar Sauce	Oz	1/2		

Pasta

	Unit	Qty	Carb	Cal
Egg Noodles	Oz	6		
Lasagna	Oz	8		
Macaroni	Oz	6		
Pizza	Oz	8		

Grocery List

	Serving Size			
	Unit	Qty	Carb	Cal
Ravioli	Oz	6		
Spaghetti	Oz	8		

Desserts

	Unit	Qty	Carb	Cal
Brownies (Cake / Fudge)	Oz	4		
Cake/Cupcakes				
Angel Food	Oz	4		
Carrot	Oz	6		

Cake/Cupcakes (Cont)

	Unit	Qty	Carb	Cal
Cheesecake	Oz	6		
Chocolate	Oz	6		
Devils Food	Oz	6		
German Chocolate	Oz	6		
Pound	Oz	6		
Red Velvet	Oz	6		
Short/Sponge Cake	Oz	4		
Spice	Oz	6		
White	Oz	6		
Yellow	Oz	6		

Candy

	Unit	Qty	Carb	Cal
3 Musketeers	Each	1/2	23g	130
Almond Joy	Each	1/2		
Baby Ruth	Each	1/2		
Kit Kat	Each	1/2		
M&Ms (Almond / Dark / Plain / Peanut)	Each	5		
Mars Bar	Each	1/2		
Peppermints	Each	2		
Reese's	Each	1		
Salted Nut Roll	Each	1/2	14g	120
Snickers (Regular / Fudge)	Each	1/2	18/16g	140/25
Tootsie Rolls (Small)	Each	1		
Werther's Original	Each	2		

Cookies

	Unit	Qty	Carb	Cal
Butter	Each	2		
Chocolate Chip	Each	2		
Oatmeal	Each	2		

	Unit	Qty	Carb	Cal
Oreos	Each	2		
Peanut Butter	Each	2		
Peanut Butter Sandwich (GS Do-Si-Dos)	Each	2		
Peanut Butter + Chocolate (GS Tagalongs)	Each	2		
Pecan	Each	2		
Shortbread (GS Tyrols)	Each	2		
Sugar	Each	2		

Doughnuts (Powdered Sugar / Chocolate / Crullers / Glazed / Holes)   DON'T EVEN ASK!!!

Jello/Pudding

	Unit	Qty	Carb	Cal
Fruit Flavored	Oz	4		
Chocolate	Oz	4		
Vanilla	Oz	4		

Pies

	Unit	Qty	Carb	Cal
Apple	Oz	4		
Blackberry	Oz	4		
Blueberry	Oz	4		
Boysenberry	Oz	4		
Cherry	Oz	4		
Key Lime	Oz	4		
Mince	Oz	4		
Peach	Oz	4		
Pecan	Oz	4		
Pecan Tassies	Each	2		
Pumpkin	Oz	4		
Raspberry	Oz	4		

Drinks

	Unit	Qty	Carb	Cal
Beer (Ice / Lite / Regular / Tap)	Oz	12		
Champagne	Oz	8		
Coffee	Oz	12		
Fruit Juice (Apple / Cranberry / Grape / Grapefruit)	Oz	12		
Ginger Ale	Oz	12		
Liquor	Oz	1		
Soda (Cola / Lemon-Lime / Orange / Root Beer)	Oz	12		
Tea (Black / Green / Herb)	Oz	12		
Vegetable Juice (Carrot / Tomato / V8)	Oz	12		
Water (Lemon / Vinegar)	Oz	12		
Wine (Red / Rosé / Port / White)	Oz	8		

HORSE SUPPLIES
[ ] Breast Collar & Crupper
[ ] Bridle w/Reins
[ ] Buckets (Feed/Water)
[ ] Brushes
[ ] Clean Rags
[ ] Electrolytes
[ ] Farrier Tools
[ ] Fly Spray
[ ] Girth
[ ] Spurs
[ ] Whip/Quirt
[ ] Grain & Grain Scoop
[ ] Hay
[ ] Hay Bags or Hay Net
[ ] Hoof Pick
[ ] Water Barrel
[ ] Lead Rope(s)
[ ] Lounge Line(s)
[ ] Manure Fork, Rake, Shovel, Broom
[ ] Rain Sheet & Blanket(s)
[ ] Reins
[ ] Red Ribbon
[ ] Saddle
[ ] Saddle Bags/Pommel Bags
[ ] Saddle Pad/Blanket(s)
[ ] Shampoo, Sponges, Sweat Scraper
[ ] Shipping Boots or Wraps

SPARE PARTS & REPAIR SUPPLIES
[ ] Clips / Snaps / Rings
[ ] Duct Tape
[ ] Girth (extra)
[ ] Halter (extra)
[ ] Leather Thongs
[ ] Reins (extra)
[ ] Saddle Soap/Leather Conditioner
[ ] Rope/Twine/Wire
[ ] Leather Punch

FOOD & SUPPLIES
[ ] Aluminum Foil
[ ] Sharp Knife
[ ] Scissors
[ ] Condiments
[ ] Cooking Utensils
[ ] Cooler & Ice
[ ] Drinks/Milk/Juice/Sports Drinks
[ ] Food for all Meals
[ ] Fruit
[ ] Matches / Lighter
[ ] Paper Cups, Plates, Bowls[ ]
[ ] Snack Items
[ ] Plastic Utensils
[ ] Propane Stove
[ ] Stove Fuel

TAKE ON TRAIL
[ ] P&R Fan

PERSONAL SUPPLIES
[ ] Alarm Clock
[ ] Deodorant, Shaving Gear, Soap
[ ] Hair Brush / Comb / Shampoo
[ ] Boots (extra pair of shoes)
[ ] Insect Repellent
[ ] Jacket/Sweatshirt/Sweater
[ ] Dirty Cloths Bag
[ ] Electrolytes
[ ] Jeans/Shorts
[ ] Long Johns/Silk Underware
[ ] Lotion, Chapstick
[ ] Medications, Poison Ivy Cream
[ ] Mud Boots
[ ] Pencils, Notepad, Permanent Marker
[ ] Reading Material
[ ] Rain Gear
[ ] Riding Boots/Mud Boots/Shoes (extra)
[ ] Riding Pants
[ ] Shirts/T-Shirts/Tank Tops
[ ] Socks
[ ] Sun-Block
[ ] Wash Cloth & Towel
[ ] Tissue, Toilet Paper
[ ] Toothbrush & Toothpaste
[ ] Tweezers
[ ] Underwear
[ ] Warm Hat & Gloves

CAMPING SUPPLIES
[ ] Batteries
[ ] Cot/Sleeping Pad
[ ] Hatchet/Hammer
[ ] Towels
[ ] Lantern & Fuel
[ ] Pillow(s) & Sleeping Bag
[ ] Propane
[ ] Tent, Tent Pegs
[ ] Trash Bags
[ ] Waterproof Tarp
[ ] Cook Stove & Fuel
[ ] Camping Chairs / Table

WITHIN EASY REACH
[ ] Coggins Papers (Original)
[ ] Health Certificate
[ ] Registration Papers (Copy)
[ ] Cell Phone
[ ] Camera
[ ] Directions and Maps
[ ] Flashlight / Batteries
[ ] Head Lamp / Batteries
[ ] Weather Radio

TRAILER SUPPLIES
[ ] Battery Chargers (camera, cell phone)
[ ] Fire Extinguisher
[ ] Trailer Ties
[ ] First Aid Kits for Human & Equine
[ ] Extension Cord

An EXTRA Ordinary Life

An Extrordinay Novel

Chapter One

The Beginning

I was born at 3 AM on the 29th day of October, 1954, in Grand Island, Nebraska after 18 hours of labor. I always use the excuse for my proclivity for procrastination that I was born running late and I haven't caught up yet, although that doesn't quite account for all of the seemingly extraordinarily ordinary (or ordinarily extraordinary) events in my unique and still evolving life.

The first memory that I can recall (age unknown) was of my new brother producing a Golden Fountain on the hardwood living room floor of our small 3 bedroom Broadwell Blvd home. My mother was changing his diaper on the living room sofa and the instant that the cool air hit his private flip-switch the fountain began to flow. My Mother didn't seem to appreciate the humor of the situation at the time, but I found the display quite entertaining. I would give the height a 9 and the trajectory an 8. He managed to clear the sofa by a wide margin and produce a prodigious puddle nearly 3 feet into the middle of the floor.

Having gotten my first memory out of the way, I can proceed to my second and significantly more important memory – my first pair of Cowboy Boots. I wasn't aware of the ominous portents this memory would introduce and the beneficial effects it would have in my future years. I remember the boots, and have pictorial proof to confirm that the memory is not imaginary. I most vividly remember the spanking I received for walking the 5 blocks to my babysitter's house (across a 4 lane boulevard) to show her my new birthday present. Needless to say, I was extremely proud of my new boots and was devastated when I outgrew them, since my parents didn't have the money nor the inclination to buy me another pair. Had they found the money and matched my enthusiasm for acquiring more Cowboy Boots, none of us would have had to endure my 3rd (and most painful) childhood memory.

One of the neighborhood boys was giving me a ride home on the luggage bar on the back of his bicycle (back when most bicycles had luggage bars), when the heel of my right foot got caught in the spokes of the rear wheel. Although the injury didn't require stitches, it did require numerous torturous treatments with a poultice like compound known as Denver Mud. The "Mud" had to be heated to a temperature beyond tolerance and then applied liberally to my injured heel. Suffice to say, voluminous screaming and pleading was involved along with my parents comments of, "Oh, quit fussing. It's not that bad." However, to a 5 year old, it was Hell on Earth. Shortly thereafter we moved to the suburbs (before they were known as suburbs, merely as "the Subdivision") and my life transitioned from the city life to the semi-country lifestyle in the "Green House".

Since both of my parents worked (Dad as a carpenter and Mom as a secretary)and I was only 6 at the time, my Brother and I were always left with a babysitter. For a merciless couple of years it was our Grandmother on my Dad's side. She was only one generation from the Old Country (Germany)and I am convinced that she learned her baby sitting techniques from Hitler himself. The phrase I most remember her for was, "Bah, Bah, spit it out!" since my brother

OOPS……Fergit What Y'all Jest SAW…..it AIN't Ready Yet !!!!!

Computer Tip of the Week 01-5 (Strong Passwords)

Strong Passwords...Strong Passwords...Everybody seems to be talking about "Strong" Passwords. Well, not wanting to be left out, I I have been asked to add my 2 Cents on the Subject of "Strong Passwords".

Computer Tip of the Week:

What is a "Strong" Password? It is a Password that is constructed in such a way that it is Easy for You to remember, but Verry Difficult for Anyone else (especially Hackers/Intruders) to Guess. There has been a lot of Info put out on How to Build a Strong Password lately, but Hopefully the Info I'm about to Provide will be just a little bit Different.

You have All Probably heard by Now that a VA Strong Password has to be at Least 8 characters in Length (up to 20 Characters) and created from at least 3 out of 4 different kinds of characters (e.g., Lowercase Letters, Uppercase Letters, Numbers, and Special Characters). However, Did You know that to build the STRONGEST Password You can't use ANY Word (or group of Letters) that can be Found in a Dictionary? Hackers use Online Dictionaries in their attempts to "Crack" Your Password. So How do You make a Password that is Easy to Remember without using any Words or Groups of Letters that can't be Found in a Dictionary? The Answer is -- ACRONYMS!

What is an Acronym? It is a Series of Letters (that "usually" forms a Word) that is built by using the First Letter from Each of the Words of a Phrase (like Central Alabama Veterans Health Care System = CAVHCS). CAVHCS would Probably Not be Found in a Dictionary, but since it is the Name of Our Organization it wouldn't be a Good Choice as part of a STRONG Password. Let me give You a few Examples that might get You thinking along the Right Lines:

Do You know much about Music? When You were First learning to Read Music, do You Remember the "Helpful Hints" You used to remember which Notes went on which Lines? For the Treble Clef, it was "Every good boy does fine" (Egbdf). This would be a Very Good start to a Strong Password. The Treble Clef sign sort of looks like a Backwards "and" sign (&), and if Your Favorite Symphony is Beethoven's Ninth (B9), Look at the Strong Password that You could Easily make -- Egbdf&B9. That would sure be a tough one to Guess (and Easy to Remember), Wouldn't it? But maybe You're Not into Music. OK, try this Next one.

Let's say that Your Life revolves around Your Children/Grand Children (or Pets, for those of Us who aren't "Blessed" with Children). How can You use that to construct a Strong Password? I'll use the Pet scenario for this Example. One of Our Chihuahuas is Named "Candy Kane" and Our Sheepdog (sort of) is Named "Rag Man". They are Both (2) really great pets. Can You see where I'm going with this? My Strong Password would look like this: CK+RM=2rgp (I Know that's 9 characters instead of 8, but it has to be AT LEAST 8 Characters -- it can be all the way up to 20 Characters). The Longer You make it, the STRONGER it is.

I Hope this has given You a few Hints for constructing Your Own Strong Password to Help Keep Our CAVHCS Network Safe and Secure. Make it a Game -- Make it FUN -- See who can construct the Strongest Password. There's Only One catch -- You can't Tell Anyone. It will have to be Your Little Secret that YOU have the Strongest Password in CAVHCS. Good Luck!

Next Week's Computer Tip: How to use Templates in Microsoft Word (Word-processing).

If You have any suggestions for Topics for the "Computer Tip of the Week", Please send them to:

WELLLL Y'all Git the Idea.........I Wrote This a LONNNGGGGG Time Ago....In Another LIFE......

Ten Commandments of "Quality" Customer Service

1. Thou Shalt Initiate a Workorder or Ticket and Contact the Customer via Phone (Using Proper Telephone Etiquette) to setup an Appointment (at the Customer's Convenience) before going to their Area to Perform a Customer Service Action. If attempting to Solve the Problem Remotely (via one of the Remote Desktop Tools), Ask the Customer if NOW is a Good Time when You Call them, otherwise Setup an Appointed Time to Call them Back (at the Customer's Convenience).

2. Thou Shalt Provide Written Explanation/Guidance for ANY "New" Hardware/Software that is to be Installed in a Private Office or Clinical Area (whether You Write it Yourself, or it is Provided to You). All Explanation/Guidance Material is to be Reviewed/Approved by Your Supervisor prior to Providing it to a Customer. And ensure that You Anticipate Any Tools, Supplies, etc. that You may Need to take with You to the Customer's Location, and ALWAYS carry a Writing device and Something to Write Upon.

3. Thou Shalt Introduce Yourself as an Information Techmology Staff Member upon Entering a Private Office or Clinical Area, and seek out the "Responsible" Person for the Office/Area to Notify them of Your Presence in Their Area. Also, be Sure to Introduce any "Assistants" that You may bring with You.

4. Thou Shalt Thoroughly and Completely Explain the Reason for Your Presence, Provide any Written Explanation/Guidance Material, and Ask if there are Any Questions or Comments (and Make the Appropriate Response) before Proceeding with the Customer Service Action.

5. Thou Shalt Allow the Customer to "Vent" Any Frustrations and Under NO Circumstances will You Retaliate! You will Appologize for Any and All Inappropriate Actions by Previous Info Tech Staff Members, and Report those Actions to Your Supervisor for Corrective Action.

6. Thou Shalt Perform the Appropriate "Wellness" Checklist (Printer, PC, Server, etc.) Prior to Attempting Any Fix Action (to ensure that the "Subject" is "Well" enough to Troubleshoot, and to ensure that You don't "Fix" something that isn't Broken).

7. Thou Shalt Perform the Appropriate Troubleshooting and Corrective Action to Fix the Customer's Problem (to the Customer's Satisfaction), being Courteous and Respectful (of the Equipment as Well as the Customer) during the Entire Process.

8. Thou Shalt Promise to Inform Your Supervisor of Any Problems encountered (whether they may have been Caused by a Previous Technician or Not), and Follow-up with an E-mail to Your Supervisor (with a Courtesy Copy to the Customer) Confirming Your Promise.

9. Thou Shalt Apologize to the Customer for Any Inconvenience Your Actions (or those of a Previous Technician) may have Caused them, and Inform them of their Opportunity to Comment on this Customer Service Action when they Receive a Copy of the Completed Action via an E-Mail Message.

10. Thou Shalt ensure that the Problem is Fixed (and No "New" Problems are Created) Prior to Leaving the Customer's Area (or Ending the Call, if Correcting Remotely). Take All Tools, Diskettes, CDs, Supplies, Trash, etc. with You when You Leave the Customer's Area, and Leave their Area at Least as Neat and Organized as You Found it (if Not More So). Closeout the Work Order (or Refer it to the Appropriate Person for Resolution), and Follow-up (if Referred) with an E-Mail to the Technician to which the Workorder is Referred (with Courtesy Copies to Your Supervisor, Their Supervisor, and to the Customer).

The wdnoreufl hmuan mnid!

Rseaearhc sniectists hvae disveocred taht it is not nceessray to hvae all of the lttreers in the crrocet oredr to uednratsnd a wrod. Its olny nceessray taht all of the ltteres are pesernt and taht the fsrit and lsat ltteres are crroect!

Now AIN'T Y'all GLAD That I Decided NOT ta Write My "Baby" Like THAT ??

The "BIG AL " Song (ReVISITed)   *WEELLLLLLL DOGGY.....YEEEEEEHAWWWWW !!!"

This HYAR's a Fable "OF" a Fella "CALLED" "BIG AL"

A Poor LAN Manager, BUTT He Kept His "Family" WELL

And THEN One Day He Was a "Shootin' fer the MOON"

And the LORD Said, "Have I Got's a JOB Fer YOU !!!"

Write Me a "BOOK"......a "Prophet" You ARE !!!

His "Family" and "Friends" Said, "He's CRAZY in the Head"

Them Thar WACO "Reps" and "Dems" Said, "We'll Leave the Man Fer DEAD."

BUTT the GOOD LORD Said, "You Will Have No LACK,

Cause the 'BIG 3' TRINITY Has Got's Yer BACK !!!"

WE Are "OMNIPOTENT".......AIN'T "NO ONE" Can STAND Agin' US !!!

He Made MegaBUCKS from a "Satire" that He Wrote.

The "BOOK" Was DeSIGNed ta Git "MOST" Folks ("Nanny") GOAT.

His KinsFolk Said, "BIG AL, 'Move ON' Outta There,

Ya KNOW that WEST Nebraska Has the Freshest AIR !!!"

Lama Ranches....and Bison Farms !!!

Now I "Don't Know" HOW This Story's Gonna "END"

BUTT I "HOPE" Along the "WAY", that I "STILL" Will BE Yer "FRIEND"

(WHAT a "FRIEND" We Have in JESUS, ALL OUR Sins and Griefs ta BEAR.....

Or Bare.....OR Bere.....OH HELL....I'M "OFF TRACK" Agin.....)

Please WISH Me GOOD "LUCK", Cause I'll be NEED'n it a "LOT".....

As I TRY ta "Fix" a BROKEN "Meltin' POT" !!!

AMERICA That IS.....Land of the "FREEE???"....And HOME of My BRAVE ("Little NIPers") !!!

Y'all READ My Little "Baby" Now.....Ya HEAR !??!!!

"Does ANY a This CRAP Make SENSE ta Ya, OR Am I Jest FUNNIN' Ya.....YOU DECIDE !!!"

(from AuthorHouse on eBook, Papaerback, and CD....Read by "BIG AL" HisSELF)

(Comin' SOON to a Book Store......OR eBook Store Near YOU)

NEW Indapandanca Party
www.GoNIPer.org

You NEED a Little PURPLE in Your LIFE

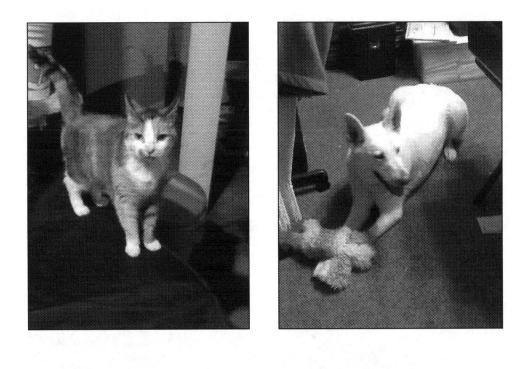